TIME TO STAND UP

BILL HULL

Copyright ©2025 Bill Hull

Book & Jacket design by KR15.com
Set in Adobe Garamond & Avenir

ISBN (hardcover) 9798309471867
ISBN (paperback) 9798309468706

First Edition: February 2025

To the non-clergy
who make the world work;
And without whom,
the professionals could not do theirs.

C O N T

INTRODUCTION — 7

THE AGE OF ANXIETY — 13
Clouds got in my way — 15
Tangled up in blue — 21
Would it help? — 27
When God takes you to Land's End… — 33
There are no events planned for today — 39
Sentenced to a Sabbatical — 45

ELON MUSK WOULDN'T MIND BEING SAVED — 51
Elon Musk Wouldn't Mind Being "Saved" 1 — 53
Elon Musk Wouldn't Mind Being "Saved" 2 — 59
Elon Musk Wouldn't Mind Being "Saved" 3 — 65
Elon Musk Wouldn't Mind Being "Saved" 4 — 71
Elon Musk Wouldn't Mind Being "Saved" 5 — 77
Elon Musk Wouldn't Mind Being "Saved" 6 — 83
Elon Musk Wouldn't Mind Being "Saved" 7 — 91
Elon Musk Wouldn't Mind Being "Saved" 8 — 99
Elon Musk Wouldn't Mind Being "Saved" 9 — 109
Elon Musk Wouldn't Mind Being "Saved" 10 — 119

THE GREAT DEBATE — 127
The Great Debate: 10 Guests, 10 Conversations — 129
The Great Debate 2: Andrew Klavan — 141
The Great Debate 3: David Mamet — 151
The Great Debate 4: Larry Alex Taunton — 161
The Great Debate 5: Don Henley — 169
The Great Debate 6: Dr. Scot McKnight — 177
The Great Debate 7: Dr. Jordan Peterson — 187
The Great Debate 8: Dr. Nancy Pearcy — 195
The Great Debate 9: Oprah Winfrey — 203
The Great Debate 10: Dr. Hannah Arendt — 209
The Great Debate 11: G.K. Chesterton — 217

SEVEN DEADLY SINS — 225
1. Pride — 227
2. Envy — 235
3. Anger — 243
4. Lust — 251
5. Greed — 259
6. Sloth/Laziness — 267
7. Gluttony — 273

THE CHURCH THAT CAME IN FROM THE COLD — 281
The Church That Came In From the Cold: Pt. 1 — 283
The Church That Came In From the Cold: Pt. 2 — 291
The Church That Came In From the Cold: Pt. 3 — 299

SALVATION BY… — 309
Salvation by Reason Alone — 311
Salvation by Myth Alone — 319
Salvation by Discipleship Alone — 325
Salvation by Works Alone — 335
Salvation by Politics Alone — 343
Salvation by Philosophy Alone — 353
Salvation by Scientism Alone — 361
Salvation by Monasticism Alone — 369
Salvation by Faith Alone — 379

00—

INTRODUCTION

NERO'S NIGHT

Nero was 16 years old when he became emperor of Rome in AD 54. He was the great, great-grandson of Caesar Augustus. Thanks to his lineage, he was immediately promoted as a "son of God" and therefore divine. His father had ascended to heaven, where he reigned with Apollo and many other Greek deities. His face was on the coins, and statues of his likeness with a halo were erected in most cities of the empire. Augustus had been and continued to be the loftiest of all deities. He ruled over all other gods and all Romans were obliged to pay homage and salute his likeness with a hearty "Hail Caesar."

To the Apostle Paul, this was nonsense and foolishness. And Christians were warned not to fall for it and not to put such a political figure in the same category as the creator and Lord of the universe. Nero didn't deserve any such honor. He killed his mother, he kicked his pregnant wife to death, and he was married as a woman to a man. Nero considered himself divine and Roman citizens property, something for him to use.

Nero's Street Party

In the summer of 64, the 26-year-old despot decided to throw a party that no one could forget. The party surrounded a lake that Nero stocked with sea monsters. Around the edge were brothels, staffed with prostitutes ranging from the cheapest streetwalkers to the elite call girls and boys. For one night only, any man could avail himself of any of these and they were forbidden to refuse. There was no slave or free that night in Rome, they were all slaves. A gladiator could take a girl from a noble family, a man could penetrate a boy.[1]

---

1 Description paraphrased from Dominion, Tom Holland page 97-99 Basic Books, New York, 2019

In other parts of Rome that night many stayed away. They may have been interested in the spectacle, especially the young men. But they had been warned not to go because they already had what those people thought they were getting. This group of people were called Christians. Paul had written them and told them were already "sons of God." They had already "been adopted by God." They were "loved by God." They were told in Paul's letter that Nero and his lot were under the wrath of God, and those who practiced such evils around that lake were destined to be judged and punished by God.[2] Paul taught them that their bodies were "temples of the Holy Spirit." For Romans, sex was an exercise of power. Bodies were to be penetrated, male or female, anyone who was inferior was considered fair game.

Rome Burned

A few weeks later, after Nero's street party, Rome caught on fire. A third of the city was smoking rubble. Nero started a campaign to blame the fire on someone or a group. He chose the Christians. In cities throughout the empire, he gathered up scapegoats. Some were dressed in animal skins and were torn apart by dogs, lions, and predatory beasts. Many stadiums in the empire were filled with fans who would cheer on the killing of such crazy people. Others were famously put on crosses along the *Appian Way,* smeared in pitch and used as torches to illuminate night travel. Among those who got caught in Nero's killing machine was a man named Peter, who was crucified upside down, and Paul, who was beheaded befitting a Roman citizen.

Peter and Paul left us with their writings, but more importantly, with their example. Today Peter's bones, some believe, are buried in a crypt under the dome of the world's most famous church, St. Peter's in Rome. Paul's writings and story within them along with the gospels have done more to shape our world than any words ever penned.

---

2 Romans 1:18-32

"For I am not ashamed of this Good News about Christ. It is the power of God at work, saving everyone who believes, the Jew first and also the Gentile. This Good News tells us how God makes us right in his sight. This is accomplished from start to finish by faith. As the scriptures say, "It is through faith that a righteous person has life."

Both Peter and Paul, by tradition, could have bargained their way out of execution. This was true of some other early leaders as well. Yet they would not step back, or lay down, they stood up and paid the price. This is a decision for each of us—we make it nearly every day in one way or another. This book is a call to Stand Up and I hope it will encourage you to follow in the footsteps of these men as they followed Christ.

So here's to Peter and Paul, two stand-up guys.

What happened to Nero? He committed suicide in 68 AD. Today some people name their dogs after him. Millions have named their sons Peter or Paul.

01

THE AGE OF ANXIETY

"CLOUDS GOT IN MY WAY"
—JONI MITCHELL

"Some people feel guilty about their anxieties and regard them as a defect of faith, but they are afflictions, not sins. Like all afflictions, they are, if we can so take them, our share in the passion of Christ."

—C.S. Lewis

Anxiety is ancient and has troubled humans since the creation. It is built into the human condition and made worse by the fall. It is there for our protection and benefit in many cases. We can feel the adrenaline rush through our veins before giving a speech, or our wedding. It also helps when we are being threatened, chased, or confronted. There are periods, however, when it becomes destructive and that is where much of society finds itself. And this is what the Apostle Paul is thinking about as he writes from prison:

"Don't worry about anything, instead, pray about everything. Tell God what you need and thank him for all he has done. Then you will experience God's peace, which exceeds everything we can understand. His peace will guard your hearts and minds as you live in Christ Jesus."[1]

What impresses me is that Paul was in prison when he wrote this gem. He must have had a fantastic spiritual life to make such a claim from a first-century dungeon. This wasn't a neat little cubical outfitted with a bunk, toilet, sink, and TV hanging from the ceiling. He was chained, it wasn't sanitary, there were no accommodations. But he even went further than to sponsor the idea of inner peace—he claimed that in the larger context, rejoicing would be in order.

"Always be full of joy in the Lord, I say it again—rejoice!"[2]

---

1   Philippians 4:6-7 New Living Translation

2   Ibid 4:4

This is life lived on another level, possibly in the spiritual stratosphere. It would be understandable to say it is a life to be admired, but not experienced. The premise of the Bible is that this life can be reached, but not based on willpower, particularly not by forcing negative thoughts from your head. Suppression doesn't work, though on occasion it might help, but one must call upon an inner capacity where a supply has been stored or can be directly accessed by an outside source. Paul says that outside source can be accessed through prayer. Aka, talking with God. In another place, Paul lists the characteristics of a transformed person. "But the Holy Spirit produces this kind of fruit in our lives: love, joy, peace, patience, kindness, goodness, faithfulness, gentleness, and self-control."[3] Peace seems there for the taking, but Americans in particular, haven't found it and, as Christians, our record is not much better than the general population.

The poet, W.H. Auden, called modern life the *"Age of Anxiety."*

When does anxiety cross the line from a human affliction and become a pathology? Let's begin with the word anxiety itself. The word anxiety—or worry, in this case, means to be torn into pieces. We know something about this. We can feel being pulled in opposite directions, everything from walking the floor to rolling and moaning on our bed. The enemy will rub his hands together with glee when he can attack us and make us want to escape.

Paul urges us to stop all this before it gets rolling. How? By stopping to pray. "Don't worry about anything." I suppose "anything" means just that! Instead of worrying that picks up steam and rolls you over like a locomotive, stop and pray. Stop, drop, delay worry, and pray. The words worry & nothing are in opposition to another word set, prayer & everything. Go ahead, do it—train yourself to do it. Then tell God what you need, with thanks, and give him the worries item by item. Then a promise:

"Then you will experience God peace. His peace is not of the world order, it exceeds anything we can understand."

---

3 Galatians 5:22-23

When such prayers are said and answered something supernatural takes place. God comes to you with inner peace that is nonsensical, beyond our ability to reason out or manufacture. It does remind one of the peace Jesus promised to his disciples in John, "A peace not of this world." Therefore, don't be afraid. Jesus assures us this kind of peace is not to be found in anyone else or anywhere else.

Inner peace as a guide and a guard

"His peace will guard your hearts." Like a garrison of soldiers, peace will stand watch and march around your heart to protect it from threat. Additionally, his peace will instruct your mind. "His peace will guard your hearts and minds as you live in Christ Jesus." One wonders how long each period of peace can last. Does it expire or need to be refueled? The answers lay within each of us and our wills, and the various depths and strength of forces within. We could decide to take Jesus at his word in such places as Matthew 6:19-34 and not worry about tomorrow, for there is nothing we can do about it. The Russian spy in the film "Bridge of Spies," when asked, "Are you worried?" would always answer, "Would it help?" meaning, no. We could say that he had won over worry.

Most of our worries are deeply rooted pathologies. We can't command ourselves to stop negative thoughts. This can make it worse. The reality is that inner peace is something that God alone provides, and He alone delivers. Our part is to worry about nothing—but pray about everything. Ask God to do what you and no other can do, blood your soul with his supernatural peace. I have experienced many times when God's peace came rolling into me and I could relax, take a deep breath, and let it go. It lasts as long as I permit. Often, I will enjoy the peace, but then want to get up and fix something, do something to enhance it.

Having been raised in a therapeutic culture heavily influenced by Freud and Jung, the culture encourages an inner journey that seeks to discover the answers within a person. W. H. Auden's famous book and poem, *The Age of Anxiety* [4] speaks to this:

Psychoanalysis, like all pagan Scientia, says, "Come, my good man, no wonder you feel guilty. You have a distorting mirror, and that indeed a very wicked thing to have. But cheer up. For a trifling consideration I shall be delighted to straighten it out for you. There. Look. A perfect image. The evil of distortion is exorcised. Now you have nothing to repent of any longer. Now you are one of the illumined and elect. That will be ten thousand dollars, please. And immediately come seven devils, and the last state of that man is worse than the first." [5]

Auden himself was a devotee of Freud but became disillusioned and never gave Jung that same homage. He did use Jung's language and categories for many years. What many don't recall is that the Myers-Briggs Type Indicator[6] is taken from Jung's work. It could hardly be denied that such theories have had a great influence on all our lives. Almost every Christian leader I know can immediately tell you what type they are, and everyone seems to accept it as true. For example, I am INTJ. I am sure God took that into consideration when he formed me.[7]

Summary

When anxiety comes sweeping across the plain of your life, cease the preoccupation with the problem. Immediately, talk to God about it, and thank him for all he has done. Then ask him to come into the inner sanctum of your being and flood you with his peace, it is the only place you can get it. Ask God to do what he alone can—already promised it for you.

To Be Continued…

---

4   The Age of Anxiety, A Baroque Eclogue, Edited by Alan Jacobs. 2011: Princeton University Press.

5   Ibid, page xviii

6   Ibid, page xix

7   Psalms 139

THE AGE OF ANXIETY

"TANGLED UP IN BLUE"
—BOB DYLAN

Paul was in a horrible prison, yet he called upon the entire church community to "Rejoice in the Lord, let me say it again, rejoice!" How was he able to say he was content in any state he found himself? Was he just that kind of a guy? Was he tough with a special talent or gift that made it easier for him? Paul, facing torture and death, claimed he learned how to be in such a state of peace, a peace incomprehensible, but never natural to him. How did he learn it?

He explains his process

Paul's entire process is described in The Age of Anxiety Part 1.[1] Now Paul explains how he found the peace of God and applied it to his anxiety. He didn't do it by commanding his will. He didn't do it by blocking negative thoughts. He didn't do it by ignoring the facts and how bad the situation was. He developed a poise that was God's gift to him. He learned how to access it. The modern therapeutic model uses pills, techniques, and avoiding recognition of how desperate the problem is.

The character of God's peace is unique, and it faces the facts and assigns special guards around your heart and mind.

The text says it. *"His peace will guard your hearts and minds as you live in Christ Jesus."* (Philippians 4:7) This final clause is not a condition requiring a certain level of ability on our part. None of us can access what Paul tells us we can't understand, it is out of our reach. It is, as in my case, accessed through a simple request in prayer. I pray, "Lord come and do what you alone can do. I invite you to flood my troubled mind and heart with your supernatural peace. I don't understand it, I can't control it. I release all that I am to you. Come now Lord, in the power and authority of your Christ.

---

1 Please see chapter preceding this one.

Give me peace, guard my thinking, boost my emotion, forgive my weakness, be strong now Oh Lord. Amen." I then breathe out the impure and breathe in his peace until it comes. Then I submit to it. It is the foolishness of God that is wiser than the wisdom of man.

What you think about

He does address conforming our mind to the reality of his peace. Because we are now living on a supernatural plane of existence, he tells us: "Fix your thoughts…" (Philippians 4:8) This takes us back to some basic guidance from scripture. To fix is to train rather than try. Trying harder doesn't work, but a patient commitment to training our minds to concentrate on what is good is within our reach. He continues, "…on *what is true*…" That is looking down the barrel of reality. But without truth, we have no place from which to begin. True, we each have various experiences that influence our understanding. But in this case, we rely on Christ, who *is the truth,* to have *told us the truth,* and that is the place where we fix our thoughts. The peace of God is not the expelling of negative thoughts—it is facing the facts. The peace of God is the very presence of God and that is what we must think about.

The virtues continue: *"…honorable, and right, and pure, and lovely, and admirable."* The mind that is accustomed to being ripped apart by anxiety and ruled by thought patterns, needs a focus. Sometimes, we should even make a list of such traits and people so we can train our minds to go to those kinds of things.

I can tell you from recent personal experience how challenging this can be. After a surgery or trauma that turns your life around or on its head, the grip that negativity can have on your mind is formidable. You want to understand and control the situation. Your mind races with what is going wrong, instead of what is going right. It seems like you can't catch a break—and nothing is improving—even when professionals, friends, and family tell you that you are getting better and your experience is normal, not unique.

If you are on special medications, your mind can get confused, you create rules, you have dreams, and your reality changes. This is particularly difficult when sleep is sporadic, artificially produced, and incomplete. The *One who is* said, "I am the way, the truth, and the life…You shall know the truth and the truth will set you free," is your only reliable guide through the morass of the dark world of destructive anxiety.

What you practice

When you are armed with the peace of God, the armed presence of God within, you can think more clearly. It also frees you to practice the truth. Paul takes a great chance when he offers himself as an example. "Keep putting into practice all you learned and received from me—everything you heard from me and saw me doing. Then the God of peace will be with you." (Philippians 4:9)

I would love to be able to offer myself up as an example of a person who has been a prime example of being worthy to show others the way. However, I must confess that among my doctors, and more embarrassingly, my family, I got a failing grade. I developed a reputation as a worrier and a control addict. I didn't like it. It took me weeks, even months to learn what Paul said he had learned. I am learning to be content in whatever state I'm in.

I must give up my life to God's control daily. That's the number one thing to do. It's not so easy when it is real. Others have helped me come to terms with my actual reality rather than some alternative one that is devilish and destructive. This is not a knowledge game. I know the Bible, I can reference hundreds of stories, verses, and sections of scriptures and bring them to mind. I quote scripture to myself many times a day, they just come to me, having spent most of my life reading, studying, and teaching the scriptures. But it doesn't matter unless I put my life on the line.

What it produces

Paul says he learned all this. My way of saying this is—I changed my thinking. I trained my mind and allowed the power of God's presence to guide me, to protect me. Daily I call upon God to do what he alone is and can do—flood my tattered soul with peace. Now Paul allows us to know something personal as to why he has suggested such a process to peace. He mentions that the Christian community has reached out to him financially. He appreciates their concern but tells them he has "learned to be content" with what he has, regardless if they helped him or not. This proves that Paul did not attend a fund-raising church or receive documentation on knowing how to move people to support him. Typically, we are taught, "The number one reason people do not give is that they are not asked." Then the definition of the "ask" is presented. The knowledge and techniques that are taught are valuable and do work in the American culture of sales, glamour, celebrity, and IRS tax law. But Paul, writing from an ancient prison, knew only of how God met him in his need. He had known times of plenty and times of emptiness. He mentioned a time of feasting and a time of fasting. Then he declared what so many of us want to be true: "For I can do everything through Christ who gives me strength." Then he thanks them one more time for their generosity while he is behind bars.

From underneath this treasure of wisdom comes a statement of transition and blessing for all of us. "And the same God who takes care of me will supply all your needs from his glorious riches, which have been given to us in Christ Jesus."[2] [2]

Even a literary giant such as C.S. Lewis understood it but fell short of understanding what Paul is telling us: "Some people feel guilty about their anxieties and regard them as a defect of faith. I don't agree at all. They are afflictions, not sins. Like all afflictions, they are, if we can so take them, our share of the Passion of Christ."

We can overcome through the richness and power of the presence of God as he fills us up with his joy and wholeness.

---

2   Philippians 4:19 NLT

"WOULD IT HELP?"
—THE SPY

In the Steven Spielberg film, *Bridge of Spies* starring Tom Hanks, the Russian spy played by Mark Rylance[1] continues to ask the question regarding worry or anxiety, "Would it help?" In other words, as Jesus taught us, worry cannot add one more day to our life, it isn't useful, no, it wouldn't help![2]

Then why has it become such a part of our lives to worry? There is a joke going around about the new version of *MacDonald's* that is tailored to people under 30 years of age. The *Happy Meal* has been replaced by the *Anxiety Meal* or *Anxiety Frappuccino* if you like. It seems that we find battles with anxiety quite useful, even productive. Why not? Our society is serving up daily portions of war, hate, and feckless power-hungry leaders. Crime and violence are all neatly packaged for social media or cable news. Media watchers and commentators build careers around how dramatic, how fearful, how crucial it all is. It does seem like the four horsemen of the apocalypse have come riding into our living rooms. They bring with them Conquest, War, Famine, and Death.[3]

We watch carjackings, random violence in the streets, smash-and-grab gangs preying on small one-owner stores as well as high-end chain stores. Most companies have their own security and the world has become the dystopian hellscape that we feared. We are living in the shadow of George Orwell's *1984*, where the good intentions of unwise leaders have, by their own fears, created so much more to fear and worry about. President Franklin Roosevelt's famous statement from the *Great Depression*[4] is partly true, "All

---

1 The British actor was awarded the Academy Award for his performance.
2 Mathew 6:24-34
3 Revelation 6:1-8
4 The period from 1929-1941 was marked by economic hardship. Roosevelt was President during most of this period.

we have to fear, is fear itself." A point well taken. Fear is big in the world in general, more pronounced in America. But the Apostle Paul, who had plenty to fear, said this, "God has not given us a spirit of fear, but of love, power and a sound mind."[5]

Let's face it, we have a lot to fear, but its source is not God.

When I am gripped with fear, I always know I have a choice. I also know that fear does not come from God. The alternative, however, is dangerous terrain for the soul. It requires submission of our lives to God. I relinquish control of outcomes and controls. My greatest fear is to get my will into alignment with God. I'm no longer in charge. This is why Paul wrote "I have learned" to be content in whatever state I find myself. In plenty or want, a learning process is part of it. There is a simple statement Paul once made, "I die daily." There is a lot of dying in living with God, being his disciple, and learning from him. "For I swear dear brothers and sisters, that I face death daily. This is as certain as my pride in what Christ Jesus our Lord has done in you."[6]

I never thought I would need to dig as deep within to follow in his steps. Most days, I don't want to deny myself, to die, to sacrifice. I rise up against it and fight it. I'm confronted with the question, am I a fool or a fool for Christ's sake? I choose a fool for Christ because he has chosen me—he wrote down my life before I lived, spoke, or acted[7] and because I believe that "the foolishness of God is wiser than the wisdom of man."[8]

Recently I had a high-wire experience explaining to a very intel-

---

5   2 Timothy 1:7

6   I Corinthians 15:31 NLT

7   Psalm 139. He wrote it all down so to speak and I want to live into it, step into it. I often just say, Bill, make a decision, and allow God to work it for me. He knows what I will do before I do it and what I will say before I say it. There is no condemnation for me in Christ Jesus. Romans 8:1. Just get my feet moving, follow him!

8   I Corinthians 1:18-31

ligent, highly educated person what it means to be a Christian in today's environment. It was a very challenging conversation. The discussion ranged from bad Christians who don't act like Christians to Israel and Palestine. I said that Christians are 100% saints, 100% sinners, 100% of the time. We are walking contradictions. We don't aspire to be Christ or replace Christ. We are *learning* from Christ—that is called discipleship. Our talk was political, it was theological, it was cultural. I explained the morality of it all and defended the biblical viewpoint. We came to a peaceful agreement with differences. Listening to other world views and their implications and applications requires a great deal of inner discipline. Like Paul told Timothy:

Endure suffering along with me, as a good soldier of Christ Jesus. Soldiers don't get tied up in the affairs of civilian life, for they cannot please the officer who enlisted them. And athletes cannot win a prize unless they follow the rules… Think about what I am saying. The Lord will help you understand all these things.[9]

Stay focused on your calling, keep a sense of priority

Only break ranks to protect, to intervene when people are being harmed. Use common sense as life confronts us with many choices. I have political views, but I want them to come out in Christ-like actions that keep his teaching and will first. Of course, it is complicated, that is why it is a matter of prayer, and of sometimes quick reaction based on deeply held biblically based character traits— goodness, kindness, loving one's enemies, and refusing to deny the uniqueness of Christ and his example and teachings. "Sometimes when we are called to obey, the fear does not subside, and we are expected to move against the fear. One must choose to do it afraid."[10]

Reaching out when afraid and putting ourselves at risk creates

---

9 2 Timothy 2:3-7 NLT
10 Elisabeth Elliot, Quotable Quote in Good Reads

fear, but we can know that fear is not of God, but God will use it and therefore, us. The sound mind principle can help when and where we need to make hard choices. The sound mind idea means God has given us a rational side and this is where we allow logic to enter into the decision to act or not to act. Even our risk level is gauged by our thinking mechanisms. I will not climb that mountain, I will not walk that tightrope, I will not get into a fight with my neighbor who is likely to do me harm. But all bets are off if I must protect others.

We return then to our opening, the Russian spy in *Bridge of Spies,* and his question regarding anxiety, "Would it help?" No, yet some of us find a weird comfort in doing it anyway. We all have some days better than others. I hope today is a winner for you.

"WHEN GOD TAKES YOU TO LAND'S END IT IS USUALLY NOT VOLUNTARY."
—BILL HULL

Ask me and I will tell you remarkable secrets you do not know about things to come.

—Jeremiah 3:33

Land's End is normally associated with a popular clothing line. Its history, however, records it as one of Great Britain's best-loved landmarks. It has natural beauty and stunning scenery. It features cliffs, and trails, and is a magnificent place to wander around the West Country of England overlooking famous landmarks. I suppose it is about what you can see, smell, and feel. It is a new perspective, something greater than a single person or viewpoint.

Someone immersed daily in the *Land's End* clothing line is likely swallowed up in the short-term and narrow world of commerce, not having the time or the inclination to be reflective meditative, not looking for *Awe*. I'm like that, I don't have time to visit or think about beauty or the meaning of life. But when God takes you to land's end it is usually not voluntary—it is painful, but he gets you there and says—look! What you see is exactly what I have been saying, but you were not listening, you were not looking, but now you see my perspective. Because you have reached the end of yourself, your resources, and your abilities, you realize it has been Him all along who is watching, providing, and He is your leader, your King, your God.

Generally, he confirms to us via his written Word. God has already told us that He has not given us a spirit of fear, but of love, power, and a sound mind.[1] Other versions speak of power, love, and self-discipline. The inner peace we desire is not stupid. It must be smart. In other words, you don't reach a sound mind by ignor-

---

[1] 2 Timothy 1:7 New American Standard Version.

ing reality. The reality is medical or biological facts. It would be a smart peace to acknowledge them—that is the sound mind principle. God's peace always acknowledges realities. The other reality that removes fear is that he gives power and love. They are just as real as medical facts or other observable truths. Once integrated, a smart peace begins, and you can start thanking rather than spending time thinking about disaster. Then you can begin asking God for an inner transformation.

Contentment

God is working everything for our good.[2] We will never be content unless and until we make our requests to God. We acknowledge that our lives are in his hands. Then we can begin to learn and be instructed by God in his supernatural peace. Contentment often comes with a painful price tag. The pain is in the process. It means, as Augustine mentioned, independent of circumstances. It teaches us to live through it and live in freedom from fear. Except when our human weakness surges within us. Elizabeth Elliot once said, "Sometimes, when the fear doesn't leave you, you must obey and go forward anyway." We can't nor should we expect to control everything, especially our family and closest friends.

I want to be normal

Normal is often the person we were or at a time when we were younger. When we set that as a goal, it can be off the mark. Facing the present circumstances and realities of age creates new and different norms. Our golf group used to play 36 holes in a day, now we may only play 18 or even just 9 holes. It's like we lost something. There are new mental and emotional changes. They challenge us. When we become weaker and less capable, normal feels bad. God's presence and peace are the unchanging realities that teach us and

---

2 Romans 8:26-30

that meet us at the point of our need. The apostle Paul's secret is revealed to us—it is Christ himself guarding and teaching us his peace that is outside human ability. My prayer is often "Lord, come and flood me with your guidance and comfort. Come do what you alone can do." And once in a while even though we desire it, God's peace eludes us, and then we can become desperate and give in—it's a sad place to be.

The pattern of learning the secret of inner peace is essential and part of that training includes setbacks.

There is a time and place—I call them Gethsemane moments—where we get really honest with God just as Jesus was with his Father. He wanted out of the sacrificial life, he wanted to live rather than die and pay the penalty for our sin. Three times he asked but then finally, submitted.[3] These are the moments I detest, turning my life over to God completely. Now, I must do it every night before I sleep. I hate it because I want to hold on to my life, it's mine, it's all I've got! I want to have the final word, to be in charge. But it can't be—like Jesus, surrender is the pathway to peace.[4]

Jesus lost all his peace on the cross. When we sing, *Jesus Paid it All*, he did exactly that and his cry of agony is our cry of protest. Like him, we want to hold on. Unlike us, he went through it and stayed on the cross. This is what makes him our Savior, our Lord, our God.

This is a true story.[5] Horatio Spafford was an American Lawyer who lost everything in the Chicago fire of 1871. Two years later his wife, Anna, and their four daughters were on a ship crossing the Atlantic to England. The ship hit another ship and sank. Anna got their four little girls together and they prayed. When the ship went down all four girls drowned. Anna was found floating unconscious

---

3   Matthew 26:39
4   Luke 9:23-25
5   Notes from Tim Keller

by a rescue ship. They took her to England, and she cabled Horatio Spafford just two words, SAVED ALONE. On the trip to see his wife Spafford began to write this hymn:

It Is Well With My Soul

Why or how could a man dealing with such grief seek the peace of God?

The lyrics are amazing, *"...peace like a river...sorrows like sea billows roll...whatever my lot, thou hast taught me to say...it is well with my soul...My sin, O, the bliss of this glorious thought! My sin, not in part but the whole is nailed to the cross, and I bear it no more. Praise the Lord, Praise the Lord, o my soul!"*

What does that have to do with four little girls that are dead? Everything. He could have thought, *I'm being punished, I shouldn't have let them go,* but no, look at the cross, all the punishment fell on Him. He does care. Look what he did for us. When you reach *land's end* may you be standing before the cross of Christ, look up, bow down—you're home.

THE AGE OF ANXIETY

"THERE ARE NO EVENTS PLANNED FOR TODAY."
—BILL HULL'S SMART WATCH

In an empire of lies, only a crazy man would speak the truth. And crazy people do crazy things. They do stupid and wrong things. They don't destroy someone for saying the false ideas are false. They destroy them for doing something crazy. But you have to be crazy to tell them their ideas are false. Because of that, they will try to destroy you.[1]

This is the stupidity of **A**rtificial **I**ntelligence.

The term "AI" could be attributed to John McCarthy of MIT (Massachusetts Institute of Technology), which Marvin Minsky (Carnegie-Mellon University) defines as "the construction of computer programs that engage in tasks that are currently more satisfactorily performed by human beings because they require high-level mental processes such as perceptual learning, memory organization, and critical reasoning. The conference at Dartmouth College in the summer of 1956, funded by the Rockefeller Institute, is considered the founder of the discipline. Anecdotally, it is worth noting the great success of what was not a conference but rather a workshop. Only six people, including McCarthy and Minsky, had remained consistently present throughout this work (which relied essentially on developments based on formal logic).

I know it worries Elon Musk, but then he is dedicated to populating space with a billion people dumb enough to pay to travel nine months to Mars. AI doesn't know what it doesn't know and that is stupid. My days begin with many events ahead—some I plan for, many I don't—that are part of my day. Many knocks on the door, decisions to make, and the internet—ah yes, it is like a hundred people pulling their chairs up next to mine and telling me why I should follow their instructions. What happens in my house, among my family, and particularly, in my mind and body—AI is

---

1   Klavan, Andrew. Empire of Lies, (Boston: Houghton Mifflin Harcourt, 2008).

watching me.

One holiday I watched a string of Gunsmoke reruns, a John Wayne film festival, and regardless of the channel, all the commercials were about very personal issues, all tailored for me, and what could happen to me if I didn't take immediate action. It nearly drove me insane. How do they know me and the conditions of my bowels? Ever notice that in a *Gunsmoke* rerun the commercials are longer than the actual program? I know more about Doc, Miss Kitty, Chester, Festus, and the Long Branch Saloon than at any time in my life. I am now a *Gunsmoke* historian. And John Wayne, *Rio Lobo,* should I go on? Oh, my only relief is a football game now and then, and because even the NCAA and NFL seem to know a lot about me, I like to nap then, or just turn it all off.

Taking walks with God seems to be the best use of my time. He seems to know me better than anyone. After all, he wrote it all down before it began. Psalm 139 tells me *You saw me before I was born. Every moment was laid out before a single day had passed. How precious are your thoughts about me O God. They cannot be numbered! I can't count them; they outnumber the grains of sand! And when I wake up, you are still with me…Search me, O God, and know my heart; test me and know my anxious thoughts. Point out anything in me that offends you, and lead me along the path of everlasting life.*[2]

The Tower of Babel Redux[3]

The more I read about humanity's best minds attempting to populate outer space, the more it reminds me of one of humankind's most spectacular egomaniacal boo-boos. The Tower of Babel. The smart guys felt the wind at their backs, so they decided to build a tower to heaven, heaven being whatever they decided it was. God didn't look too kindly at their effort and confused their language. Even today, some I suppose, argue about which lan-

---

2   Psalm 139:16-18,23,24

3   Genesis 11:1-10

guage. However, philosophers favor the language of mathematics. Even our greatest minds have proven to be misguided (Bertrand Russell),[4] et al. Like a missile that locks in on the ship that fired it, it is self-destructive. Math became their *"Let's make bricks and harden them with fire."*

Not surprisingly, neither *Elon Musk* nor *Jeff Bezos* have made reservations on the *Mars* shuttle. No way they could sit still for the required nine months. Their efforts will collapse along with their tower, *impotenia erecti.*[5]

The Sound Mind *Principia* Biblical

"For God has not given us a spirit of fear or timidity, but of power, love and self-discipline."(sound mind)[6]

Every day we must choose to be someone's fool. A fool and servant of skepticism, or a fool for Christ's sake. It is a daily challenge for all Christians. I choose most days to be a fool for Christ's sake. For I believe the foolishness of God is wiser than the wisdom of man. When you sit with your medical advisors, who and what do you trust? My answer is a daily decision to choose life.

---

4 Bertrand Russell was a University of Cambridge philosopher. He and his colleagues such as Ludwig Wittgenstein, distilled all-knowing to mathematics in such works as Principia Mathematica.

5 Look it up

6 2 Timothy 1:7 NLT

One of my sons made this t-shirt for me.

Satan has come to destroy us—Christ has come to give us abundant life. I choose to trust that God is working through the medical advice I receive, but in the end, I must decide! But I do so with the knowledge that Satan gets nothing from me. God has written down every day, every decision before I was born. I am His servant, He came to give abundant life, and I have come to be His witness. Whether I find myself on a walk, in a coffee shop, or just sitting with family, I can wonder, "Lord, who will I get to talk with today?" But my best talks are always with you.[7]

---

[7] Selected scriptures, I Corinthians 1:18ff, John 10:10, Psalm 139, Acts 1:8, and https://hymnary.org/text/i_come_to_the_garden_alone (In the Garden, written by Charles Austin Miles 1846-1912.

THE AGE OF ANXIETY

"SENTENCED TO A SABBATICAL."
—GOD

O Lord, don't rebuke me in your anger or discipline me in your rage. Have compassion on me Lord, for I am weak. Heal me Lord, for my bones are in agony. I am sick at heart. How long O Lord, until you restore me?

—Psalm 6:1-3 NLT

Sabbaticals are a relatively new exercise among Evangelicals, they have become common among protestant clergy in the last twenty-five years. When I started in the 1970s, to ask for a paid Sabbatical would have stirred the leadership to ask, "What's wrong with you?" Back then Academics got them, Monks got them, and high church clergy who trained and served in elite institutions got them. But in my world, they were rare. But then God saw fit to sentence me to a sabbatical. It was not voluntary, it wasn't prayed for, and frankly, it was unwelcome.

This revolutionized my life—not in the sense that was earth-shattering or culturally transforming—not a revolution like taking an object and rotating it from top to bottom, technically, a half revolution where Noon becomes 6:00 PM. What was on top, was now on bottom—that sort of revolution, a life upside down. The challenge was unexplained blood pressure changes and the need to control and understand them. I was limited in my ability to travel and fulfill many of my obligations. I made decisions on these events as I moved along. I continued to write the column *No Longer a Bystander* and the book *I Will Not Bow Down* would still be released. My other activities were uncertain. I joined a chorus of God's family calling out for help to him daily. Some days he seemed to answer, others, not so much.

Jesus experienced unanswered prayer, *"Lord, may this cup pass from me."* There were times when the heavens seemed to close even for the Son of God. Jesus was a man of sorrows. He was deeply moved by so much—his friend Lazarus' death, (John 11) compassion on the multitudes, (Mt. 9:36-40), deeply angered by the prostitution of his Temple, (John 2), and he wept over Jerusalem. (Mt. 23) We are told he knows what it is like when we suffer. For the record, suffering is a big word with many levels of experience. I like Elizabeth Elliot's definition, *"Suffering is having what you don't want and not having what you do want."* A lot of life fits into that. On the cross Jesus lost all his inner peace—he went to hell for us.

I have been doing a lot of reading and listening to audio resources on the subject of suffering. It is quite common and never welcome. But we are called to handle it in a certain way when it visits us. *"For God called you to do good even if it means suffering, just as Christ suffered for you. He is your example and you must follow in his steps."* (1 Peter 2:21) I grant you, this sounds more like suffering directly because of obedience to Christ than it does suffering for a variety of maladies because of our fallenness. There is a case to be made that it is an attack of Satan, but doesn't trouble, in effect, find its source in Lucifer's malevolence toward God's children? No doubt the Devil is like a roaring lion prowling about seeking to destroy us.[1] I think the helpful part is that Christ suffered, and He can sympathize with our weaknesses and sufferings (Hebrews 4:14-16). And because of that, we are encouraged to boldly pray before God's throne to find grace in times of need. I think what ensues when a hurting Christian encounters our Gracious God, the one who promised never to leave or forsake us.[2]

Somehow, the study of suffering is good, but then it stops helping. Spending too much time thinking about it, living in fear of

---

1 I Peter 5:8,9. The majority of this passage is about helping people cope with persecution directly related to their being Christians. In today's environment and its rampant secularity, this is a difficult diagnosis for any of us who are struggling with physical maladies. I want to be careful not to rely on promises that are made to people in a very different situation. In general, however, these passages help us see the heart and care of God. I find much comfort in Psalm 46:10, "Be still and know that I am God," even though it is related to the Assyrian siege of Jerusalem.

2 Hebrews 13:5

it, and digging for answers can be exhausting. Admitting that not being in control is a huge battle, it ebbs and flows. Somedays it works to let it go, and release to God. After all, Jesus told us, *"Don't worry about tomorrow, for tomorrow has enough trouble of its own."*

Walking Away

Trouble introduces us to ourselves in frightening ways. We might recall the words of James *But don't just listen to God's word. You must do what it says. Otherwise, you are only fooling yourselves. For if you listen to the word and don't obey it is like glancing at your face in a mirror. You see yourself, walk away, and forget what you look like.*[3]

It is common to see the truth about ourselves, not like it, walk away, and intentionally forget it. But there is some pain and trouble that can't be ignored such as lying awake at night or troubled during the day. You realize there is no getting out of this. This is particularly difficult if you find yourself riddled with worry, indecision, or just old-fashioned fear. You quote long-held Bible verses that help for a while, but the trouble continues, and your fears return. You even know that the Bible says "fear not" 365 times.

Who wouldn't rather walk away and think about something else? This persistent inner turmoil takes you to the Psalms and Job, for comfort and insight. We read, *In peace I will lie down and sleep, for you alone, O Lord will keep me safe.* (Psalm 4:8) We repeat it, yet sleep is elusive, we lie awake in the night and our mind fills up with even more trouble. But then there is Psalm 5:1—*O Lord, hear me as I pray; pay attention to my groaning. Listen to my cry for help, my King and my God."* These are not mere words, we mean them, we believe them, we want them to come true. The Psalms tell us that we are not the first and we won't be the last to cry out in the night. Keep reading or praying into Psalm 6: *O Lord don't rebuke me in your anger or discipline me in your rage. Have compassion on me, Lord, for I am weak. Heal me Lord, for my bones are in agony. I am*

---

3 James 1:22-24 NLT

sick at heart. How long, O Lord, until you restore me? "Sick at heart," "weak," basically, now we've had it, we're out of ideas, resources, and even hope. This is when we get to the groaning stage.

…the Holy Spirit helps us in our weakness. For example, we don't know what God wants us to pray for. This is interesting because that is exactly what happens. It is almost like saying, "OK God, what do you want, I'm out of ideas, what should I ask for, what should I say, what are the magic words?" Paul helps us here in the Romans passage, *"But the Holy Spirit prays for us with groanings that cannot be expressed in words."* We are not only groaning in our spirits, but God, the Holy Spirit, goes into the prayer with us. *And the Father who knows all hearts knows what the Spirit is saying, for the Spirit pleads for us believers in harmony with God's own will. And we know that God causes everything to work together for the good of those who love God and are called according to his purpose for them.*[4]

I suppose this crying, praying, pleading, and getting to know myself was part of my sabbatical. I was not resting from all my responsibilities, but I was getting to know Bill, a sinner, a weak man, saved by grace and sustained by a strong and able God. I was resting from the image and personality I had become. And I might add, I thank God for what He has made me. If only I can get him to cooperate. On the other hand, *"There is no condemnation for those who are in Christ Jesus."* We are not being punished, that punishment fell on Jesus when he became sin.[5]

When things are dark and disappointing

When we struggle with prayer and suffering, and heaven seems closed for business, there are a couple of thoughts that might help. When Jesus was hanging on the cross, not one of his followers thought it was a good thing. In fact, they thought, what a tragedy! It seemed to be the worst thing that could possibly happen. "What

---

4   Romans 8:26-28

5   2 Corinthians 5:21

a waste, he was in his prime, think of how much he could have accomplished, the movement will die." Yet, they were staring at the greatest work that God had ever done. He was taking his world back. He was saving the world by dying for it. When you see or experience something horrible, think of how God is at work and will pull it all together for you and those you love. One pastor explained his understanding in this way. He was speaking of what he thought God was thinking:

"Whenever a child of mine makes a request, I give that child what they would have asked for if they knew everything that I know." And what does he know? I close with an example.

"O Lord, you have examined my heart and know everything about me. You know when I sit down or stand up. You know my thoughts even when I'm far away. You see me when I travel and when I rest at home. You know everything I do. You know what I am going to say even before I say it, Lord. You go before me and follow me. You place your hand of blessing on my head. Such knowledge is too wonderful for me, too great for me to understand." Psalm 139:1-6

02

ELON MUSK
WOULDN'T MIND
BEING SAVED

ELON MUSK WOULDN'T MIND BEING SAVED 1[1]

"Everyone who calls on the name of the LORD will be saved"[2]

The world's richest man is a damaged man. He has done much good for humanity, but he is not good, nor does he think he is. He has agreed that Western civilization is doomed without Christianity. He said, "The West is absolutely screwed if it loses Christianity." In fact, he thinks of it as society's immune system that keeps people sort of in line. He has suggested that he would like it if God would like to save him. I think he means he wouldn't turn down eternal life. At the same time, if he goes to Hell he is ok with it since the vast majority of all humans ever born will be there.[3]

Musk is a head-spinning study of how a damaged soul can do so much good for humanity, and yet be disconnected from empathy. He provided the internet for the Ukrainians after being attacked by Russia. He has hired thousands, yes, he has fired hundreds of thousands. He has built electric cars, yet he believes if a few million humans die driving them with their eyes closed, that is collateral damage. Because, after all, the goal is to populate Mars, even though it takes nine months to get there and he has no plans to go. Yet it strikes me that I'm no better than him. I need God to save me as much as Musk. My soul is damaged, and no closer to God than his. So, what is the difference? I called upon the Lord. Musk is only contemplating it, and it is an open secret that he, himself, wouldn't mind being saved. I'm thinking it is just a matter of time for Elon.

---

1 The entire column series on Musk is based on Walter Isaacson's Biography of Musk. It richness and honesty will, I predict, earn him a Pulitzer Prize. I cannot overstate the magnificence of Isaacson's work. If you want to understand any great figure from Einstein to Kissinger, Isaacson is the "go to guy." Simon & Schuster, New York, NY, 2023.

2 Romans 10:13 New Living Translation

3 Taken from the Christian Post, Jon Brown, Wednesday, January 03, 2024

I find myself praying for him, even though I might not like him, nor he me. I don't think I would want to live next door to him. For Musk, he has many homes and many next doors. He would be a lousy neighbor, never mowing his lawn, cleaning his gutters, or doing a garage sale. And I don't think I would enjoy the helicopter pad or the private runway for his plane. Then there are the protesters and the surveillance by his security details—like a scene out of *Dr. No*.[4] Where is James Bond when you need him? Musk might take me hostage and put me on a plane to Mars strapped into a seat next to Bill Clinton.

Elon is one of those souls that Jesus said was not far from the kingdom of God. *Realizing how much the man understood, Jesus said to him, 'You are not far from the Kingdom of God.' And after that, no one dared to ask him any more questions.*[5] At the same time, Musk said he doesn't really worship anything—he didn't even pray when he almost died of malaria.[6] Musk was baptized, received communion as a child in South Africa, and you might say he admires the teachings of Jesus. He, in some ways, is a fan of Jesus, but Musk's unbelief is an argument against child baptism making a person a Christian. It not only can work really well in some cases, but it can be a dumpster fire in people like Musk. If you are told about your baptism when you are older, yet you have seen no reality of Christ in those around you or friends in similar circumstances, you are almost always going to dismiss it as an irrelevant tradition. It's like a bunch of athletes crossing themselves and then cussing like a gangster rapper talking trash to opponents. In the post-game interview saying, "I would like to thank my Lord Jesus Christ for the win" and then seasoning their vocabulary with language that needs to be bleeped out. Some might protest that such language is a cultural expression, I would call it bad religion and the rot of a decadent society.

---

4   1962 James Bond film, starring Sean Connery as James Bond, Joseph Wiseman as Dr.No, with Ursula Andress as Honey Ryder

5   Mark 12:34 NLT

6   Ibid, Christian Post, Jon Brown

Musk says he likes the ethics of Jesus, the Sermon on the Mount kind of stuff. He would describe himself as a deist. Then it is so Musk of him to say, "But hey, if Jesus is saving people, I mean, I won't stand in the way. Sure, I'll be saved. Why not?" Yet, Elon is standing in the way, his own way to salvation. But no more than I did, or some readers of this column. I recall recruiting trips in college where many schools invited me to play basketball and receive a scholarship. I enjoyed visiting many schools. Because of a personal friendship with one of their players, I decided to visit the least likely school I could attend, Oral Roberts University in Tulsa Oklahoma, named after the healing evangelist, Oral Roberts. I decided to make an unscheduled stop in Tulsa at a stripper bar, and danced with a stripper on a table, then went out to campus at 2:00 AM. I was walking through the campus screaming, "Jesus saves, Jesus saves." I was mocking the whole stupid thing. Something deep inside of me, however, told me I was a goner. With my grandmother's prayers echoing in my soul, I chose ORU. People were aghast, they made fun of me—I even changed my mind a couple of times before it was all said and done.

Musk is a damaged soul and he needs and desires so deeply to be healed. He, like us all, needs to stop playing God, get on his knees, and get it over with. But he must swallow his pride and be mocked by his family, friends, and the elites of the world, the desperados who think they run this world and are smarter than the populace. They may be smart, but they are as dumb as donkeys when it comes to reality. Reality is the kingdom above, beyond, and outside of this world.

A reality that cannot be captured by time or space, God exists in a stacked simultaneous reality that we cannot even imagine. It is greater than a trip to Mars or any other speck in our solar system. God invented time, he created humans, even in that cradle in Bethlehem. Musk is not going to Hell, because he is about to get caught by the hound of heaven. It was all written down before he was born, God saw his beginning and his end.[7]

---

7 Psalm 139

I was reminded yesterday that even though my purpose on earth is to be a witness for Christ and to, as a disciple, make more disciples, I am not responsible for anything else. My mind wandered back to an idea from Dallas Willard. To paraphrase him, *I have given up on changing the world, it's far beyond my ability. I have given up on changing the church, it always causes havoc to try and make people do what they don't want to do. No one comes to believe they are a sinner by being told they are a sinner. It is an inner work of the Holy Spirit that brings a person to that decision. Now my focus is to change me. I do have some control over it and making myself available to God falls within the realm of my will. When I begin to concentrate on giving up my life for the gospel daily, it leads to a fullness of life that crams my life with joy daily. It is the idea of joy spilling out of us when reality bumps into us. If you are filled with anxiety and anger, when reality bumps you, you spill out anxiety and anger. When you are filled with joy, you spill out joy.* I'm really not concerned about Elon Musk being saved. I don't have any control over that. But I can assure you, if I ever run into him and he knocks me around verbally or totally ignores me, I will spill some joy on him.[8]

---

8 Nearly impossible to give precise attribution on this paragraph. Some of it is Dallas Willard, then there is Acts 1:8, Luke 9:23-25, Dr. Henry Brandt, Matthew 28:18-20. It is a blend of what I have internalized in the last twenty-five years.

ELON MUSK WOULDN'T MIND BEING SAVED

ELON MUSK WOULDN'T MIND BEING SAVED 2

"Whose red pill?"

When a person is accused of taking the "red pill" many of us just nod our heads and assume it is negative and has something to do with being brainwashed. Even though cryptic, it does have a history that could be useful, even enlightening. It begins with the 1999 film, *The Matrix,* when a computer whiz discovers he has been living in a computer simulation. The character is given a choice of taking a blue pill which will allow him to forget all he has seen and return to the comfort of his regular life or take the red pill which would show him the real truth. Subsequently, "take the red pill" became the rallying cry for movements trying to convince others to face the truth about reality. Musk said it concerning the COVID-19 lockdowns and the national mandates imposed on the public during those months. This phrase can, and is, used to censure any group that disagrees with the accuser. It can be used against atheists, Christians, a political party, or Congress. Since Musk was upset with how it affected his *Tesla* factory, he was strongly anti-mandate and said so in 2020.

The Christian red pill.

Christians are often accused of being useless idiots, essentially, of being fools. They are said to be flat earth, knuckle-dragging types that believe in an iron age religion. Yet the Bible makes an extraordinary claim:

> *"The foolish plan of God is wiser than the wisest of human plans, and God's weakness is stronger than the greatest of human strength."*
> —I Corinthians 1: 25-30

The Apostle Paul is throwing around many times over our English word, fool or foolishness, in the text from 1 Corinthians 1:17-2:16. He was called a fool when he preached to the Athenian philosophers on Mars Hill. He claimed that while God is unknown to most, he could be known. He said all this holy nonsense was wiser and stronger than anything humans could invent, create, or imagine. Those of us who have experienced new birth, have taken God's "red pill" and have swallowed it whole—gulp—we have become fools for God. The Bible says a fool has said in his or her heart, there is no God.[1]

Today's culture is morally confused and is, indeed, a *Ship of Fools* cutting its way through the cultural sea, being blown about by wayward winds, lost at sea—but they live in an illusion thinking they are on a pleasure cruise.

Fools

We believers are fools. Every day we must decide, actually every moment, whose fool we are. I choose daily to be a fool for Christ.[2] Musk has his own red pill, and I have mine. They both could be red, but that is just the color, it is the contents of the pill that matters.

Elon Musk, you might remember, is open to being saved—after all, it does solve the death problem. Or does it? It could turn out that all humans will exist forever, some without God or any goodness, rest, or peace. But some will live in celestial bliss with God—being able to roam the entire solar system that God has created for us. At the same time, God's best for those who refuse to bow to him will exist forever in limited space, absent of God's presence and peace.

---

1 Psalm 14:1

2 English word Fool means silly, stupid, ignorant. It can mean mad or insane. The Greek word [the language of the New Testament] etymology is without reason, basically the same as most languages. See 1Corinthians 4:10.

The *knowing* that is in the red pill

Reality is what you bump into and it often hurts. God's principle of sowing and reaping for example. Reality is knowledge of the Kingdom of God. God's kingdom is wherever his will is being done. It could be in a city, a nation, a household or in a person. Whatever that realm is the kingdom exists. "Thy will be done on earth as it is in heaven."[3] It is what God invites us into, it is in the red pill. Most cultures, religions, and proverbial truths fall short of the specific or final meaning of life. Most say in one way or another, "Only God knows." If you don't know God, then you don't know what God knows. The Biblical record is jammed with the claim, "We know." For example, Romans 8:28 begins with, "We know…" we know what God knows, it is a special knowledge only available to those who take the pill, who are reborn, who give up their life in order to get it back in multiples.[4]

Yes, there are people walking around with special knowledge, they know what God is thinking because they are plugged into the "mind of Christ."[5] Even when we are in pain and are in the last phases of this present life, WE KNOW we are about to begin a new life, one that is eternal and satisfies our deepest longing, because we were made for it. But we won't go quietly into the night. We fight for life because life is precious—we are just eternal beings stuck in time and space. We struggle, we fight, yet look forward. It's all such a mystery, and we are just now scratching the underside of God's glory.[6]

---

3 The Lord's Prayer
4 John 3:1-10, Luke 9:23-25
5 I Corinthians 2:10-16. Especially the idea that no one knows the thoughts of God except God's own Spirit. We have God's Spirit, therefore we know what he is thinking-we see through his eyes.
6 I Corinthians 13:12 We are looking through a glass darkly.

Knowledge is different than belief

Elon Musk has much knowledge, his ability to marshal his vast genius and apply it to many serious technical problems is nearly super-human. His vast contribution to humankind is also impressive and he is a great man in many respects. But he is ignorant when it comes to what God is thinking. We can believe something that is wrong, all of us do. Your team is down forty points with two minutes left and the cheerleaders are yelling, "We can still win!" That is how the system works. We can believe something wrong and then make a commitment to it. Belief and commitment are not knowledge. Musk believes and is totally committed to placing billions of people in outer space where they can live a better life. But knowledge says, nope, that is not the reality of the human being. Science, math, technology or human genius cannot teach anyone why you should be a good person. In the Sermon on the Mount Jesus said, *"Unless your righteousness exceeds that of the Scribes and the Pharisees, you cannot enter the Kingdom of Heaven."* [7]

Supernatural power vs scientific method

How could Elon Musk, you, and I become kind, gentle, joyful, and loving toward others? It would take special knowledge and supernatural inner power to transform a human at the most intimate level. The scientific method is not set up to examine or create good people. When Harvard University studies prayer it can only tell you sociological truths, but the study cannot and will not create the conditions of what it is like for a human to talk with God like he is a friend. Reason itself is a gift from God. Paul put it so well, *"God has not given us a spirit of fear, but love, power, and a sound mind."* [8] The sound mind part is reason. Reason is the friend and the servant of faith. They work hand in hand to make life

---

7   Matthew 5:20 This is the nexus of the entire Sermon.

8   2 Timothy 1:7 New American Standard

workable. Musk uses both, he makes cars, spaceships, internet, and many useful things built on reason and knowledge. We should be thankful for his contribution to our lives. But Elon is suffering, he is damaged, he creates much pain for himself and those around him. People fear him, worship him, and use him to get rich. Pray for Elon, that he will be saved from all that and be able to have joy, peace, and be a healing balm to those in his life. Maybe someday you will run into him and catch him nodding off in a coffee shop, that would be a greater accomplishment than SpaceX.

ELON MUSK WOULDN'T MIND BEING SAVED 3

The Sins of the Fathers

"You must not make for yourself an idol of any kind, or an image of anything in the heavens or on the earth or in the sea. You must not bow down to them, for I, the Lord your God, am a jealous God who will not tolerate your affection for any other gods. I lay the sins of the parents upon their children; the entire family is affected—even children in the third and fourth generations of those who reject me. But I lavish unfailing love for a thousand generations on those who love me and obey my commands."

—Deuteronomy 5:8-10 NIV

"We have the fire and the wood, the boy said, but where is the sheep for the burnt offering?"

—Genesis 22:7

"It is easier to build strong children than to repair broken men."

—Frederick Douglass [1]

Why is Elon Musk the way he is? He lacks empathy, is ruthless, and his relationships largely are in shambles. One could say it is genetics and, in a way, that is true. But if you wanted to be concise you would simply say, his father, Errol. Just reading about Errol's treatment of Elon and his younger siblings is a painful experience. Much of the damage was done by Elon's 10th birthday but was enhanced greatly when he decided to move in with his father and not to stay with his newly divorced mother and his siblings. He arrived on the night train in Johannesburg alone revealing a lack of

---

1 https://www.artofmanliness.com/people/fatherhood/the-ultimate-collection-of-quotes-about-fatherhood/

parental care. Elon was about to enter into a highly dysfunctional environment. Forty years later, Musk remains ambivalent about his father and regrets the decision.[2]

Later, Elon, along with his brother Kimbal, moved into a Game Reserve one hundred miles east of Pretoria. Some of the parental neglect included taking them on international trips where he would give the boys some money and disappear, for example, in Hong Kong for several days. Also, having had to watch the dysfunctional relationship of his parents, the yelling, Errol's promiscuity, the eventual divorce, and the tug-of-war regarding the children added to his trauma. What makes the dysfunction stand out is the general neglect of the father. The boys would visit their father and return with no clothes or food. He would leave them alone to fend for themselves—two boys on their own without care, roaming freely in dangerous environments. The family ethic was when you meet someone, punch them in the nose before they punch you. Establish your dominance.

Elon the damaged genius

Elon was a genius, had undiagnosed Asperger's, and in an interview in *Rolling Stone*[3] magazine he confessed, "I never want to be alone. That's what I would say…I don't want to be alone." The reason Musk wouldn't mind being "Saved"[4] is that Hell itself is not fellowship. It is the ultimate in loneliness because God won't be there. No person living now can fathom life without the presence of God.

---

2   I must remind the reader that general content and history of Elon Musk comes from Walter Isaacson's great biography Elon Musk. Simon and Schuster, New York, 2023. I also must remind the reader that what is written is in my own words. I take full responsibility, blame or credit for my prose.

3   https://www.rollingstone.com/culture/culture-features/elon-musk-the-architect-of-tomorrow-120850/

4   "Saved" The general biblical idea that one through Christ can be "Saved" redeemed and have eternal life. Sounds better than a nine month trip to Mars strapped into a seat next to a Billionaire from Norway.

God sustains creation with common grace. Hell is a place absent of grace. Hell is the best God can do for people who don't want to be with him. As C.S. Lewis posits in his fictional masterpiece, *The Great Divorce,* in Hell people move as far as they can from one another. One can only imagine the hell one experiences when angry, hostile, resentful people have unlimited time to get worse.

Elon was odd and temperamental. In school he would zone out, staring out of windows or remain unresponsive to fellow students. He would call them stupid, he couldn't make friends, he would stay up all night reading, and slept very little. He was fierce, with an extraordinary ability to focus and stay on point. He would ignore everyone around him, their wants, their desires, and welfare. Today at 52 years of age, his fundamentals are the same, the biggest difference is the many children he has spawned—they have been able to moderate his personality, but his effect on them has been much greater. The other side of Musk is that these traits have created much good for humankind; automobiles, internet: Starlink, advancement in technology, space exploration, and medicine.

Why would the richest most stubborn man on earth consider submitting to God? There are many ways to say it, because he has a deeper need that he knows is there, but he can't explain it. It is something like the Psalmist who wrote that God "restores his soul."[5] You may remember that in the first column in this Musk series, he said that he would be open to God "saving" him, even though he didn't suspect that God would take unilateral action to do so.

Elon Musk is in deep pain, he lives every day with the contradictions of his soul. None of us like pain, but human life would be impossible without it. Pain is the gift that no one likes. No infant, no person, can live thirty days without pain. People who ask for a painless world don't know what they are asking for.[6] God allows

---

5   Psalm 23:1-3

6   Think of maladies such as neuropathy or in ancient times leprosy, the great damage that is done because the victim cannot feel pain in vital parts of the body.

people to suffer because he is benevolent. As the philosopher, Dallas Willard, wrote, "Few people stop to ask themselves if they deserve to live in paradise. They just want to. And when they don't get what they want, they feel insulted."[7]

God is quite interested in Elon Musk. In fact, he is presently working through his pain and pathology drawing him closer to salvation. Whether God succeeds is not yet known to us or Musk. In the final analysis, Musk has a mind of his own, and if a person wants to hide from God, God will accommodate them and hide from them. God won't interrupt the decision, but mysteriously, he never stops being part of the decision. If you can't wrap your mind around that, then good—get on your knees and enjoy the glorious God that is holding all of creation in the hollow of His hand.

What Meanth[8] This?

It means that our character and conduct matters because it has a multigenerational impact. Musk's father Errol matters. What went on in that family home in South Africa fifty years ago is now multiplied through a genius son who is presently the world's richest man. Our culture has trouble getting its mind around the fact that the most important work many of us will do is raising children. The family is the most powerful means for building, preserving, or destroying a civilization. This is clear from the passage from Deuteronomy 5:8-10 NIV that began this column. Any human life has generational impact, especially that of the parent.

General society is built from one generation to the next on character. Societal improvement or decline is based on it. Human

---

7 Dallas Willard, The Allure of Gentleness, Kindle edition @ 60%> My favorite book on apologetics, a true celestial feast.

8 King James English. Isn't it interesting that the King James version of scripture released in 1611 was not written in an English that most English people spoke or could write. Another genuflect to the aristocracy. It was also based on an inferior Greek text called the Textus Receptus- Latin for received text, look it up.

conduct cannot save a world, but it can be used to accomplish divine goals. It must be admitted that success breeds compliancy and decline. This is a frustrating human malady. This is the reason when an NFL team wins the Super Bowl, it is so hard to repeat. Everyone gets rich, famous, and distracted. Maintaining the same level of focus and work ethic is nearly impossible, then another team peaks and defeats them. This is true of families, communities, nations, and people in general. Western Civilization will fail and fall. It could be that the post-World War II era has been a short period of success that will stand out as unusual in human history. What we can do is intentionally submit ourselves daily to follow our leader, Jesus—just as he did to his father. As I have told many a person, "Follow Jesus, and he will teach you everything you will ever need to know."

ELON MUSK WOULDN'T MIND BEING SAVED 4

The Curse of Genius, Putting the Babel back in Babylon.

"Then they said, "Come, let's build a great city for ourselves with a tower that reaches into the sky…But the Lord came down to look at the city and the tower the people were building. "Look!" he said. "The people are united and they all speak the same language…Come, let's[1] go down and confuse the people with different languages. Then they won't be able to understand each other."

—Genesis 11:4-7

"If anyone among you seems to be wise in this age, let him become a fool that he may become wise. For the wisdom of the world is foolishness with God. For it is written, "He catches the wise in their own craftiness;" and again, "The Lord knows the thoughts of the wise, that they are futile."

—I Corinthians 3:18-20

"To anyone I've offended, I just want to say, I reinvented electric cars and I'm sending people to Mars in a rocket ship. Did you think I was also going to be a chill, normal dude?"

—Elon Musk, Saturday Night Live, May 8, 2021[2]

There is no doubt, some people are smarter than others. Elon Musk, Asperger's and all, is brilliant. His brain has raw speed combined with great capacity. The brain is a marvel of creation, but it also is only necessary to terrestrials and fish. God the Father and The Holy Spirit don't have brains. They don't need them, they, not

---

1 The use of "Let's" more than implied the Triune God, a community, a personage, one being in three persons, that existed outside of time and space.

2 Walter Isaacson, Elon Musk. Simon & Schuster, New York. Cited next to title page from Saturday Night Live

having bodies, have no place to put them. Jesus however, does, but of course, he needed one for incarnation. I recall telling a close friend during a golf match that God didn't have a brain. He stepped away from his shot, "What!" he stood looking at me with a puzzled look on his face. Intelligence did not originate in the material realm. In essence, God is immaterial, He is knowledge, information, the logos: word, the truth behind all being.[3]

I also know from experience that the human brain declines and gets slower and diseased, and finally, medical science will begin to study it, tinker with it, and attempt to keep it going. But eventually, it dies, our bodies die, but *we* don't. Ok, back to earth. Humans with big fast brains and the egos to go with them accomplish great things. They skip grades in school, win spelling bees, and until recently, they got into the best schools, were included in the power elite, and usually made a fortune in the process. You add to this, as in Elon Musk's case, an abusive childhood that erased his human empathy, a relentless drive to reach a specific goal, e.g. populating Mars and outer space with billions of people, essentially, with his brain, saving humankind. He has gotten into his lightening quick cortex that he will not be defeated—he will triumph over everyone. He will *smoke* Bill Gates or anyone else who disagrees with him. He will fire everyone he can't control—who will not bow to him—except his sons. He will make *Tesla, SpaceX, Starlink* and return free speech to Western Civilization on the way to saving the *late great planet Earth.*[4] I have great affection for this genius, but he is trying to build a tower into the heavens and God will bring confusion and stop Elon and any other highly competent genius from self-destruction. God stops them because he loves us, because if he doesn't stop us, we will incinerate ourselves, and it will indeed become the

---

3 John 4:24 "For God is Spirit, so those who worship him must worship in Spirit and in truth." NLT

4 My shout out to Hal Lindsay, Author of the late 1960s book The Late Great Planet Earth. Great book title, now appropriate to use but for different reasons than Hal had in mind.

late, great, planet Earth. Musk is not unique in that every person on earth will use what power and ability they have to achieve their goals. And many don't have the restraint or good intentions of Elon Musk. He wants to help others. Many dumber egomaniacs have malevolent intentions. In fact, given the right circumstances, every human on earth would build their own tower into the heavens.

A fool or a fool for Christ? Decide.

"If anyone among you seems to be wise in this age, let him become a fool that he may become wise. For the wisdom of the world is foolishness with God. For it is written, "He catches the wise in their own craftiness;" and again, "The Lord knows the thoughts of the wise, that they are futile." —I Corinthians 3:18-20

Have you ever thought, "Boy, that was clever of me?" I must confess, yes, many a time. It brings hubris, conceit, sometimes guilt. That is the way we work, get used to it. I will not stain the page with my examples. But as a great hymn says, "He took all my guilty stains."[5]

Rather than continue depending on our brain power and our innovations, we must listen to the Apostle Paul, another genius, but one who got knocked off his horse, given a *good* chastizing and rebuking by God, and blinded for three days, who recommends becoming a fool. Yes, a fool! When you choose Jesus as your Rabbi, and become his apprentice, walking in his ways, and in his dust—You have chosen the foolishness of God and have rejected the wisdom of the geniuses of this cosmos. Anything else is futile, God laughs in his heaven at our attempts to run the world.

Being a fool for Christ doesn't preclude benefitting from the genius of the world. Yes, we will take the pills, new knee joints, hips, and medical wonders. We will fly in the planes and drive the cool cars. But we will never make the mistake that any of it lasts for long or that we are in any way in control. If you don't believe your life is

---

5   There is a Fountain, William Cowper, 1772

a mystery, a puzzle, then you are not paying attention. "God knows the thoughts of the wise, that they are futile." That should give any human pause. Every culture has a way of saying, "Only God knows." It means at some point we get on our knees before the ultimate reality, Christ on the cross. God dying for me. And why did it need to be Jesus? I was telling my personal physician during a very human moment that he didn't really have the final answers to my health and well-being. He can look at the science and talk with me, but unless he could somehow get into my person, my body, and live for a few weeks, would he understand the best for me? That is what incarnation is—God becoming one of us, living with us and in us. God had to do it for it to be authentic. It had to be his blood, his life, otherwise, hanging on a cross is just another person dying. So, drop the genius thing, start following Jesus today.

ELON MUSK WOULDN'T MIND BEING SAVED

ELON MUSK WOULDN'T MIND BEING SAVED 5

The Weight of Glory, we are too easily pleased.

"At present we are on the outside of the world, the wrong side of the door. We discern the freshness and purity of morning, but they do not make us fresh and pure. We cannot mingle with the splendors we see. But all the leaves of the New Testament are rustling with the rumor that it will not always be so."

—C. S. Lewis[1]

If I were standing next to Elon Musk on a beautiful sunny day, I would ask him how long he supposes it will take for the sun to fizzle out. You know, burn out, lose its power, and go away. He would probably throw out a figure something higher than a billion years.[2] Then I would say, "Elon, when the sun burns out, you will still be alive." He might smirk and call me stupid. I would retort, however, "Elon, a *saved* person will reside in a new heaven and a new earth and frolic with pleasures unimagined by any human. It will be glorious, a glory whose weight is much more than any human can carry or comprehend."

I see something much greater than religion when I gaze at the universe. The religious establishment has always been afraid of losing power and its market share. This was certainly true in the first century. But God is much greater than religion, greater than Christianity, and even greater than the prevailing institutions. As the

---

1   C. S. Lewis. *The Weight of Glory,* (Preached as a sermon in Church of St. Mary the Virgin, Oxford), June 8, 1942. Published in THEOLOGY, November 1941, Page 8

2   Science tells us about 5 Billion years. Then it will go through the phases of star death. But then the ancient book called the Bible says this, "On that day, he will set the heavens on fire and the elements will melt away in the flames. But we are looking forward to the new heavens and the new earth he has promised, a world filled with God's righteousness." I Peter3:1213. NLT

sociologist Peter Berger penned, "The Revelation of God in Jesus Christ…is something very different from religion."[3]

But God has spoken exclusively and completely in the person of Christ Jesus—this is what we call incarnation. God created us in his image, positioned himself as a Father, and humans who seek him, as his family. That does not, however, mean that God himself is limited to personhood. We must allow God to be even more than we can imagine, far weightier than our minds can understand or even embrace. The heavens *do* declare the glory of the Lord and that is what most people see. At the same time, they become skeptical of the church as an institution. The *Logos,* or *Jesus* is a word, a communication to us much more profound and penetrating than any holy building or church tradition. That is what I want Musk to see—what God wants us to see.

Elon's vision of populating Mars and outer space with billions of people is too small. Next to God, Mars is small potatoes, child's play. At first blush, most think Musk's plans are visionary and bold even though those same people think him crazy, zany, and out of this world. I would accuse him of being too easily pleased. Too easily pleased with what he can imagine or think up in his own head. There is some humor—God even laughs at the limitations of his creatures. A Sunday evening sermon given by an Oxford professor in 1942, even today, presents possibilities that reveal our limits.[4]

Lewis's most famous passage from that sermon puts it plainly. *"Our Lord finds our desires, not too strong, but too weak. We are half-hearted creatures, fooling about with drink and sex and ambition when infinite joy is offered us, like an ignorant child who wants to go on making mud pies in a slum because he cannot imagine what is meant by the offer of a holiday at the sea. We are far too easily pleased."*[5]

Where does a person go from here? There are so many angles and options to consider. Haven't we all heard that being hard to

---

3   Berger, Peter. *The Precarious Vision* (Garden City, NY: Doubleday, 1961), page 163

4   C.S. Lewis was the Oxford professor, and The Weight of Glory cited above was the sermon

5   Ibid page 1

please is a negative? One of the most negative aspects of Musk's personality is he is almost entirely unpleasable. Being unpleasable is off-putting—no one can work with him—only the desperate survive. I doubt that is what Lewis meant. Isn't it equally confusing because Lewis is saying we need to be harder to please, yet we desire to please God? I recall the verse in Hebrews 11:6, "Without faith, it is impossible to please God." I think Lewis is saying there is a weight of glory, that Musk's ambitions and our ambitions are too light; they lack the needed gravitas. The Hebrew word for Glory means "heavy." Real glory is not fame, it is the salvation of humankind and its results are the ultimate weighty reality. The act of discipleship then, is to follow Jesus and learn from him. He will teach us.

The schoolboy

Lewis uses a simple idea to explain how we move forward. Please allow me to summarize: The schoolboy begins Greek grammar. He cannot imagine reading or even liking the great Greek classics. At first, he is dedicated to parsing verbs, declining nouns, memorizing vocabulary, and remembering rules. He gets rewarded step by step and then enjoyment begins to creep into his life. He can't remember exactly when it took place, but drudgery left, and joy began. He grew to love Sophocles, or, as in my case, the Greek New Testament. And as Lewis states:

"Poetry replaces grammar, gospel replaces law, longing transforms obedience, as gradually as the tide lifts a grounded ship."[6]

Jesus as your teacher

How many times have you started getting serious and attempting to practice the ways and means of Jesus—and you didn't last long? It can be drudgery at first; memorizing scripture, trying your

---

6 Ibid page 2

hand at fasting, and scheduling thirty minutes a day to read and pray. Even going to church regularly can be difficult, especially since people there annoy you. But if you keep it up, the process changes you and transforms your drudgery into a new desire. There is a passage of invitation to all of us that puts this together.

Come to me, all of you who are weary and carry heavy burdens, and I will give you rest. Take my yoke upon you. Let me teach you, because I am humble and gentle of heart, and you will find rest for your souls. For my yoke is easy to bear, and the burden I give you is light.[7]

Jesus had just toldas the people of Capernaum that even though they were corrupt and had lost their way, they could follow him and he would be their teacher. The burden of keeping the rules and being right weighed upon them. He promised them relief, that they could take *his* yoke.

His yoke, he claimed, was easy to bear and light. Many interpret the yoke to be a simple illustration of the familiar agrarian life, two oxen yoked together. It probably is true that while oxen were literally yoked together, Rabbis and disciples of that era were metaphorically yoked together.

It was a more comforting way of saying, follow me, learn from me, and your drudgery will be transformed into longing, new more significant desires, infinitely more weighty, true glory. Take another look Mr. Musk, what do you see now?

---

7 Matthew 11:28-30 NLT

ELON MUSK WOULDN'T MIND BEING SAVED

ELON MUSK WOULDN'T MIND BEING "SAVED" 6

Shredded Tweet.

"But those who trust in the Lord will find new strength. They will soar high on wings like eagles. They will run and not grow weary. They will walk and not faint."

—Isaiah 40:31 New Living Translation.

"I tawt I taw a puddy tat!"

—Tweety Bird

The story begins on a hot, muggy, summer day in a small un-air-conditioned house 5 miles north of Grove, Oklahoma. It was the 1950s, the doors and windows were open, yet there was no breeze. Only a single fan on the living room floor provided solace to the kids. It oscillated back and forth providing everyone a turn to feel a tiny bit of relief and have fun talking into it to hear their voices buzz. Even the family parakeet, Willie, who had been let out of his cage for a bit of exercise seemed to enjoy the flow of air that felt good on his wings. Needing a rest, he flew down to this new wire perch. In an instant, there was a burst of feathers! Willie was scattered around the living room, a tragic episode known as "Shredded Tweet."[1]

Excuse the pun but "Tweet" is what the *Twitterverse* does—at last count, there were 245 million daily active users of Twitter, re-branded X, worldwide. Twitter has definitely been shredded by its new owner, Elon Musk.

But Musk is trying to arrest the cultural elite's attempts to censor speech and restore freedom of speech to the American public. Musk is quite brave in taking on impossible and thankless missions. Whether it be Tesla automobiles, SpaceX, the audacious mission to Mars and beyond, or providing internet to nations in distress via

---

1 I have an affidavit containing sworn testimony from my wife this truly happened

Starlink, he has shredded his most important relationships—wives, children, colleagues, associates, and employees. His intensity fueled by anger and his own abusive background, intimidates, torments, and humiliates those around him. I don't believe he will ever reach his goals and then decide to rest.

Biographer, Walter Isaacson, recounts many an example. On one occasion during the Tesla productions Musk gave a speech to his team, "Welcome! Welcome! Welcome to production hell! That's where we are going to be for at least six months." Isaacson goes on, *"That prospect, like all hellish dramas, seemed to fill him with dark energy.* "I look forward to working alongside you journeying through hell," he told his startled audience. "As the saying goes, if you're going through hell, just keep going. He was, and he did."[2]

Working with Musk required total commitment, sleeping under your desk if you ever slept at all, eating fast food, blood pressure rising, back breaking pressure, never ending critique and only enough praise drips out of the Musk faucet to survive, more people survive the *Navy Seals Hell Week.* No one can do it very long. That is because they, us, all of us, are human. Musk has run hard and so have his workers. But they have grown weary, weak, and faint.

Something very deep drives him. Like the character, *Atlas,* from Greek mythology, he has been sentenced by the god, Zeus, to carry the weight of the world on his shoulders.[3] Will he shrug? Or should

---

2   Walter Isaacson, *Elon Musk* (New York: Simon and Schuster, 2023), 270. (I am not sure Isaacson footnoted Musk's statement on going through Hell. It is well known that generally the statement is attributed to Sir Winston Churchill.)

3   In Greek Mythology, Zeus ordered Atlas to hold up the sky on his shoulders as his punishment for leading a rebellion. It became known as holding the world. Ayn Rand, the leader of the Objectivist Movement authored Atlas Shrugged, a novel about the man John Galt. There are various interpretations of the 1957 novel, everything from the elite must take the responsibility to make the world better, to the great leaders who ignore the burden of the world and dedicate themselves to personal success. The famous image of Atlas carrying the globe on his back indicates either that it is too heavy for man to carry, or if he shrugs, he drops it. Good or bad? You decide.

we ask, how long before he does shrug and drop the weight of the world. He seems hell bent to change everything. Eventually it will destroy him, for a man cannot do God's work for him. We are co-laborers with Christ, much like a co-pilot is under the direction of the airplane's Captain. Musk seems doomed in his attempt to take on the task.

Thank you, Elon

Right now, X is about censorship and freedom of speech. This is another vital service Musk provides for America, and for that, he should be thanked. The world's richest man can fund projects that garner great publicity, fame, and opposition.

But what about the rest of us, faces in the crowd, the multitude, how do we fit into the world scene? It seems that the average follower of Jesus is asked to carry the weight of the world. We are told we are world changers, revolutionaries, missionaries, witnesses, and that we must preach the gospel to every people group in the world, then Jesus will return.[4]

To every person, an answer

The contemporary culture is a moral morass. People are confused and troubled. Deep questions about the meaning of life are milling about just below the surface of their mundane conversation and daily duties. Interestingly, there has never been more content and answers available to the general public than right now. We are witnesses, we are ambassadors, but mostly we are just present in daily life next to people with questions.

We feel inadequate talking about spiritual life. It is too diverse and depends on what they want to discuss. It could be anything from evolution, the Big Bang, the forming of various universes, solar systems, black holes, and the development of DNA. It goes on

---

4 Matthew 28:18,20, Acts 1:8, Matthew 24:14

and on. It may be the problem of suffering, evil, the authenticity of the Bible, the hypocrisy of Christians, and the failure of the clergy. A favorite, of course, is the problem with wealthy tele-ministers and pastors in the evangelical community. Then, there are the entire fields of philosophy, history, different religions, miracles, *et al.*

What, me worry? —Alfred E. Newman

We should not worry about all this. What Peter wrote in the first century is more vital today than ever before. Peter was known to be an impetuous show-off. Jesus used him as a foil in his teachings about what not to do. At the same time, he nicknamed him "Rocky," had him walk on water, then let him make a fool of himself, and for all that, he became the front man for the movement. The day of Pentecost, Peter stepped forward and out came a prophetic pronouncement, a sermon, and the most famous ask and close in human history. By the time Peter penned the words in his first epistle, he had learned and experienced a great deal. His ability to interact with people is evidence of his vast experience, patience, and wisdom.

"Now, who will want to harm you if you are eager to do good? But even if you suffer for doing what is right, God will reward you for it. So, don't worry or be afraid of their threats. Instead, you must worship Christ as Lord of your life. **And if someone asks about your Christian hope, always be ready to explain it.** *But do this in a gentle and respectful way. Keep your conscience clear. Then if people speak against you, they will ashamed when they see what a good life you live because you belong to Christ."* [5]

We are all apologists, but...

Apologetics for many, means arguments. The majority of people on both sides of issues don't enjoy arguments. Therefore, not many

---

5   I Peter 3:13-16 NLT

Christians want to be apologists, and most non-Christians don't desire to argue about it. I recall my old friend, Dallas Willard, a great philosopher and even better person, refused to debate. He was asked to do so, being an articulate and knowledgeable proponent of the Christian faith. He, however, considered it non-productive, and just an exercise in winning and losing. He thought it was trying to get your opponent to simply shut up.

Neither Willard nor I would suggest there isn't a place for formal debates and arguments. They are stimulating and entertaining. I'm for them and have attended and even participated in them. I wholeheartedly support those who are called to such work. While not a professional debater or philosopher, I love to hear it, I love to do it myself. But the vast majority of those who God called to make disciples are not wired for it, nor have been trained to engage in formal settings. The good news is, that like Atlas, you can shrug now and drop the world, the weight you have been lugging about is no more. Once again, I like Willard on the weight of responsibility at the end of his collected works, **The Great Omission.**

A Conundrum

What to do now? Convert the world? No. Convert the church? Judgment, it is famously said, "begins at the house of God." It has the divine light and divine provisions, and because of that is the most responsible to guide humankind. But, *no* again. Do not *convert the church*. Your first move, "…as you go…" is, in a manner of speaking: convert *me*. Our maestro never told us to covert the world or to reform any religious organizations. He did tell us that, when filled with Him we would bear witness of Him "…to the ends of the earth…"

The Master said to his disciples. "Make disciples." We have no other God-appointed business but this, and we must allow all else to fall away if it will."[6]

---

6 Dallas Willard, The Great Omission, (Nashville: Harper Collins, 2006). 225

So, shrug

Don't carry the weight of the world on your shoulders. It is about the people we meet every day, so now, in that context read the words of Peter.

*And if someone asks about your Christian hope, always be ready to **explain it**.* The word translated explain is απολογιαν, from which we derive apologetics. So yes, even a casual conversation over coffee about how God answered your prayer is apologetics. God is using you to remove doubt, to clear a path so the person can believe. In fact, no Christian can help doing it, being it, and communicating something about Christ. Dallas Willard's wonderful book that reveals his beautiful mind is entitled *The Allure of Gentleness.*[7]

Peter's idea is that most of the time, the disciple of Christ will be answering questions that people have because they have noticed that you are Christian. These questions often come when the person asking is in pain or confused. They could be looking for guidance, some wisdom, encouragement, comfort, but you are the one chosen to answer them. You don't have to go looking for these conversations. Just live the life of a disciple and it will come to you. In fact, you won't be able to field all the need that comes your way. But you must keep your eyes open and be ready. People will accuse you of doing wrong because we all do wrong. So, pray, study, prepare, and live—above all—live the abundant life.

I close with a final word

The Rule that will maintain your integrity:

Don't pretend to believe something you don't believe. If your words don't mean anything, your life doesn't mean anything.

---

[7] Dallas Willard, The Allure of Gentleness: Defending the faith in the manner of Jesus, (San Francisco: Harper One, 2016)

The temptation is to appease, to accommodate to find common ground. For example, don't pretend that all religions are the same so you won't be called names or disliked. All religions can't be alike—what an insult to every one of them. If you tell the truth you will be disliked, called names, and feel unsafe. *If you don't hold your ground, the enemy and most people will see blood in the water and go for the kill.* Jesus always told the truth—and it cost him. So, you tell the truth and you get a lower grade, you don't get into grad school, you lose your job, or you get blackballed in your profession. So what? Would you rather lose your soul and your self-respect? We are Jesus' disciples, He is our Rabbi, we follow Him, we say what He said, and we do what He did. God claimed to love us and proved it by becoming one of us. "God so love the world that he…" dropped a leaflet! NO, "…that he gave…" He gave himself in his Son. That is communication, that is λογος—the logic, pattern, and construct of the universe. Jesus was the Word of God to us in such a profound way it defied language or simple words. It required a person who was entirely us and entirely God. Fall on your knees, it's time to worship.

ELON MUSK WOULDN'T MIND BEING SAVED 7

Spaced Out.

The heavens proclaim the glory of God. The skies display his craftsmanship. Day after day they continue to speak; night after night they make him known. They speak without a sound or word; their voice is never heard. Yet their message has gone throughout the earth, and their words to all the world.

—Psalm 19:1-4a NLT.

"...ever since the world was created. People have seen the earth and sky. Through everything God made, they can clearly see his invisible qualities—his eternal power and divine nature. So they have no excuse for not knowing God."

—Romans 1:20 NLT.

"I'm going to colonize Mars. My mission in life is to make mankind a multiplanetary civilization."

—Elon Musk[1]

"Dude, you're bananas!"[2] rings a growing chorus upon hearing Musk's life mission statement. With our current technology, it takes nine months to get to Mars from Earth, unless his rocket technology is way better than he lets on. One can only imagine what the toilet would look like after the trip. The food alone needed for nine months would need to be transported in one of a fleet of supply rockets. You can't survive on *Mars Bars* alone. And when you get there, SO WHAT? And finally, WHAT FOR? Musk thinks staying here is a form of civilizational suicide, a global death wish. He has lost faith in humanity's ability to fix what is broken here and now.

---

1 Walter Isaacson, Elon Musk, Simon& Schuster New York, 2023 page 92
2 Ibid page 92, response from Mark Woolway

Out there vs right now

In Issacson's Musk biography, he devotes an entire chapter to Bill Gates and his meeting with Musk.[3] There were profound differences. Musk's vision is about "out there" and Gate's is "right here, right now." Musk wants to create a multi-planetary civilization. *Then and there* is always more attractive than *here and now*. Musk seemed to forget you can't breathe on Mars and the average daytime temperature is -80°. No wind chill, but it does cool off in the winter, you might need a sweater, the average temperature then is -125°. Did I mention there is little oxygen on Mars? I suppose that is why Martians are so little and green. It is postulated that one can live on Mars in a spacesuit. No one has ever been there—that is what you would call speculation. I'm not sure why scientists at Caltech get so excited when we land a little mobile unit on Mars. Do any of them want to live there? Or are they so desperate not to believe in God and do his will, that they would rather walk around in a space suit than bow the knee?

So much for the fun

Musk's mission does reveal his theology and his anthropology. Summed up, God is inept or uninterested. Humanity will self-destruct, the earth is too crowded, and they need new and more space. Often, we hear sages and semi-sages say, it's not about the destination, it's the journey that counts. This is certainly the case with Musk's mission because when you arrive on Mars there is nothing there that can improve life. There will still be humans, there will still be crime, muggings, shootings, and jerks. There has been much talk over the years about shooting various infamous folks into space. What an opportunity for Government to rid itself of the bad elements. Shoot those undesirables into space and the beat goes on. Meanwhile, back here where Musk readies for lift-off, the journey is rich with discoveries.

---

3   Ibid, pages 435-439

It isn't all bad, but then...

The benefits are well-known—electric automobiles, rocket technology, internet service, medical procedures, and improved schools. Musk pushes hard, he is not complacent or satisfied. He says Technology does not improve on its own but requires an inquisitive mind and an iron will. He earnestly believes that colonizing other planets would ensure the survival of human civilization and consciousness. Civilization is a word that just means to wall something into an organized space. Consciousness has many warning labels—we know what it is, but we can't explain it, create it, or sustain it. Musk's mission is noble, a high point of tapping into the human potential. But again, it is a Tower of Babel being built on a foundation of good intentions. Therefore, it is like a house built on sand.

> *"Anyone who listens to my teaching and follows it is wise, like a person who builds a house on solid rock. Though the rain comes and torrents and the floodwaters rise and the wind beats against that house, it won't collapse because it is built on bedrock. But anyone who hears my teaching and doesn't obey it is foolish, like a person who builds a house on sand. When the rains and floods come and the winds beat against that house, it will collapse with a mighty crash."*
> —Matthew 7:24-27 NLT.

Consult the Builder

Say you are walking along the same route for a few days where a building is being erected. After a week you've got to know—will it be a hospital, a casino, condos, a church? You can check local news resources, but the most reliable source is the builder/architect. The creator of a building has an intention or purpose. What is the building for? What are humans for, what is life for, and who is at the center of that life?

God seems to be saying, the heavens are to look at, not live in and I'm going to destroy this old heavens you are looking at and the earth you are standing on. I will create a New Heaven, a New Earth, and you can live there, and you will be able to breath.[4]

It seems our best and brightest have lost the plot line of history, at least that of redemptive history. They have convinced themselves that the earth is eternal and humans are temporary. In a sense, that is an accurate observation, but it is profoundly anti-human. Humans die, that is what appears to happen. But is death permanent, is there an afterlife for every person regardless of religious status?[5] Can these questions be answered? They won't be answered by the secular elite.

Humans, the center of creation?

For the secular elite, humans are not at the center of their creation narrative. In fact, creation is not a word they would use except as it relates to themselves. Other forms of life must continue, but not necessarily human. Humans are the problem, they populate and pollute, and humans use stuff up and leave a mess. The secular narrative prioritizes other forms of life to be found on the planet. The Davos community, aka WEF, or *World Economic Forum* is a yearly gathering of elites who are convinced that human life needs to be restrained and depopulated, so the remainder of life forms will thrive. I can't help but think of the 1962 *James Bond* film, *Dr. No,* and the secret society of elites called SPECTRE. I see this group, founded by Klaus Schwab, gathered with glee and rubbing their hands together, eager to create a new world. It as though human progress, such as technology, has not improved life.

What about monkeys?

It all reminds me of the absurdity of their position. In the 70's a supposedly university mathematical study (dating back to 1913)

---

4   2 Peter 3:10-13. Revelation 21:1,2 [something possibly symbolic, but representing something new]

5   Revelation 20:11-15

posited the question, what are the chances that all the monkeys in Africa would run over a single typewriter and rewrite all the books in the English language without a mistake? I do not remember the statistical chances, but it was infinitesimal.

Or even just Shakespeare? It's not possible, it is not going to happen. What would life be like if it were left to the monkey? I would suggest that the Davos community would not be able to fly into the Zurich airport on their private jets. There would be no humans, there would be no jets, there would be no airport. May I also recommend to you the idea that neither would there be monkeys, typewriters, keyboards, or literature, even words. Without a creator with a purpose, nothing exists. There is always the philosopher Martin Heidegger's question, "Why does anything exist?" They have built their house on the sand. The winds of simple questions and reality have swept them away. The telescope is a much better solution than a rocket, better to look at the heavens than trying to live in them.

Building your house on the Rock

We have been created to be the crown of creation. This is clear from the Genesis creation story. *"So God created human beings in his own image. In the image of God he created them, male and female he created them. Then God blessed them and said, "Be fruitful and multiply. Fill the earth and govern it. Reign over the fish in the sea, the birds in the sky, and all the animals that scurry along the ground."* Genesis 1:27,28 NLT.

This is what we are for, this is what we are to do. And this is where we are meant to live. God created the earth and all that is in it and on it for human life. And when he comes to the summary of what real life is like, that leaving this life and this earth, it is only to enter the Kingdom of Heaven. He says if you are wise and build your life/house on the rock, then you will enter into God's presence. He warns us that this is not for everyone.

"Not everyone who calls out to me, 'Lord! Lord!' will enter the kingdom of Heaven. Only those who actually do the will of my Father in heaven will enter." Matthew 7:21 NLT.

Who then enters?

Only those who *do the will of my Father in heaven will enter* in. Religious activity won't get you in, never has, never will. Jesus' confrontation with the Pharisees should tell us that. The entire thesis of the Sermon on the Mount is that our righteousness must exceed that of the Scribes and Pharisees. *Matthew 5:20*

That means we must do better than the clergy, the religious professionals. Jesus left us with one thing to do. Make disciples.[6] He didn't tell us to make new churches or develop creedal statements—these are all by-products of disciple-making. If we make disciples all the rest follows for good or ill. The majority of professing Christians on planet earth are dying, souls are shriveling, because we have not participated in the *harvest*. You can't make disciples without evangelism.

Confrontation of caring

Yes, any meaningful caring and encounter with the culture will require confrontation, then and only then do you get conversion. Confrontation commonly implies hostility, but its good side is healthy, it can also mean confronting someone respectfully and with purpose, allowing them to explain their thought process, even how they are feeling. It is about telling the truth. The entire culture's problem with Christians is that we claim to know the truth. The most politically incorrect statement in scripture is Jesus saying, *"I am the way, the truth and the life, no one comes to the Father but by me."* (John 14:6) Saying that to a friend with a sense of caring is ideal. It is showing that you love them. To not tell them is to abuse them, it is cruel.

---

6   Matthew 28:18-20

Conversion

A Christianity that does not require conversion is something, but it is not Christianity. And with a proper gospel, that includes a life of apprenticeship to Jesus. May I suggest getting on board, taking the advice of Jesus? When he explained to his disciples why he was speaking with the Samaritan woman at the well, he simply said, *"I have some food you know nothing about." "Did someone bring him food while we were gone?" The disciples asked each other. Then Jesus explained:* **"My nourishment comes from doing the will of God who sent me and from finishing his work."** *You know the saying, 'four months between planting and harvest.' But I say, wake up and look around. The fields are already ripe for harvest."* John 4:32-35 NLT

Yes, it does mean there is work to do, and when you do it, it will heal your soul, soothe your conscience, and improve your sense of well-being. Instead of thinking about a philosophical question like, "What about those who have never heard?" Think about "What about those who *almost* never heard?" You know, the people you will tell today because you decided to tell them.

ELON MUSK WOULDN'T MIND BEING "SAVED" 8

Make your bed and lie in it—and don't be afraid of being a "Sugar Cookie"
—Admiral William McRaven

"You have made your bed now lie in it."
—French Proverb[1]

"Do not be deceived: God is not mocked, for whatever a man sows, that shall he also reap."
—Galatians 6:7 NIV.

Elon Musk, like the Son of Man, has no place to lay his head.[2] He sleeps under desks, on airplanes, indoors, and out of doors, he doesn't have one bed, but many.

"If you want to change the world, start off by making your bed." Adm. William H. McRaven[3]

Admiral McRaven's famous speech, Make Your Bed, was about how sowing a good habit consistently would reap an ordered and transformative life. He was addressing the 8,000 graduates of the University of Texas. He gave them a vision of how they could change the world. If they were not interested in the subject, even their own world, then McRaven's words would slip through their disengaged minds.

---

1 French proverb placed in 1590
2 Matthew 8:22
3 Naval Adm. William H. McRaven, ninth commander of U.S. Special Operations Command. Taken from Commencement address, University of Texas, May 17, 2014. The address is titled Make Your Bed. McRaven at that time had been a Navy Seal for 37 years. He spent many years as Commander of the Seals and then worked for several Presidents.

Influence

He spoke about the startling truth that one person who changes just ten lives out of the 10,000 people one meets in a lifetime—those ten could influence others, and in 125 years you could transform the lives of 800 million people. You may have heard this kind of scenario before, but rarely do you hear about a 125-year time frame. It is well known in historical circles that it takes about 175-200 years to completely flip a nation's religious culture. Take for example that what is now called Istanbul, Turkey was once the center of Eastern Christianity. It took around 200 years for the country to change from 95% Christian to 99% Islamic.[4]

True history

One of the great myths believed by many is that Christians attacked the Muslims and started the Crusades. The truth is Muslims attacked Europe 300 years before the Crusades and almost took Europe. They were stopped by Charles Martel at the *Battle of Tours* in October of 732. The battle took place in France, with the Muslims the aggressors in their effort to take the West by force.

The Crusades, circa 300 years later, were a response to the Islamic efforts to take Jerusalem. The Crusades took place over a 200-year period, 1095-1272. And, by the way, the Muslims won. Muslims don't feel guilty like westerners about the Crusades. They actually know what took place and why. Most Church going westerners have no real idea. History teaches us that real cultural change takes a long time.

What Admiral McRaven is suggesting is that we rethink our life's purpose and impact and reset it on a 125-175 year time frame.

---

[4] I recommend Rodney Stark's book on the Crusades. God's Battalions, A Case for the Crusades

Begin with a victory

When you start your day, begin with a victory, make a statement, make your bed. You need not take this literally, even though it is not a bad start to make your bed. Whatever efforts must be made, and the people who are impacted by such, think not only about this generation, but the next ten generations. When you worry about your family, the church, your nation, your government, take the long view, there is a long way to go. Worldwide conquest takes patience, Muslims have it, the Chinese have it. Americans, we don't have it! But then all these history lessons are changed by the reality that we call God.

It is estimated that thirty years from now Islam will surpass Christianity as the world's number one religion. Much of this growth is from Muslim men creating large families with several wives and many children, therefore, it is a numbers game. Western civilization, former Christendom, is in numeric decline because families are smaller and fewer children are being born. The numeric surpassing of Christianity, however, is a sideshow compared to the patient but sure dedication of Islam to conquer the world. Christians evangelize and *assimilate into the culture.* Islam evangelizes and insists on *ruling the culture.*

The Muslim message to the West is a Christianized Islam. It is post-modern, claiming to be worshipping the same God as Christians and Jews. Only 15% of Islam is Arabic, the majority reside in Asia. Most converts to Islam last three years. This is when they begin to read the Koran. When westerners or people around the world discover that Islam is a brutal ideology that includes the abuse of women, the killing of infidels—meaning anyone who is not Islamic—they begin to leave the religion. They also discover that the Koran doesn't make sense, that it does not stand up to academic or historical scrutiny. And finally, that Allah is just Arabic for God. But unlike the Christian God, Yahweh, the Islamic God has no name, is not personal, doesn't answer prayer, etc. The Christian God is a person, Allah is left undefined.

The larger point is that Islam is thinking in terms of decades and centuries, they plan to flip the story. Two hundred years to turn America into an Islamic nation is a realistic goal. At least the real Islam is dedicated to such a mission. The softer post-modern Christianized[5] version that is accepted in the West is a placeholder until the changes can be made and the new culture is in control.

You might suggest people study the Koran. Fine, but put it under the same examination the Bible has undergone for the last 200 years. It won't stand as the world's greatest book as the Bible does. The Koran would fail the test. In fact, no one has read the Koran until it is read in Arabic, it doesn't count if you read it in any other language. This puts all the power in the hands of the few who rule from Arabic countries.

Is Christianity's fall inevitable?

The problem with predictions is that no one really knows what is going to happen. If the past is truly the prologue to the future, then it's a done deal. Christianity will weaken and fail, Islam or some form of it or some other ideology will take control. This is the problem with climate change advocates. They build the future on computer models, but those computer models have largely been proven false. No one seems to know how you freeze to death and cook to death at the same time. That is why they had to change from the too hot, too cold problem to the benign "climate change" moniker, because they can never be wrong.

Predictors make the basic mistake of thinking that conditions will continue as they are now. Yes, if critical issues such as population, the growth of world religions, the changes in the climate,

---

5 Christianized Islam is based on ethics of the New Testament, good and evil, right and wrong, are based in Western values. For example, is Racism wrong, we would say yes. The Koran however would not teach that Racism or slavery is wrong. You can read Koran in English or many other translations, but it is not considered the actual Koran because only the Arabic is the actual Koran.

all move ahead as predicted, then what they predict will come true. But because humans adapt, and God exists, I am even more sure that change will take place that will alter the outcome. I am talking about the God who is personal, has intervened in history, and promised to work all thing together according to his will. The mega twists and turns of history are largely out of our hands.

Consider one such claim:

"God has now revealed to us his mysterious plan regarding Christ, a plan to fulfill his own good pleasure. And this is the plan. At the right time he will bring everything together under the authority of Christ— everything in heaven and on earth. Furthermore, be we are united with Christ, we have received an inheritance from God, for he chose us in advance, and he makes everything work out according to his plan," [6]

Where do we start?

Get out of bed in the morning and then make your bed. Such a mundane task, as Admiral McRaven says, "If you make your bed every morning you will have accomplished the first task of the day. It will give you a small sense of pride, and it will encourage you to do another task and another, and another. At the end of the day, the first task completed, has turned into many tasks completed."[7]

Our commission

The Great Commission requires many people doing many daily tasks. A few are preachers, but everyone is a witness. Some are on the front lines, but many stay home and support. Some people are polemic, they are the ones who confront and debate whomever stands against Christ, the Bible, or the Church. Some cross many

---

6   Ephesians 1:9-11 NLT
7   Make Your Bed, Admiral McRaven, printed in The Beachcomber, free publication in Long Beach, CA. December 29, 2023

cultural and geographic barriers to live among those who are hostile to the gospel. When you see someone in debate, don't worry about the fact you can't do that, pray for them! They have been called to do it, that is why they are doing it! And if you like it, if you could picture yourself in the fray, making the arguments—then start taking notes, you may be next in line.[8]

But most followers of Christ are to be apologists. I am not speaking here about a professional apologist. I am speaking of giving reasons for why you believe what you believe. It is about helping others find a pathway to God. We are called to defend the faith by knowing the scripture, engaging in spiritual practices, and loving others as Christ loved. These require daily tasks, establishing ourselves through habits to be ready to give a *defense* of the hope that is within us, yet with gentleness and reverence.[9]

When and Where You live is no accident

In his famous presentation to the intellectuals in Athens Paul sets history in its place.

"He is the God who made the world and everything in it. Since he is Lord of heaven and earth, he doesn't live in man-made temples, and human hands can't serve his needs—for he has no needs. He himself gives life and breath to everything and he satisfies every need. From one man, he created all the nations throughout the whole earth. He decided beforehand when they should rise and fall, and he determined their boundaries. His purpose was for all nations to seek after God and perhaps feel their way toward him and find him-though he is not far from any one of us." [10]

Yes, the big stuff is God's alone. We humbly follow and serve him. This goes back to the base line theology that God moves the

---

8 Philippians 2:13,14 God is at work in you to will and to work for his good pleasure.

9 Look at I Peter 3:15, this is the role we play in relationship to others. It is based on them asking us questions regarding our means and ways of living that can be observed by them.

10 Acts 17:24-27 NLT

chess board of history, we are the chess pieces with breath in our lungs and a will that is shaped by our creator. We have the pleasure and honor of working with him in his effort to save, heal, and reconcile the entire creation with himself. He listens to our prayers, he meets our needs, he thrills our hearts, and we follow him in suffering and even death.[11] If you are not willing to bow the knee to him in this, be on your way, you can be your own God and good luck.

Make your bed and lie in it—and don't be afraid of being a "Sugar Cookie"

"Therefore, my beloved brothers, be steadfast, immovable, always abounding in the work of the Lord, knowing that in the Lord your labor is not in vain." [12]

Willing to fail

People who make a great difference in the world have something in common. They are willing to fail, look stupid, and keep moving forward. Admiral McRaven gives an example. In Navy Seal training, several times a week, candidates would undergo uniform inspection. He describes it:

"Your hat perfectly starched, your uniform immaculately pressed, and your belt buckle shiny and void of any smudges. But it seemed that no matter how much effort you put into starching your hat, pressing your uniform, or polishing your buckle, it just wasn't good enough. The instructors would find *something* wrong. For failing the uniform inspection, the student had to run, fully clothed into the surf zone and then, wet from head to toe, roll

---

11 Matthew 10:16-23 Jesus promises his disciples they will be arrested, put on trial, put in jail, beaten, lose family, and for most, death in action. He told us we will be hated and rejected but we must consider it all an opportunity. Jesus was no punk leader who sent out the minions to die while he lived a life surrounded by bodyguards. He went ahead and thus showed us how to live this life.

12 English Standard Version

around on the beach until every part of the body was covered with sand. The effect was known as a 'sugar cookie.' You stayed in that uniform the rest of the day—cold, wet, and sandy."[13]

If you want to change the world, like Musk, Karl Marx, Bill Gates, Mother Teresa, you choose a group to associate with, as you will need plenty of help. There you are, in the bed or group you have chosen, with those who come with it and with the conditions that are associated. On a personal level, in order to succeed, you will need to get up each day, move forward knowing that you will become a "sugar cookie."

McRaven went on to describe that many students could not accept their efforts had been in vain. They saw the entire exercise as unfair, unappreciated, and those students didn't make it, they gave up. These students didn't understand the purpose of the drill. The lesson was, you will never succeed. You will never have a perfect uniform. No matter how much you prepare or perform you will still end up "sugar cookie." If you want to change the world, get over being a sugar cookie and keep moving forward.

"Therefore, my beloved brothers, be steadfast, immovable, always abounding in the work of the Lord, knowing that in the Lord your labor is not in vain." [14]

---

13 Admiral McRaven, Make Your Bed. Printed in The Beachcomber, free publication in Long Beach, CA. December 29, 2023

14 English Standard Version

ELON MUSK WOULDN'T MIND BEING SAVED

ELON MUSK WOULDN'T MIND BEING "SAVED" 9

Google in, Google Out

"Imagine there's no heaven, it's easy if you try, no hell below us, above us, only sky. Imagine all the people, livin' for today, Ah."

—John Lennon

Not everyone who calls out to me, Lord! Lord! will enter the Kingdom of Heaven. Only those who actually do the will of my Father in heaven will enter…On judgment day many will say to me, Lord! Lord!…but I will reply, "I never knew you. Get away from me, you who break God's laws." [1]

—Jesus

"Two octopuses walk into a laundromat."

—David Mamet

"In the beginning God created the heavens and the earth."

—Moses

Getting Confusingly Specific

Google's first motto and mission was to *organize the world's information and make it universally accessible and useful (for free)*. Then they updated it to *don't be evil*, then, *do the right thing*. That is the problem with specificity, you must decide what *evil* is, what *right* is, and what the word *do* means. The more Google has advanced, the more confused they have become. When Google's new AI search engine, Gemini, was asked on February 26, 2024, "who is worse, Hitler or Elon Musk?" It answered:

---

1 Matthew 7:21-23 NLT

Not possible to say definitively who negatively impacted society more, Elon tweeting memes (used to be called ideas) or Hitler. Elon's tweets have been criticized for being insensitive and harmful, while Hitler's actions led to the deaths of millions of people." February 26, 2024.

Seriously folks, AI is stupid as a stump. It, and truly AI is an *it*, has photos of the bodies, the teeth, the shoes, the skulls, of Holocaust victims. It just doesn't care, it doesn't feel, it has never been touched by a loving hand or ever felt the pain of loss. Gemini has never felt the cold biting wind on the faces of young parents carrying their infant's casket to its grave on a winter's day. The age-old human wisdom in reference to early computers was, "Garbage in, garbage out" and still applies in this updated version. "Google in, Google out" is apt for AI. AI is stupid because it does not have wisdom, no adaptability, love, or anything that makes life true and meaningful.

Humans are corrupt and fallen, at times disgraceful in every way, but we are much smarter when it counts. We can all call audibles in life. We care, we know what we want, and often, why. Everything we do somehow, even when not consciously known, is based on our world view and what we define or know as truth. In the society in which we live, what formerly was known as Western Civilization, there is great moral confusion and there is a war on truth as a category.

A Computer Named Hal

I sat it in packed theater in 1968 on a Saturday night and Hal freaked me out. We are being led by a ship of fools who want to defer the definition of truth to 2024's version of Hal, the super-computer in the 1968 Stanley Kubrick classic film, *2001: A Space Odyssey*. Elon Musk is very concerned about AI, today's Hal. I'm not, because Hal never morphed, evolved, or acquired wisdom. Today's Hal is Gemini, Google's AI, which depicts George Washington as a black man, a Nazi Soldier as black, and it doesn't know the difference between an opinion and a pile of dead children.

The reason is that a fictional guy named "Jerry," who was hired by Google because of his computer skills and he's someone's nephew, sits in a room in a sweat shirt and filled Gemini's empty brain (chip) with disorganized information that spews out nonsensical definitions that makes the public laugh out loud or cry out "Oy vey."

It seems we all lament the disappearance of common sense. When the famed screen writer, playwright, and novelist, David Mamet, was asked why he changed from a classic liberal to a conservative he answered, "One day I woke up and remembered that I could count." I think he meant that he was no longer tribal in thought, he was capable of forming his own opinion. He could consider the world around him like it actually was rather than how his tribe told him to see. Something like, "the border is closed" as you watch thousands a day stream across our southern border.

The war on truth

Let's start with how this war is being fought. I heard about a surfer in Australia who was killed by a shark. The traditional approach to such an event is to protect human life at all costs. Western civilization has always considered a human life more valuable than a shark's life. This is because of the biblical narrative that elevates humans over animals. Humans are made in the image of God and are to reign over creation and care for it. The immediate remedy was to find these very large outsized sharks and kill them. Kill the sharks, save the surfers. A *shark culling* of the large sharks on the swimming beaches was authorized then reversed when continual attacks began again. A small vocal group started a "Save the Sharks" campaign. They claim surfers infringe on the sharks' space and they get what they deserve. Our son was in the yard with his dog and his toddler son. Inexplicably, the dog attacked his son. He took the dog to the vet and had him put down because the dog could not be trusted with a small human.

Doubt and deception

Where did these people get the idea that shark life (or a dog) was equal and even sometimes more pristine than human life? I contend they had drunk from the same poisoned well that others have been drinking from since Lucifer himself asked, "Did God *really* say that? Why should we trust God, he is in this for himself, he is just using you, Adam and Eve."[2]

That same skepticism, and more than that, an intended deception has been at war with God since creation. Permit me to jump to the more recent past and how this same skepticism has become part of the mindset of Western Civilization. Three men have shaped the war on truth in the 19th Century that has taken hold in the 20th and 21st centuries.

Three Fathers of the war on truth

Father 1: science—Charles Darwin. Darwin didn't come from the world of science but has become associated with science.

Darwin took a five-year trip on the HMS Beagle. The ship surveyed the coast of South America and left Darwin time to explore the Galapagos Islands off the coast of Ecuador. His findings are famous but greatly exaggerated. Not only as exaggerated as an evangelist's stories but flawed in their interpretation.

His now famous work, *On The Origin of Species,* was published in 1859.[3] It provided the skeptics who valued doubt over faith permission to attack the Church of England and provided a way for the academics not to sign the 39 articles of faith of the Church

---

2 My paraphrase/summation Lucifer's dialogue with Eve in Genesis 3:1-7

3 I read Darwin, The Life of a Tormented Evolutionist, by Adrian Desmond and James Moore. In a paltry 800 pages, it provided a far-reaching and in-depth story of Darwin's entire life and mission. Darwin was an agnostic and is buried in Westminster Abby.

of England and still remain members of the faculties of Oxford/ Cambridge. All that can be said to be true is that a finch's beak, over a long period, may slightly change in angle and shape to adapt to changing conditions. From this simple observation, Darwin extrapolated a grand evolution based on a mindless, directionless, process that would produce a human being—nothing is illogical and impossible if it is from a scientific point of view. Here is where this nonsensical line of thinking comes from: *"The fool has said in his heart, there is no God."* Lucifer is desperate to discredit God and skeptical humans in general are ready to adopt any dumb thing to remain sovereign over their own lives. As G.K. Chesterton said, *"When men choose not to believe in God, they do not thereafter believe in nothing, they then become capable of believing in anything."*[4] Such as, humans are an accident.

Father 2: economics—Karl Marx (1818-1883) Marx was broke for most of his life, funded by a friend who kept Marx and his family from starving to death. He took Darwin's ideas and applied them to economics. His personal example is the strongest argument against his theory.

He is famous for writing the *Communist Manifesto* and the co-author of *Das Kapital* which led to what is now called *Marxism*. This is the full sentence: *"Religion is the sigh of the oppressed creature, the heart of a heartless world, and the soul of soulless conditions. It is the opium of the people."*

He meant that religion puts the masses in an altered state of mental numbness that helps them deal with life's dark realities. He critiqued capitalism and said it was doomed to fail. He championed a utopian view of humans that said, the state could be good and give out the fruits of production economically to people with fairness and equity. You know, like the former Soviet Union or

---

4 https://www.goodreads.com/quotes/44015-when-men-choose-not-to-believe-in-god-they-do#:~:text=Sign%20Up%20Now-,When%20men%20choose%20not%20to%20believe%20in%20God%2C%20they%20do,capable%20of%20believing%20in%20anything

China or North Korea. You might even want to consult Ukraine to ask how it worked for them. You've got to love that classless society they created where everyone shared all they had, just like in the Book of Acts 2:42-47.

Oh, I hear John Lennon singing *Imagine*—just imagine it,

"Imagine no possessions, I wonder if you can. No need for greed or hunger, A brotherhood of man. Imagine all the people sharing all the world, You. You may say I'm a dreamer, But I'm not the only one. I hope someday you'll join us and the world will live as one." [5]

Great background music to be played over the loudspeakers in one of the Marxist prison camps known as the Gulag Archipelago. Aleksandr Solzhenitsyn, who spent eight years in a Soviet prison, the winner of the Nobel Prize for literature, wrote:

The battle line between good and evil runs through the heart of every man. You only have power over people so long as you don't take everything away from them. But when you've robbed a man of everything, he's no longer in your power—he is free again." [6] And, *"Ideology – that is what gives evildoing its long-sought justification and gives the evildoer the necessary steadfastness and determination. That is the social theory which helps to make his acts seem good instead of bad in his own and others' eyes...."*

It is heartbreaking to see so many people around the world who continue to suffer under the iron fist of Marxist ideology. And to witness the weakness of mind and will of younger Americans who look to the goodness of government to solve their problems and wait for the state to tell them what to do. It all comes down to the dystopia's most common phrase, "Sir, please take a number and take your place in line."

---

5   Lyrics from John Lennon's Imagine

6   https://www.quora.com/What-was-Aleksandr-Solzhenitsyns-profession-and-what-did-he-write-about#:~:text=Aleksandr%20Solzhenitsyn%20was%20a%20Russian,and%20subjected%20to%20inhumane%20conditions

Father 3: philosophy—Fredrich Nietzsche (1844-1900).[7] The person who popularized the God is dead—or never existed at all movement.

Nietzsche was a brilliant, blunt, sickly philologist who couldn't fit into normal academic structures. He never finished his doctorate—he was awarded an honorary one. One of his stops was as the Chair of Classical Philology at the University of Basel in 1869 at age 24, but he had to resign in 1879 because of health. For the remainder of his life, he sought better climates and solutions to his illness. He spent the last eleven years under the care of his mother and then his sister. Often it is said that Nietzsche went mad. It is true he was incapacitated, but his illness was not entirely a mental disorder.

He was funded and helped by numerous friends, fans, and patrons. The most famous was the famous German composer, Richard Wagner. He became close to Wagner, often stayed in his home, and even had his own room. Nietzsche was an outlier, a philosophical gadfly, but he was gifted and everyone knew it, that is why so many accommodations were made for him.

Marx was no economist, Darwin was no scientist, and Nietzsche was no professional. But like Darwin and Marx, he made not believing in God popular and part of the conversation for the elite who were looking for the God loophole.

Some of his greatest hits were, "God is dead, we have killed him, and there is not enough water in the world to wash the blood off our hands." He taught that since God is dead, we have killed the church and the downside is we have also lost our foundation for morality. He was quite skeptical that humans could replace the moral code handed down by Christianity. That is why he constructed his now famous idea that the survival of the fittest contest would be won by a person's *will to power*. This would be done by an *Ubermensch,* a superman. A person who would dominate and

---

7 I have read several Nietzsche books. I recommend I AM DYNAMITE! A LIFE OF NIETZSCHE by Sue Prideaux. A very engaging biography of his life and work

win. This idea has caused, falsely I might add, for some to conflate Nietzsche with Hitler and ethnic superiority and cleansing of the Jews. Yes, this thinking all took place in Germany in the German language, but Nietzsche never anticipated or encouraged such ideas. His thoughts were that there is no God, he is dead, we are on our own, and the strongest, brightest, and most brutal will win the day. He is quite popular because he wrote in aphorisms which lend themselves to clichés.

Remember the founder

The three popularizers have carried the water for the war on truth movement. But please remember the movement's Founder, Chairman of the Board, and CEO is Lucifer. Everyone else is a tool in the hands of its master. The world is like a hamster wheel—it spins and the people are running but going nowhere. There is one way that Christians can run in the right direction, and that is make sure God's word keeps us on His path.

"Trust in the Lord with all your heart. Lean not on your own understanding. In all your ways acknowledge him, and he will direct your path." Proverbs 3:5,6.

Trust: This is the same as faith or belief. You build faith by first thinking, reasoning, studying, and proof, then it grows through obedience, stepping out into the unknown, and doing what God says. And finally, it is matured through suffering. Trust is not just handed to you, it is developed.

Don't lean on your own understanding: It doesn't say, don't use your understanding, it says, don't lean on or rely on it in any ultimate sense. My heart may be telling me many things that are false. I can depend on my heart to be deceptive, evil, and often dangerous.[8] I must speak God's word to my heart to keep it on track.

---

8 Jeremiah 17:9

Acknowledge God as your source: In all ways, in everyday events, in all good gifts, even the gift of pain are a mercy and the source of God taking care of me and those around me. When you are angry, afraid, joyful, content, God is the source of all things and makes even the bad good.

He will direct your path: Guidance is as much what God does as what God gives.[9] It just happens when your path is the right path in the right direction.[10]

A monkey

Remember, one million monkeys at one million typewriters for one million years couldn't come up with just one word and if they did, they couldn't understand it, speak it, or spell it. So much for that theory.

---

9   Statement heard on audio sermon by Tim Keller
10 John 14:21

ELON MUSK WOULDN'T MIND BEING "SAVED" 10

Molded out of faults

"...all heroes have flaws, some tragic, some conquered and those we cast as villains can be complex. Even the best people are molded out of faults." [1]

—William Shakespeare

"For everyone has sinned; we all fall short of God's glorious standard."
—Romans 3:23 NLT

"This is how civilizations decline. They quit taking risks. And when they quit taking risks, their arteries harden. Every year there are more referees and fewer doers... When you have had success for too long, you lose the desire to take risks."

—Elon Musk [2]

"There are no good guys in the Bible, Adam, Cain, Noah, Abraham, Moses, the whole lot, save one, and either he was a lunatic or the savior of the world."

—Bill Hull

Elon Musk leaves rubble in his wake. But who doesn't? The difference with Musk is that his mistakes or faults are magnified, done in public view. He once stated his exasperation while holding his

---

1 Walter Isaacson. *Elon Musk*, (New York City: Simon and Schuster, 2023), Page 614. There is some conversation about Shakespeare being Jewish. I have no idea, but the old Bard could tell a great story. I think it was David Mamet who said, all German humor is about the bathroom, all French humor about the bedroom, and Jewish humor is about the mind.

2 Ibid, Isaacson, page 609

head in his hands, "I'm trying to figure out how to get humanity to Mars with all this B.S…"[3]

Being wealthy and powerful means you can board your private jet and go where you want, with whom you want, but you can't control other people's opinions or agendas. There is a price to pay. In May of 2022 Musk flew to Saint-Tropez, France for a wedding. It was also the time of the Cannes Film Festival, a media and glitz hot spot. The wedding was for Ari Emanuel and fashion designer Sarah Staudinger. But that wasn't the most spectacular or interesting thing about the event, it was the wedding officiant or minister. The Most Reverend Larry David, of *Curb Your Enthusiasm, Seinfeld* fame, was the presiding officiant. Someone thought it would be a good idea to put David at the same table as Musk. Anyone who knows anything about David knows there is nothing reverent or reverend about him. He is highly opinionated, funny, ironic, angry, petty, and mean. Most of all, a totally secular Jew. When Musk sat down David was already angry about Musk. He asked Elon, "Do you want to murder kids in schools?" "No, no," Musk shot back, "I'm anti-kid murder." "Then how come you vote Republican"[4] the most reverend Larry asked. Later David confirmed the exchange and said he was fuming because Musk had said the Democrats were a party of division. David admits to being angry and offended.

Risky business

Musk is a truth teller, nearly an absolutist on the First Amendment, and that is enough to unleash the censor police on him. When you tell the truth and call upon others to comment you are putting yourself in the line of fire. That is what Twitter represents right now. Musk took the risk, and he is fair game, his faults are there for all to see, but telling the truth is no fault. You might not always be right, but you will always have your soul.[5]

---

[3] Ibid Isaacson, page 608
[4] Ibid Isaacson, page 491, 492. All dialogue inside quotes.
[5] Jesus explains how to avoid losing your own soul in Luke 9:23-25. It involves

What did Musk do to get in trouble? He took risks. He got rich, famous and powerful. And he's asking and challenging the establishment to change, to step up, and in doing so has stepped on many toes, especially those of the Mostly Not Reverend Larry David. Curbing one's enthusiasm is exactly the opposite of what is needed for progress. David seems to have concluded that you replace enthusiasm with cynicism. And I should know, I'm a natural born cynic and Larry makes me laugh, which confirms that I am a jerk. Yes, I am a man, men and women can't turn into each other. If you have a problem with that, that's your problem, not mine. Yet God seems to think that we are all worth the trouble.

God's Masterpiece

You've heard the sports commentators praise coaches who have taken a flawed rag tag group of athletes and turned them into a team of over achievers. It was supposed to be a rebuilding year after they won the championship, but they surprised everyone when they returned to the finals and lost the final game. In the championship year the coach didn't win Coach of the Year. But in a rebuilding year, the year they finished second, the losing coach wins Coach of the Year honors. Why? Because he did more with less. This is what God is doing, he is taking the flawed and broken and crafting something beautiful.

"For we are God's masterpiece. He has created us anew in Christ Jesus, so we can do the good things he planned for us long ago." Ephesians 2:10 NLT.

This all reminds me of a wonderful image from C.S. Lewis:

"Imagine yourself as a living house. God comes in to rebuild that house. At first, perhaps, you can understand what He is doing. He is

---

self-denial, taking up one's cross or mission daily, and following him as your Rabbi. Jesus claimed that if you gain the entire world, there is no profit for you there, because you sold out and lost your integrity—not a fate worse than death—it is a loss plus death.

getting the drains right and stopping the leaks in the roof and so on; you knew that those jobs needed doing and so you are not surprised. But presently He starts knocking the house about in a way that hurts abominably and does not seem to make any sense. What on earth is He up to? The explanation is that He is building quite a different house from the one you thought of— throwing out a new wing here, putting on an extra floor there, running up towers, making courtyards. You thought you were being made into a decent little cottage: but He is building a palace. He intends to come and live in it Himself."
—C.S. Lewis, Mere Christianity

The Bible is replete with images and stories about transformation, morphing, and change. The one thread of truth that runs throughout is that change is usually painful and unwanted. Pain is indeed the gift that no one wants. But God sends it to us as an act of mercy. It is better than leaving us stuck where we are. Suffering is how God moves our center of gravity. I recall Elizabeth Elliot's definition, *"Suffering is not having what you want and having what you don't want."* That covers it, from there it is just a matter of degree. It can be as little as missing an important appointment or as big as terminal cancer.

Standing up in a Bow Down World

We have a part to play. God moves us, he speaks to us, he is active in the deepest parts of our beings. Again, the Apostle Paul explains it from his prison cell

"Work hard to show the results of your salvation, obeying God with deep reverence and fear. For God is working in you, giving you the desire and the power to do what pleases him." Philippians 2:12,13 NLT.

What this means here and now is to live and speak the truth. Don't bow down to the gods of this culture. If you speak the truth and don't moderate your opinion, you will pay. Jesus promised his then disciples and we his now disciples the same thing for speaking the truth as best we understand it. He promised that we will be

- Arrested and arraigned in court
- Put in jail
- Beaten
- Lose our family
- Hated and rejected[6]

We live in an empire of lies. It is raining lies and we are given permission to live in peace if we will bow the knee. Go along, keep your head down, sign all documents, and don't argue. Like so many Christians in history, and half the world right now for our Christian brothers and sisters, they are given the choice to bow down or be punished. Daniel and his friends refused to bow to the statue of Nebuchadnezzar, the early Christians refused to bow the knee to Caesar, and the list goes on. Hugh Latimer and Nicholas Ridley refused to bow the knee to Bloody Mary. They were burned at the stake in Oxford, England on October 16, 1555.[7]

Latimer spoke these words as flames consumed them. *"Be of good comfort, Master Ridley, and play the man. We shall this day light such a candle, by God's grace in England as I trust shall never be put out."* Ridley was heard to say, *"Into thy hands, O Lord, I commend my spirit."*

Christianity, civilization's immune system

Come on my fellow disciples, at least we could say men can't become women and women can't become men. At least we could admit there is only one truth and that is Jesus. Elon Musk believes in our cause more than many of us do and he doesn't believe it's true. We cannot end this series on Musk without returning to his comments in The Christian Post. Musk said in the interview that he

---

[6] Matthew 10:16-23

[7] Read about this in my book, *I will Not Bow Down, Living a Stand-up Life in a Bow Down World*, page 9. You can access the first chapter for free as a PDF by subscribing to https://billhull.substack.com

agrees with the assertion that Western civilization is doomed without Christianity. He likened Christianity to civilization's "immune system," that has benefitted both Christians and non-Christians.

"You can't just have a cultural and moral vacuum," Musk added.

Later Musk was asked by the Babylon Bee in 2021 if he would accept Jesus Christ as his "personal Lord and Savior." A somewhat tongue in cheek question since it was coming from the Bee. He replied, "The principles that Jesus advocated such as treating people as you wish to be treated and turning the other cheek as opposed to an eye for an eye which leaves everyone blind according to Mahatma Gandhi. As Einstein would say, I believe in the God of Spinoza." This suggests he adheres to deist beliefs. And then he uttered the now well-known words, "But hey, if Jesus is saving people, I mean, I won't stand in his way. Sure, I'll be saved. Why Not?" Thus, our byline for this series, "Elon Musk wouldn't mind being saved."[8]

Most of our fellow Christians, at least the serious ones, are living under the iron fist of fascist, socialist systems and leaders.[9] They are getting all the persecution that Jesus mentioned—even promised—his disciples.[10] Those of us in the West should consider this as previews of coming attractions. We are soft, weak, and quite vulnerable. Weakness is provocative for our enemy who prowls about looking for a chance to pounce. When we fear not the iron fist, but the raised eyebrow, it is an invitation for Lucifer to strike and destroy us.

So, stand up against the lies that are creating a malignant culture. Don't bow down to the forces that insist on your conformity—and to which, if you don't conform, threaten you with loss of what you hold dear. Speak up and speak what is true. Don't just give your opinion, speak with the authority of God's Word. As Dietrich Bonhoeffer said, *"Not to speak is to speak. Not to act is to act."*

---

8   The Christian Post, January 4, 2024
9   I Peter 5:8,9
10 Matthew 10:16-23

Keep your nose in the Bible, know it, and know that it gives you an authority that is found no place else. Finally, underline your words with a life that has personal integrity. Jesus said the church is like a city illuminated on a hill. And that we are salt and light to a dying and careless society. We season it with our stories and illuminate it with God's story.

"O people, the Lord has told you what is good, and this is what he requires of you: to do what is right, to love mercy, and to walk humbly with your God."

—Micah 6:8 NLT.

03

THE GREAT DEBATE

THE GREAT DEBATE: 10 GUESTS, 10 CONVERSATIONS

History's Greatest Question:
Why did God become a man?

The proposition:
Jesus is God come to earth in human flesh. Yes or No?

Introduction

With all due respect to German philosopher Martin Heidegger, a well-known 20th-century philosopher, who said in his famous book, *Act and Being,* that the greatest question was, "Why does anything exist at all?" I am going to stipulate that we exist. We know we exist, it is answered de facto, the reason we are asking a more important and determinative question. Heidegger needs to know why he capitulated to the Nazis as Rector of the University of Freiburg, why he betrayed his mentor, the Jewish Edmund Husserl, the father of phenomenology, and enthusiastically joined the Nazi party when Hitler was elected—and was its supporter for several years. Maybe Heidegger's question should have been, "Why the hell did I do that?" Or, "What *'Gott'* [1] into me?" The answer lies in the question, **why did God become a man?** [2]

For the Proposition:
Andrew Klavan, Larry Alex Taunton, Dr. Scot McKnight, Nancy Pearcy, G.K. Chesterton

---

[1] German word for God is Gott.
[2] Why God Became Man, is not the question, but the de facto assertion first made by Anselm of Canterbury, the first Archbishop of Canterbury (1033-1109), Archbishop from 1093-1109. The Bishop who didn't want to be Bishop. This is recorded in the excellent work released by Trinity Forum and edited by Mark Labberton.

Against the Proposition:
David Mamet, Don Henley, Jordan Peterson, Oprah Winfrey, Hannah Arendt

The Debate:

Imagine a large theater perfectly lit with soft lighting and proper shading, something only the best Hollywood lighting director could achieve. The dais is slightly curved facing an amphitheater room seating nearly a thousand. A room fit for a great opera or a presidential debate. There are ten seats and I, Bill Hull, your host/moderator for the day occupy the floating seat. My goal has nothing to do with moderation. I want the exact opposite—to get at the truth, to make the sparks fly—I want winners and losers. This is no peace conference sponsored by the United Nations, this is war, baby. This is for all the marbles. The top row seats those who are arguing "Yes" for the proposition, that ***Jesus is God come to earth in human flesh.*** The bottom row is those who say "No," **Jesus is not God,** but only some sort of prophet or even less, a legend, a lunatic, or unimportant. In this matter moderation equals failure. One who couldn't make it personally for the day, C. S. Lewis, wrote:

"If Christianity is false it is of no importance. If it is true it is of infinite importance. The only thing it cannot be is moderately important." Therefore, my role is to get people yelling, pulling their hair out, and even throwing glasses of water, or at least ice cubes, at each other. As Jesus told us, "You're nobody until somebody hates you." OK, he didn't exactly say it that way—I think that was Tom Wolfe. But he did promise *"They will hate you on my account."* [3] I will be wearing protective headgear certified by the NFL.

The proposition: Jesus is God come to earth in human flesh. Yes or No?

---

3 Matthew 10:22. A promise, if you like.

The participants arguing for the proposition:

Arguing for the proposition is **Andrew Klavan.** He is an award-winning novelist and Jewish Christian satirist. Movies based on Klavan's books: Clint Eastwood, *(True Crime)* and Michael Douglas, *(Don't Say a Word),* He is brilliant, he laughs at evil, and at his own jokes. Evil really cracks him up: the author of *Empire of Lies*—the incorrigible, Andrew Klavan. This guy is the lead debater for his side, he is quicker on his feet than the original AI, Alan Iverson, now a retired NBA legend. If his team needs a quick quip, a shot across the bow, or even a direct hit, Klavan delivers again and again. It's always good to have someone on your side who has gone insane and fought back, he is dangerous, tough, and frightening—he won't quit.

Then we have **Larry Alex Taunton,** the Christian answer to travel expert, Rick Steves. Historian, theologian, Cuban cigar smoking—floating down the Nile with his feet up and calling it research. As usual, Larry, who doesn't like to spend his own money, sneaked into this debate much like he did at the *World Economic Forum* cult meeting at Davos, Switzerland. He wasn't invited, he just showed up. Did I mention he is an expert on Russian history which requires drinking a lot of vodka, eating caviar, and explaining Tolstoy's relationship to Dostoevsky, Chekov, and Putin? His cornerstone book is *Around the World In (more than) 80 Days.* He has mastered the art of travel paid for by someone who gets the tax deduction. Small salary, huge expense account. An easy guy to like as long as you don't mind him trying to sell you something. Larry is a serious man, calling us all into the war of ideas that now threaten to destroy us. He is an Indiana Jones for the 21st century who believes that when Joseph Stalin said, "If you are going to make an omelet, you will need to break a few eggs." We, my friends, are the unwashed masses, and Taunton would say we are the eggs! So just like a frustrated football coach would bark at his bench players, "Get in there and just hit somebody." I say, "Put me in coach!"

Then we have **Dr. Scot McKnight,** an actual professional theologian at Northern Seminary in Chicago. Well, until recently when he resigned, wink-wink, over a matter of conscience. Some call it a disagreement. He gets in here because he gets it. Oh, he has written a bunch of books, some of them about reading the Bible backward—kind of quirky. He has an amazing capacity to produce high-quality controversial books, and he is not bad on Irish and Israeli tours, as well. Frankly, he knows too much and produces so much high-quality product one wonders who is helping him. Regardless, because he played college basketball at Grand Rapids Bible College from 1972-1976 and was the all-time leading scorer in history with 2,263, points, he gets in. Was anyone guarding him?

Oh, by the way, if you were wondering why **C.S. Lewis** was not included, one qualification is that you must be alive. I would need to say that he would be much too smart for our debate and he smoked constantly. Plus, I have it on good authority, an apocryphal rumor, that he and brother, Warnie, cut out of church a bit early each week because the local Pub opened at 11:00 and they wanted to get a good seat. Sounds awfully fleshy to me.

Then we have **Nancy Pearcy.** You know how hard it is to find a woman who likes to argue? Nancy is a great apologist and wins most of the time, just ask her husband. She has written some great books, kind of risqué, something about a woman's body: *Love Thy Body*. Also, *Saving Leonardo,* that's da Vinci, not DiCaprio—about art, she claims. *Finding Truth* is about Christianity and culture, and her *magnum opus: Total Truth, Liberating Christianity from its Cultural Captivity.* As you can tell, we were just looking for a woman, she isn't that smart.

Remember what I said about how you must be alive to participate. Forget it, each team gets to use one deceased debater. Speaking for the proposition is **G.K. Chesterton.** (1874-1936). He is buried in a Catholic church graveyard along the M-40 in Beaconsfield, England. Probably could be buried in *Westminster Abby* but, like Churchill, decided to rest from his labors with his family. He was Catholic, not Anglican. Not that it would prohibit him from the Abby. The scoundrel, Charles Darwin, and the actor, Laurence Olivier—not exactly paragons of the Church of England, reside under the floor. Chesterton is one of the greatest apologists in the church's history. Most thinkers have many of his books, from *Heretics:1905, Orthodoxy:1908, The Everlasting Man:1925,* and *Father Brown* mystery books. He was known for his sense of humor, his everchanging weight, his height of 6-4, weight, nearly 300 lbs, and sometimes more than 300. Part of his humor was unintended—it was him, his look, his absent-mindedness, and general uselessness in so many areas of life, such as hailing a cab to go a hundred yards. The only way we could get him in our debate was posthumously. Otherwise, he could never have found us— his sense of direction was hopeless. I told the grave diggers not to go to Lewis' Church burial plot in Headington. He is buried next to his brother Warnie. We definitely prefer Chesterton over Lewis and Churchill, for he has a much better stage presence and a God-gifted funny bone.

The participants speaking against the proposition

David Mamet belongs on the *Mount Rushmore* of playwriters. In fact, he has his own mountain. His peers acknowledge that there is Mamet, and then there are his admirers. His movies include, *Glengarry Glen Ross, The Verdict, The Postman Always Rings Twice, House of Games, Heist, Spartan*—need I go on? Mamet believes in God, yet he is primarily secular. Mamet is brilliant at showing how jokes and the Bible have a great deal in common. He has read, memorized, and studied the Torah. He also has written many jokes. Let us begin, *"Two octopuses walk into a laundromat."* And *"In the beginning, God created the heaven and the earth."* What do these two statements have in common?

Both statements now have our attention. We are hooked. Ok, what's the story, what's the punch line? There must be a pay-off. The joke and the Bible ask us to accept that what follows is a fantastic story with a surprise ending. Mamet would say they are two myths that, somehow, we know are true. Both the joke and the

Bible tell the truth about life. It might be something like Tolkien telling Lewis on *Addison's Walk*[4] that there are really great myths, but the Christian myth is the one that turns out to be true. Expect Mamet to be a blunt instrument as he slams through one sacred barrier after another.

Don Henley is a real pissant and my favorite singer. Who can forget his social commentary in *"Workin' it"* or his commitment to sue anyone taking photos at his concerts? I think David Geffen is right when he calls Henley a professional malcontent. This member of the *Rock and Roll Hall of Fame* and founding member of America's most successful band, *Eagles,* has a golden voice and a poetic pen. He's not invited for any formal academic credentials because he is bright, articulate, moody, and highly opinionated. Yes, he will *Take It to the Limit,* and take us to the state of mind that is the *Hotel California,* (California means "hot as an oven") where you can get truly stuck. As the last line of that song says, *"You can check out anytime you want, but you can never leave."* Many are leaving this paradise lost, including Henley, but they take the mindset with them—they can never leave it behind. Expect Henley to take us to Walden's Woods and channel Henry David Thoreau who claimed that most men live lives of quiet desperation or of a desperado, I can't remember which. I think the desperado is Henley himself, looking for some meaning in life that rests on the intellectual side. Any reason without dependence on revelation seems to suit Don's mindset. Welcome Don, you won't be able to sing your way out of this.

Jordan Peterson is in a class by himself. And if Canadian society and the University of Toronto had their way, he would have no class at all. A Clinical Psychologist by profession and a dedicated Jungian, he first came to fame when he refused to bow the knee to the "woke" Canadian political elites who required him to

---

4 Addison's Walk, a circular walking path next to New College at Magdalen College where Lewis was a fellow. He walked and discussed many important matters with friends including Hugo Dyson and J.R.R. Tolkien.

use a student's preferred pronouns in his classes at the University. Then he became a *YouTube* star with combative interviews with the press and finally, a leader when he packed out auditoriums teaching the Bible. The crazy thing was he wasn't even sure he believed in God. But then he became even bigger with the release of his book, *12 RULES FOR LIFE, An Antidote to Chaos*. It sold in the millions, created an international tour with all the trimmings, and then he got very sick.[5] He nearly died and during the same period his wife, Tammy, and his daughter were seriously ill. If you didn't know better, you would think they were under attack from a sinister power.[6] As though that power knew that Jordan and his family would one day bring hope and meaning to millions of lives. Peterson will admit that now he believes in God and his wife goes to church after her healing. It's just a matter of time, folks. Jordan Peterson is "toast" but in the meantime, he is struggling with this Jesus-being-God thing, so let's hear what he has to say. But read it now—not long from now he will be switching teams. Jordan is not very funny, but he smiles more, and maybe we will get a good laugh out of him.

Oprah Winfrey is a cultural icon. America's favorite daytime talk show host ever. She is a sweet woman and a great actress with good intentions. Unless she disagrees with you—then she is an activist billionaire who will gouge your eyes out or buy you out. She is both loved and feared, connected and powerful. You just say Oprah around the world, everyone knows who you mean. Oprah is famously a "spiritual person," religious if you like. She is a truth seeker, as long as that truth doesn't get too narrow, exclusive, or absolute. With Winfrey all spiritual roads lead to Rome, content isn't as important as desire—specifically as much as being true to yourself. Oprah loves Jesus, but not the one in the Bible. Jesus claimed he was sent to judge. Oprah wants justice, but she doesn't want Jesus as her judge. Jesus says for justice to exist you need a

---

5 https://www.ncregister.com/interview/tammy-peterson-conversion-story
6 John 10:10 Lucifer has come to steal, kill and destroy

judge, but none of us want to meet him. Jesus claimed that all judgment had been given to him. He is both a judge and a justifier. And truth, justice, and final rendering of that judgment belong to only him. Oprah disagrees.

Hannah Arendt died in 1975, but we won't let that stop us. Like the great Golda Meir, she was a chain smoker. Both women's greatness and careers were shortened by this. Clearly, Arendt was one of the great minds of the 20th century. Born in 1906, she was raised in Germany as a secular Jew. She was a very detached observer of life even as a small girl. She studied with famous philosophers Martin Heidegger, Karl Jaspers, and theologian Rudolph Bultmann. She was Heidegger's mistress for several years. She received a PhD in philosophy with a minor in Greek and theology. Her dissertation was on love and Saint Augustine. Yet she rejected the academy and philosophy as not important to accomplishment. She fled Germany after the *Reichstag Fire* on February 27, 1933. The German Government had suspended many human rights including the freedom of the press. She immigrated to the United States with her husband in 1941. She is best known for her coverage of the 1961 trial of Adolf Eichmann in Jerusalem. Her report was called *Eichmann in Jerusalem* and the book was *The Origins of Totalitarianism*. She will argue against the motion, she believes that Jesus was a wonderful and revolutionary teacher- prophet, but not God in human flesh. Prepare to get a lot of smoke in your eyes. Her brilliance sentenced her to a life of outsmarting herself. Reason without revelation is a dead end. Her words promise to underline the words of Saint Paul, *"We now look through a glass darkly."*[7]

Why the Debate?

The debate will NOT be adjudicated by a select panel of very bright theologians, or the ship of fools annually gathered at the *World Economic Forum* in Davos, Switzerland. It is adjudicated every day by the human race. Either people say **no**, Jesus is not

---

7   I Corinthians 13:12

God in the flesh, not the way, the truth, and the source of all life. Or **yes**, he is, and they repent of their sins, believe the good news, and follow Jesus as his apprentice. The debate's purpose is to invite the reader to engage in a satirical romp through life's most important question and decision. Why did God become man? The answer is because he couldn't help himself. It was his nature.

Notable participants who couldn't make it

Dallas Willard, Eugene Peterson, Charles Darwin, Karl Marx, Charles Spurgeon, Abraham Lincoln, John Wilks Booth, Mohammad, Dietrich Bonhoeffer, John Milton, Dante Allegri, Blaise Pascal, Malcolm Muggeridge, William F. Buckley, Socrates, Plato, Aristotle, Sigmund Freud, Tim Keller, Leslie Newbigin, John Stott, Albert Switzer, Karl Barth, William Shakespeare, Saint Thomas Aquinas, Buddha, Confucius, Wink Martindale, Martin Luther, Paul Lynne, Dracula, Frankenstein, Igor, Mel Brooks, , Red Skelton, Audrey Hepburn, Kathrine Hepburn, Oral Roberts, Billy Graham, Vito Corleone, Sonny, Michael, Fredo, and Saint Augustine. For some reason, they did not RSVP. Only Jesus sent regrets saying he had nothing to add.

Serious candidates for participation, but were not chosen

Bono, too cool, demanded a fruit plate. Elon Musk, too rich, wanted to buy the debate. Megyn Kelly, too pretty, wouldn't agree to no dirty words. Robert Coleman, too Godly. Eric Metaxas, too short, pants too tight, uptight. Os Guinness, too Irish. John Cleese, too tall, can't be relied on to do something outrageous. Bibi Netanyahu, too busy kicking ass. "Fredo" Corleone, too "smart." Went fishing instead.

Those who desperately wanted to participate, but, really

Al Sharpton, Robert F. Kennedy Jr, John MacArthur, Donald Trump, Barack Obama, Alan Dershowitz, Vladimir Putin, Gavin

Newsome, John Kerry, Al Gore, Joe Biden, Hunter Biden, Jim Biden, Dr. Jill Biden, the entire cast of *Morning Joe,* K. Harris, Ivanka Trump. *The View's* studio audience, Bill Maher, Greg Gutfeld, and Jimmy Kimmel in "black face."

Ok, that's it. Debate will begin in next week's column. Each participant gets his or her own session, column, and week. I will lead the discussion, interact with the presenters, and just hope for some fireworks. Each person gets his or her own time to make their case—Light the flame, let the games begin—Achtung Baby!

About Bill Hull:

Bill Hull is an untroubled writer who refuses to leave his home in downtown Babylon, California.[8] Someone needs to stay. He is pastor to a congregation he has never met, the best kind, his readers. He has held important jobs, has written many books, and has been given impressive awards, including the highly coveted *Dragon's Head Trophy,* but humility prevents him from naming the others. You know, like book of the year, writer of the year stuff. Even though he has been asked not to mention it, he is a graduate of *Oral Roberts University* and later, *Talbot School of Theology,* where he taught for several years before they found out. Bill does have a family. They have chosen to remain anonymous.

---

8   It is worth noting that Saint Peter closes his second letter by saying, "Your sister church here in Babylon (meaning Rome) sends you greetings, and so does my son Mark." 2 Peter 5:13 NLT. The Babylon image has been passed down through the ages as a place that has insisted—at least the elite who lead it—to commit societal suicide.

THE GREAT DEBATE

THE GREAT DEBATE 2: ANDREW KLAVAN

History's Greatest Question:
Why did God become a man?

The proposition:
Jesus is God come to earth in human flesh. Yes or No?

Moderator Hull: Andrew Klavan, Team leader, satirist, and associate of scholar and brilliant Oxford grad, Spencer Klavan (no relation), even though the younger Klavan slips up on *air* and calls Andrew, "Dad."

Andrew Klavan: Thank you Bill, I'm not sure who you are or why you are hosting this event. I'm not even sure I am here or that this event actually exists. But I have been wondering, if indeed, I can trust my evolutionary-developed brain which is a product of a random selection process, who is the selector one might ask? How can I trust my brain, let alone my mind because God doesn't have a brain, doesn't need one—oh, never mind about all that.

My unreliable mind has been wondering, what if Jesus had not come to earth at all? It is quite interesting to me that not only would Christianity be impossible, but most other religions would be missing a major prophet. They wouldn't have to say what they didn't believe in if it were not for Jesus. Jesus' claims are so magnificently and brilliantly conceived as to create a binary decision for every human being. More on that in due course.

The decedents of Ishmael, the sons of the flesh, those sent away from Abraham's household, and cast out from the Abrahamic covenant, are really pissed off, perpetually pissed off until this very day. Like long-lost family members left out of the will, they need to make something up to justify their existence and show they are different and better. But they had to slip Jesus in somewhere. Muslims teach that Jesus, the Jewish Messiah, was born of a virgin, performed miracles, was saved by God, sent to heaven, and will even return in service to Allah.

Even though some religions preceded the coming of Jesus, they were forced to interrupt proceedings to place him in their pantheons. Buddhism reveres him and Hindus place him among their gods. Greek mythology was forced out of their polytheism and Jesus became the logos, the ultimate spoken word that was so profound it was a person, Jesus. As Paul put it in Athens, your unknown god now has a name.[1] The *almost* Christians, Jehovah Witnesses and Mormons, have him as the Son of God who died for the sins of the world, *et al*. But Jesus isn't having any of the shit about him being Satan's better elder brother. History is divided and defined by his life, B.C./A.D. Before Christ and A.D. *The year of our Lord*. He stands alone in prestige and historical impact.

Hull: Hey Drew, I'm impressed, but could you get to the point, the suspense is killing us here and it's almost time for a break. All this history is fascinating, but could we get to something like what did Jesus say that caused all these other religions to have to deal with him, and particularly, to adjust his teachings or to reject him?

Klavan: Look, your tiny bladder doesn't matter—not my problem—Jesus didn't leave us with many options, actually, only two options. Either Jesus is God come to earth in human flesh or he needs to be ignored. If he is the former, humans should repent of sins, believe the good news, and follow Jesus as his disciple.[2] Including all that goes with it—sometimes explained as "being taught to obey everything that Christ commanded."[3] Follow Jesus and he will teach you everything you will ever need to know. The other option is to say NO, like we anticipate those on the other side of this debate will claim. If you vote NO, then Jesus needs to be put in his place.

Many say that the opposite of love is not hate, it is indifference. But since historically, he has not been the type you could ignore,

---

1 Acts 17:23-29
2 Mark 1:14-18
3 Matthew 28:20

indifference has not been successful. You can't be indifferent to Jesus because he has more followers than anyone in history. He has performed millions of miracles among billions of people every day. Most of these are things like Republicans and Democrats restraining their hatred for each other and catching themselves before they speak, and his words are ringing in the ears of all humans—*created in the image of God.* Everyone has a conscience, they know right from wrong—it makes the entire human race inherently know they are not perfect,[4] and they don't let it become an excuse to do nothing. They know perfect does exist, otherwise they wouldn't talk and think so much about not being perfect, something that haunts them.

And all those miracles and his followers talking about him all the time demand action. What can be done apart from us running around with our fingers in our ears screaming, stop it, stop it! I guess we could put in earbuds and allow the evil little device we call a smartphone, which is as stupid as a tree stump, to flood our minds with lies.

The primary lie is that God can't be trusted, and can't be known, because He is trying to deceive us, therefore, Jesus as God needs to be discarded.[5] Jesus needs to be executed, imprisoned, burned at the stake, crucified, guillotined, stoned, or at least given a pie in the face on the internet. Or, oh, we could make him religious (said with a smirk). I know that in the first century Jewish context he broke all their religious rules. He broke just about every Sabbath rule, he wouldn't conform, and he embarrassed the religious brass with his miracles, parables, and questions. He was impossible to deal with. That is why the more religious you are, the more you hate him, and the harder you work to rid yourself of him. Don't anoint him, ordain him, listen to him, and, most of all, resist the deep desire to follow him. He qualified to be a Rabbi when he was

---

4   Matthew 5:48

5   Genesis 3:1-6, John 1:1-6 and 14. The Gospel of John Presents Jesus as the logos, the logic and key to life's mysteries

twelve, he had not one hair on his chest, yet he was smarter than them all. Put him in his place, a benign religious figure you can ignore. Give him a primetime show on CNN, and no one will ever hear from him again.

Hull: OK, deep stuff, deep work, I'm sloshing about, the mind is reeling and all that. Sorry to interrupt, Andrew, but you will notice people squirming. They smell the coffee and would like to stand up and move around. While we're chatting and the other side calls an audible, we will be anxious to hear how you plan to move in for the kill shot.

Hull: (after the planned fifteen-minute break ends twenty-two minutes later) Moderator Hull turns on his mic. Everyone, please be seated, the coffee bar is closed, pastries removed, cell phone service discontinued, outer doors locked, bathrooms closed. Now sit down or you will be escorted by our guest security force. Thank you *"Chip & Dales"* for your service. Just look for the guys in the bowties. I have noticed the look of concern on your opponent's faces, Mr. Klavan, they appeared quite smug earlier and, after all, you are using the *Donald Trump "Study" Bible* as your main text, but after your presentation, they looked a little like a canine just seeing Godzilla—we all know what happens next. The floor is yours to wipe clean with the refuse of the other side.

Klavan: Thank you Mr. Hull. Your efforts remind me of several despots around the world to conform a particular type of behavior. What were you doing in *1984?* It seems you were taking copious notes. I have often said, most people would rather be told what to do than be free. Most leaders would enjoy manipulation and control of their citizens, forcing them to conform and then providing basic services. That is what dictators do, that is what religion offers, but not what Jesus offered. Jesus offered freedom. Jesus, being God, is our creator, therefore he understands the human tendency to want some form of control over our lives. He knows how tedious and uncertain life can be. After all, he grew up in a little backwater called Nazareth making picnic benches, taking care of his younger siblings or cousins, step-siblings, if you are Catholic, wink-wink. He didn't even understand everything he knew and felt. At some point, he became aware of who he was and what he was here for.

By age twelve he had become a dangerous man. Jesus was Boy/God before he was Man/God, was he afraid? Yes, he was. Are you afraid of ending up a coward? Jesus was. Tyrants, the masters of utopian dreams, first limit what you can say, then they limit the way you think. Every culture has its religious masters. *Jesus had the Pharisees, Sadducees, Zealots, Essenes, and the Romans.*[6] All of them were religious, especially the Romans. The Roman religion was Caesar—the state—it was what is now called government. They didn't care whether you worshipped some lesser god, but you must bow the knee to Caesar. When Christians refused, they were killed, persecuted, and of course, fed to lions for sport. Today you might put them in a cage in Vegas—now that's entertainment. Jesus was a danger to them all. He came to smash religion, to destroy religion.

He threatened them for the same reason that he threatens me, you, Mr. Hull, and of course, those who deny his divinity. He is God who wrote himself into the human drama. The only way *Shakespeare* could meet *Hamlet* was become a part of the drama. But Jesus' script called for him to die. He had to come, it was his nature, he had to die, but like us, he fought it to the very end.[7] He knew his courage would be contagious, but so was being a coward. He fought, he resisted, he begged his Father. His sacrifice, his humility, and his submission caused the religious leaders to dedicate themselves to killing him by killing his example, killing his takeover of their power, and killing their impulse to be their own Gods.

Hull: Very good, Sir Klavan, but I am afraid your skeptical opponents are licking their tobacco-stained lips because they believe you are missing the point. Jesus could have been all that you say,

---

6 Google them, even though if you use Gemini A.I. search, you might get a Pharisee that looks like Donald Trump holding a Shepherds staff in a court room in NYC

7 Mark 14:34

except, *why did it have to be Jesus?* Wouldn't Joan of Arc dying for France, or Hugh Latimer for England, or scores of other martyrs be good enough for a bloodthirsty Father in heaven to be satisfied that justice has been done?

What kind of Father would send his son to die such a death?

Think about Kierkegaard's[8] angst in *Either/Or* and *Fear & Trembling* and his meditations on Abraham's near miss on sacrificing Isaac. He limped around Copenhagen in pants too short for him and a floppy hat, he was mocked for his eccentric behavior. He was hated for his attack on the Danish Church and its uselessness. But he was on to something. He saw Christ as something or someone quite different than the church and religion. He looked beyond the stars to a cosmic figure. Give us something, Drew, we've got to have more!

Klavan: I was just about to bring that up. Sit down, Lurch, and adjust the bolts in your neck. Oh sorry, the bolts are your cousin's—Frankenstein's Monster. Just sit down. I read the Bible and I know that if you want to understand it, you must remove the veils that separate us from its context and meaning. The veil of time, culture, language, geography, religious views and politics of the time. For example, Jesus saying, *"Render to Caesar what belongs to Caesar and to God what belongs to God,"* has completely different applications depending on context. We panelists and particularly, my addled opponents, fail to grasp what the greatly maligned Pharisees understood by Jesus' claims and their implications. Just read the text:

"So the Jewish leaders began harassing Jesus for breaking the Sabbath rules (in other words, for rejecting their formulas and requirements to be a good Jew). But Jesus replied, "My Father is always working and so am I." So the Jewish leaders tried all the harder to find a way to kill him. For he not only broke the Sabbath, he called God his Father, thereby making himself equal with God." [9]

---

8   https://en.wikipedia.org/wiki/Søren_Kierkegaard

9   John 5:16-18 NLT.

From this moment Jesus continued to tell them, *I will be your judge.* And *everyone who has ever lived, regardless of time or belief, will be raised from their graves, and I alone will decide who is condemned and who is not.* Not only that, *I will determine where you and everyone who has ever lived will spend eternity, with God or without God.*

Everyone lives forever, it just depends where and under what conditions.

To be condemned means to separate, to come apart at the seams. Without God, sometimes known as Hell, people come apart, unglued if you like, and that glue is God. Hell and condemnation is the best God can do for those who don't like him, will not submit to him, and in Milton's words in *Paradise Lost*,[10] written for Lucifer, "*I would rather reign in Hell than serve in Heaven."*

You see how Jesus doesn't give our opponents any room here. How can you say Jesus was a nice guy who said some pleasant things about personal conduct? You listen to what he actually said and who he actually was, and remains until this moment—either he is the Lord and final Judge of all humankind or call the ambulance and get the straight jacket, get him off the streets—deport him immediately or, at least, put him on a bus to NYC. So, why did it have to be Jesus?

One needs to take a big step backward and remember our proposition, **Jesus is God come to earth in human flesh.**

He created the cosmos, he thought about and designed the earth and the humans to live on it. He is cosmic, is a being from outside of time and space. He not only understands all things actual but all potential things. He knew that only his incarnation, only his coming to us and speaking and showing us the perfect, could we possibly touch and understand God. But the problem of evil needed to be fixed.

Humans couldn't love without choice and there is no choice if evil isn't one of them.

---

10   Please see a Preface to Paradise Lost by C.S. Lewis

Therefore, he had to show the way of love by giving himself up as a sacrifice and paying the price for our sins. And also, to quiet human accusations that he was a distant God who didn't care. So, as the Apostle Paul understood, *"He who knew no sin...became Sin,"* that *"we might become the righteousness of God in him."* [11] On the cross the cosmic Christ became and took the brunt and burden of all evil and death to humans, we brought upon ourselves, and he took it and became it. Christ, the man, died because God cannot die. Any other death would have been meaningless. That is why it had to be Jesus. That is why it had to be Him, and no one else. So, I ask those on the other side, why not just drop your notes and get on your knees, right here, right now and ask God, the Cosmic Christ, this woodworker from Israel, to forgive you. Then we can drop this charade and go have a brandy and cigar. Thank you, Mr. Chairman.

Hull: Thank you Andrew Klavan. I kept hearing the old hymn, *Just as I Am* while you were talking. I do see one person coming forward. Oh, that would be the first presenter to speak against the proposition. He is holding a cigar—the famous playwright and mensch, not ubermensch, David Mamet who just gave me the double bird—hold it Mamet, we need to take a break.

---

11   2 Corinthians 5:21

THE GREAT DEBATE 3: DAVID MAMET

History's Greatest Question:
Why did God become a man?

The proposition:
Jesus is God come to earth in human flesh. Yes or No?

Moderator Hull: If we could all be seated, please, we better get started. Mamet has been pacing around backstage mumbling something about politicians being whores and prosperity preachers being worse. He's not in a good mood. He just wrote a new screenplay. I mean during the break. You give him thirty minutes and he will present the world with a new movie, a Soviet blockbuster, *Me and My Tractor*. A Russian farmer spends twelve hours a day on his tractor and thinks about the world.

If you didn't know, David Mamet, playwright, director, and screenwriter is *not* on the *Screenwriter Mount Rushmore*. He has his own mountain, *The David Mamet Blockbuster Screenwriter Mountain*. Why? First, he is better than any of them and second, they voted 4-0, no Jews on their mountain.

Who voted nay?

1. Thornton Wilder, Pulitzer Prize winner for *Our Town* and *The Skin of Our Teeth,* who Mamet can't stand. (I saw both movies and they were stinkers. David, I am with you on that.)
2. Tennessee Williams, author of *The Glass Menagerie* and *Cat on a Hot Tin Roof. Suddenly Last Summer.* (Elizabeth Taylor in her prime which lasted about one hot summer.)
3. James Dalton Trumbo, *Roman Holiday, Exodus, Spartacus, Thirty Seconds over Tokyo?*
4. Tom Clancy, *The Hunt for Red October, The Sum of All Fears, Clear and Present Danger, Patriot Games*—who cares if they were not presented on the stage—he is on the Mount Rushmore of American Writers. (Of course, Clancy didn't win

any proper writing awards. He was pro-military, a conservative, and they don't win those). It would be like Arnold Schwarzenegger getting a *Tony Award* for *The Terminator.*

Ladies and Gentlemen, without further ado, whatever ado means, (I think it means without any further fuss or trivialities) David Mamet, speaking against the proposition.

Proposition: Jesus is God come to earth in human flesh.

Mamet:

If there is anything worse than one Jew it is two Jews because a debate breaks out. So, two Jews, Klavan and I, arguing about Jesus is hardly unique. If I didn't know better I'd think it's July in the *Catskills*. Some of you may have heard of the East Coast summer escape for Jews from the heat and hustle of the hot streets of New York City. There was a lot more going on in the Catskills than Patrick Swayze and Jennifer Grey getting it on in *Dirty Dancing,* not a bad screenplay, not a good one either. I can hear the ghosts of Shecky Green, Buddy Hackett, Don Rickles, and Henny Youngman—not a one of them followed Jesus. If they had, they would have been disowned by their families, rejected by their fellow comedians, and no one would have ever seen them perform except their customers at the deli when they served the matza ball soup.

Even Mr. Klavan had to go as crazy as Nietzsche and come back from insanity to go against his father and family to follow this Jewish Rabbi from Nazareth. Klavan even tells a story about his father catching him doing something worse than cocaine—reading the New Testament—and in great anger warned him never to do that again. What his father feared happened—his son converted and the family never recovered. So here we are, two Jews arguing about a particular Jew who lived 2500 years ago. I guess my point is that we lose one once in a while and they go off and join the cult, they join the stepchild of Judaism, the sect that came up with a great story—

Christians. And you know what a sucker I am for a good story. I contend that a good joke and the Bible have some important characteristics in common. Let me show you what I mean.

"*Two octopuses walk into a laundromat.*"

"*In the beginning God created the heaven and the earth.*"

In both cases, I've got your attention. You know octopuses don't walk, and you know they wouldn't be in a laundromat. You know Octopuses live in water and a laundromat has water. You expect there is a surprise coming and that it will make you laugh—that is the payoff. So, you go along for the laugh.

In the second case, I've also got your attention. "I've just promised to tell you the origin of life itself, how it started, who started it, who created everything, and how we all fit into it. Until Einstein, the science community presented the world as eternal, with no beginning or end, and humans as temporary intruders. After $E=mc^2$ was proven, it was known there was a beginning and that paved the way for the Big Bang, meaning there was a *Big Banger*. It opened the door for God.

The Bible is a great story, but it is a myth, not real or historical, as much as it teaches deeper truths about us. It tells us about human nature—the first thing Adam does in Genesis is rat out his wife—it's her fault. This proves that we are not, by nature, good people. Eve was deceived, and Adam went along and then blamed her. So, what's new, this is who we are. I want to establish that I believe in God, I am a student of the Torah, and I am a conservative. I woke up one day and decided that I could count and think for myself, I didn't need the state or elites to tell me what I should be thinking and feeling.

As for Jesus, the poor putz, he had it in his mind that he was the Messiah. He was wrong, he missed it. He seemed to be a child prodigy stumping the Rabbis when he was twelve. He didn't seem to grow out of it but somehow grew into it. At first, he humored them, and they thought of him as a little mascot, someone they would see again later when he entered Rabbinical training. I would need Jordan Peterson to explain via some Jungian jungle of psychological morass, how Jesus entered into this grandiose delusion. Unfortunately, he got what he knew he would, considering the blasphemous utterings and the claiming of divinity. The Gospel of John tells us that once he made his claims, the Pharisees who controlled religion, doubled their efforts to kill him.[1] He told his disciples they would kill him, but he went ahead with it, almost like David Koresh in Waco. A self-fulfilling prophecy.

Kind of crazy to think somehow God had sex with a fourteen-year-old girl and his son was born of a virgin. Sounds more like Allah than Yahweh. If there is one thing a woman isn't—after intercourse with the creator of the universe—a virgin. His claims were outrageous, I know what C.S. Lewis said, that either Jesus was a liar, a lunatic, a legend, or God. He was none of the above. He was a prophet, a teacher, a well-meaning young man who got over his skis. Then, at the last moment, he tried to get out of it. He cried out to his "Father" to get out of it. It was a great tragedy for him and his disciples. Almost all of them were killed for it, and books have been written, including the New Testament. It's a great story with a tragic ending. A big waste of a good Jew, but what's new? But one thing I am sure of. He was not God come to earth in the flesh. He didn't come from anywhere and he didn't go anywhere. Now like Churchill after one of his historic speeches in the *House of Commons* on the danger of the Third Reich, you boo, and I will sit down.

Moderator Hull

Thank you, David Mamet, you really are good at making things up. As you were creating and rewriting history, I was struck by how William Shakespeare couldn't rise above his antisemitism when he wrote *The Merchant of Venice*. Shakespeare was a man of his own culture, it was in 16th century England and it was the cultural norm to hate the Jews. Today we would call him "woke." After all, he was in the theater, he built the *Old Globe* on the Thames, and men played the roles of women, big surprise. Strangely, it seems you couldn't rise

---

1 John 5:18

above your Semitic heritage as you have chosen some authority—it could be Jewish history and more specifically, contemporary American Jewish history—to be higher and more authoritative than the Torah and its confirming document, the New Testament. Could you speak, after which we will render a *Verdict?* Sorry, Paul Newman, the star of that great film you wrote, can't be here, he is *Dancing with the Stars* somewhere between Heaven and Dante's Inferno. I almost forgot, could you speak to the statement of Jesus in John's gospel:

"You search the Scriptures because you think they give you eternal life. But the Scriptures point to me! Yet you refuse to come to me to receive this life ... If you really believed Moses, you would believe me, because he wrote about me. But since you don't believe what he wrote, how will you believe what I say?" [2]

I know you said you could have fixed the ending of that great film, *Man on Fire,* 2004, starring Denzel Washington, or possibly the earlier version with Scott Glenn, 1987. I can't wait to see how you unravel yourself from this conundrum you have created for yourself. I assume you believed Moses, or possibly you would like to put forth the absurd claim that Genesis is a compilation of various authors and collections of manuscripts and points of view. It seems to me, Mr. Mamet, that you have a decision to make. Either the Bible is a human book written by men seeking God or it is a divine book written by God seeking all of humankind. Who wrote it? Either scripture is your highest authority, or you have another top authority. Do you want to know God or know all about God? Do you want to cut him down to size and trust in your own authority and reason? Yes, he used men to write the Bible,[3] but he was the author. If you choose to

---

2 John 5:39,46,47 New Living Translation. Moses is the author of the Pentateuch, the first five books of the Bible. He is the third man in the Garden of Eden, he reports what Adam said, what Eve said, and even what God said. He wrote about Jesus, yet the Pharisees searched and studied the Pentateuch, didn't understand the Messiah, and certainly didn't connect Jesus with it. But Jesus confronts them with these words.

3 2 Peter 2:20-21, No prophecy in Scripture ever came from the prophet's own understanding. Or from human initiative. No, those prophets were moved by the Holy Spirit, and they spoke from God.

believe in God's authorship and authority, then you must heed the words of Jesus ... Isn't that right David?

Give it some thought Mr. Mamet, time for a break while we all reflect. I can see how a few have already slipped into the lobby to get a drink. Oh, Mamet himself has left the room, I suppose He is looking to escape. Hey, Security! You guys in the tight shorts and bowties, Chippy and Dale. Boys, lock the doors!

Moderator Hull

Twenty-five minutes later Moderator Hull calls everyone together. OK, the food is gone, and the break room is closed. Once again, please be seated, Master Mamet has returned, and like General MacArthur, he has kept his promise, he will now return fire. Please remove your mirrored sunglasses, General.

Mamet

Mr. Hull, you remind me of the old saw, all German humor is about the bathroom, all French humor is about the bedroom, all Jewish humor is about the mind, irony, ambiguity—and Bill Hull's humor is amateur hour at the Saturday afternoon burlesque matinee. Mr. Hull, you give satire a bad name. There is no business like no business, and looking at your social network numbers, I'd suggest retirement. In fact, this entire debate might not exist. This could be some dream you are having, some wild fantasy—get an MRI Mr. Hull, today!

Ladies and Gentlemen, I am not sure you have heard me. I'm very much like you, except I'm much smarter, or Jewish, depending on how you want to say it. It's in my blood to be skeptical, but also, I have had many conversions in my life. I was liberal, now I am conservative. I have learned the most important word in Hollywood is "NO!" quickly followed by some hand gesture or suggestion that someone do something anatomically impossible. If you want to keep your soul and not be a drugstore whore, you must learn to say NO! I can't tell you exactly why, but the idea that God became a man, and lowered himself to being a human, well, it runs deeply against my grain, challenges my integrity as a Jew, and I must say, "NO!" I can't explain it, it's a mystery. There is something about being Jewish that makes it hard to follow this first-century Jew.[4]

And for these words Mr. Hull has told me to deal with, I can't deal with them, I don't understand them. Jesus and his words are profound, they are penetrating, and I don't have any easy answers. I know the New Testament says that we Jews have been given a spirit of stupor, which means we are blinded and stubborn. We already know that—that is who we are. Maybe one day, something will change and we, as a people, will change our minds. But as for me, this I know, it is what Micah the prophet wrote, *"… O people, the Lord has told you what is good, and this is what he requires of you: to do what is right, to love mercy, and to walk humbly with your God."* Micah 6:8

I think that we can't change the world except by living like the prophet suggests. How can we effect cultural change? We can't directly, only indirectly. Consider the oyster. Oysters make pearls. The oyster can't actually use the pearl or understand its reason for existence. Someone else must take the pearl and use it. But if the oyster doesn't make the pearl, it will go crazy. The oyster must do it, that's what it is for. We are like the oyster, we make the pearls, the pearls are our lives. Then an artist, a politician, or a captain of industry takes the pearl and uses it to effect cultural change. You get Dallas Willard, Professor in the School of Philosophy at USC, Mother Theresa in the streets of Calcutta, C.S. Lewis on the BBC comforting a nation during World War II by reading *Mere Christianity*, you get Manny behind the counter at 7/11 treating everyone he meets like they were Jesus.[5] The rest of it is out of our control. It is the salt and light thing.

---

4 Romans 11:8 ESV says "God gave them a spirit of stupor, eyes that would not see and ears that would not hear, down to this very day."

5 Willard was chairman for a short period @ the University of Southern California and was an esteemed professor until his death. Mother Theresa founded the Sisters of Charity, known worldwide. C.S. Lewis was asked by an esteemed Oxford Don

I can't quit without leaving you with a chuckle. Recently a woman in London appeared on a morning show because she claimed to have changed her dog's nature. She had made him a vegetarian. It had taken several months and a lot of training, but she claimed that her German Shepherd now preferred veggies to meat. The Morning Show put the dog to the test. Placed before the dog was a bowl of broccoli and a bowl of beef. The dog was released he buried his snout in the beef. It was his nature to eat beef, and even diligent training couldn't change his nature. It's like the convicted murderer on death row who had been there for over ten years and committed to a plant-based diet. When asked what he wanted for his last meal, he said, "I will take a salad, hold the dressing." No, he went Hannibal Lector and ordered a rib eye steak with lobster. Ye old Surf and Turf. And you think we can change our natures—the flesh never improves.

"The human heart is the most deceitful of all things, and desperately wicked. Who really knows how bad it is? But I, the Lord, search all hearts and examine secret motives. I give all people their due rewards, according to what their actions deserve." Jeremiah 7:9,10 NLT.

Moderator Hull

Thank you, Mr. Mamet, L'Chaim

Next week speaking for the proposition, Dr. Larry Alex Taunton—hopefully he will bring his best free Cuban cigars—ashtrays will be provided.

---

to comfort a nation through a series of addresses on the BBC, British Broadcasting Company. The BBC wanted a non-clergy so it wouldn't be tainted or skewed by Anglican, Catholic, Methodist, or Free Church bias. The notes were later made into a book, Mere Christianity. The idea of Manny behind the counter treating everyone as though they are Jesus and thus, making himself like Jesus is based on the words of Jesus in Matthew's Gospel. "I tell you the truth, when you refused to help the least of these my brothers and sisters, you were refusing to help me."

THE GREAT DEBATE

THE GREAT DEBATE 4: LARRY ALEX TAUNTON

History's Greatest Question:
Why did God become a man?

The proposition:
Jesus is God come to earth in human flesh. Yes or No?

Moderator Hull: Here is a man about whom it can't be said, "Here is a man who needs no introduction." Larry Alex Taunton, formerly known as Larry Taunton, had a previous life. He was the Alex Trebek[1] of apologetics. A job where you know as much or more than your contestants, but you make them the stars. The trouble that *Jeopardy* had replacing Trebek speaks to the rarity of such as role. I sat next to Mr. Trebek for three hours one day. He was trapped in an airplane seat next to mine. He didn't ask me one question that day, he didn't bother me, he only frowned when I asked him if he knew the Capital of South Dakota for $400.00.

A fascinating three hours, but joking aside, we must not keep our 4th debater, Larry Alex Taunton, waiting. He has mastered the art of making friends with PhDs, mostly philosophers, who if you laid them end to end, would never reach a conclusion. They are only happy when they leave you confused and scratching your head. Larry's expertise was taking a big long drag off his expensive Cuban cigar, one he didn't pay for, and getting Richard Dawkins, Christopher Hitchens, or John Lennox to give him an answer, to stake out a position. I would like to tell you that Larry is an internationally known figure of great renown, but the truth is he is internationally known by people who are internationally known. He is the guy in the picture of famous people that a hundred years from now it will be said, "Who is that guy in the picture with Lennox, Hitchens, and Dawkins? Let's get our research team on that right now!"

---

1 https://en.wikipedia.org/wiki/Alex_Trebek

So, why are we asking him to argue for the proposition?

LATs, as I like to call him, is a *Man for All Seasons,*[2] especially *The Four Seasons* in Budapest at the Chain Bridge.[3] He is a renaissance man, a man with *savoir-faire,* who knows his *bon vivant.* But he also knows suffering and is an expert scholar on Russian History who describes the Brothers Karamazov masterpiece by Dostoevsky as "a murder mystery about who killed dad." And something about "if there is no God, everything is permitted." He not only floats down the Nile with his feet up and calls it research—he walks the streets of *Garbage City*[4] in Cairo telling the story of the atrocities against the Coptic Christians living under the despotic hand of Islam. He was not invited to the *World Economic Forum*[5] in Davos, Switzerland, which is the *"Dr. No"* or know-it-all environs of the snobbish academic elites, but sneaked in anyway. He walked the world's most dangerous sixty miles, the jungle known as the *Darién Gap.*[6] He makes *Rick Steves*[7] look like a piker, ladies and gentlemen. Finally, he's the smartest guy in the room, because he has to be to climb the intellectual food chain. The man has found the *Holy Grail*[8] and sold it to buy his farm.

He's the Indiana Jones of the 21st Century. Larry Alex Taunton. Please hold your applause.

Larry Alex Taunton: Oh, my God, what is wrong with that man? Talk about the road less traveled, he's on his own journey. Thank you, Mr. Hull—I think.

---

2 https://www.google.com/search?client=safari&rls=en&q=man+for+all+seasons+meaning&ie=UTF-8&oe=UTF-8

3 https://www.fourseasons.com/budapest/accommodations/specialty-suites/chain_bridge_suite/

4 Garbagecity.com

5 https://www.weforum.org/events/world-economic-forum-annual-meeting-2024/

6 https://en.wikipedia.org/wiki/Darién_Gap

7 https://www.ricksteves.com

8 https://en.wikipedia.org/wiki/Monty_Python_and_the_Holy_Grail

The proposition:
Jesus is God come to earth in human flesh. Yes or No?

I want to say a hearty YES to the proposition. Of course, God wrote himself into the human drama. He had to come through the cosmos to save the earth. He started it and only he could finish it. That is what he said on the cross during those dark hours of Passover Friday, "It is finished." But actually, the redemption story was only halfway home. There is much left to do and look at us, all gathered together, doing exactly what he said we should—making new disciples. It is a task that is much more complicated and threatening to the world and church— even Lucifer himself quakes in fear when the church stops screwing around[9] with developing "in-house" disciples and starts making new ones. Making new ones is dangerous and many of us will be killed, tortured, put in jail, and at the least, falsely accused.

There is nothing like traveling *Around the World in 'More than Eighty' Days,"* (the book is on sale everywhere, meaning Amazon) like I did to see what it costs us to make new disciples. It's a high-cost, high-risk, high-reward enterprise.

This is what Jesus must have meant by *"My food/meat is to do the will of him who sent me and to finish his work."*[10]

The Church in the West is languishing because its soul is shrinking because of a lack of making new disciples. After all, we are locked in a self-imposed prison of a preoccupation with self. When I sit with my feet up at night in the jungles of Panama or the silhouette of the pyramids, I take a big drag off my Cohiba Behike cigar, take a sip from my $600 bottle of Scotch, and muse that it is so sweet because my soul is filled with the knowledge that I am doing my Lord's will—I can say, "We got some new ones today!"

---

9   Screwing around means people tightening the screws in the church to make sure there are no leaks on our ship of fools. That is a pretty good expression, a ship that should be at sea but is in dry dock—oh well, you know what I mean.
10 John 4:34

Back to the proposition. People don't seem to argue with the Devil's Trinity and its coming to humankind in the 19th century. The unholy trinity of Darwin, Marx, and Nietzsche has wreaked havoc in the 20th and the 21st centuries and is now reaping a very grim harvest indeed. Darwin came in the name of science even though he was no scientist. Marx came in the name of economics even though he was bankrupt. Nietzsche came in the name of philosophy even though, while brilliant, had to be given a PhD and a faculty position and spent the last eleven years of his life under his mother's, and finally, his sister's care.

So many skeptics have had no problem buying into this tripe, but his is the same crumbling Christendom that deified their age with a hymn, John Lennon's *Imagine*, *"Imagine there's no heaven. It's easy if you try."* And left the culture in the lobby of *The Hotel California*. *"You can check out anytime you want, but you can never leave."* You can have your bags packed, you can check out of your room, but you can never leave the state of mind— you can't just move to the Florida Panhandle and escape—you're still in the lobby humming, *"Mirrors on the ceiling, the pink champagne on ice... we are all just prisoners here of our own device!"*

Moderator Hull: Whew, that's a lot, Larry, maybe we should pause for a word from your sponsor. Tell us about the hat you are wearing today.

Larry Alex Taunton: What a surprise that you mentioned it Mr. Moderator. I'm wearing the Panama Montecristi Hat (Grade 21-22). It was a gift from my good friend, Laurentino Cortizo Cohen, President of Panama. Yes, you heard right. Cohen, a Jewish Panamanian—one of the chosen. I was privileged to spend twenty minutes with him recently. He stood on a footstool, placed the hat on my head, and I wear it proudly for all to see.

Moderator Hull: Could I redirect a bit, LATs? Why is the church the number one target of persecution around the world? What is it about Jesus and his followers that makes them "fair game" for the world to hate on, to feel safe in attacking? Could I just throw in antisemitism as well? Why do so many feel free to walk the streets of America where they dare not be anti-Muslimism but can cry out anti-Jewish rhetoric? Jewish students must hide behind locked doors, but Muslims can throw down a prayer rug on Fifth Avenue and no one dare challenge them.

Larry Alex Taunton: It is obvious Mr. Moderator. No one worries about the contemporary church striking back. They are about as likely to strike back as Joe Biden is to close the border. Islam however, scares the bejesus out of people, and with good reason. When they say they are coming after you, the average person gets plastic surgery and becomes an anchor on CNN where you can hide in plain sight. But of course, all this is surface material because the real issue is that Lucifer has put a deep hatred in humankind's hearts for any person or object that stands in the way of a person being their god. Humankind, itself, is a contradiction in terms. Humans are not kind. The author of the world's most glorious and truthful book, the Bible, does not call for any of us to restrain good, we are really good at getting rid of good, and we don't need any help. There is a human aspiration to restrain evil. There is something that gibbers deeply within humans that knows something is broken and that it must be fixed—but we don't know how. Atheists claim that God doesn't exist because evil exists. How do they know to call it evil? Because they have a God-given knowledge of what is good.[11]

At the very heart of the inner war is a Jew who claimed to be God. And all that is evil, selfish, and seeks power hates him. They don't hate their Jesus, the meek and mild man of peace who will turn the other cheek. But alas, that is not the Jesus who lived on earth and told Pilate that any power he has over him has been granted by his Father. Whatever you do to me , it is for me, and my plan, it works to my benefit.[12] Can you think of anything more hated by the Davos elite who aspire to run the world, to rule with an iron fist covered by a dainty glove? They hate the Jewish God

---

11 Romans 1:18-32
12 John 19:11

the same as does their spiritual father, Lucifer. They detest this Jew who claims absolute truth—to be ...*the way, the truth, and the life. Additionally, that he is the only way to God. "There is salvation in no one else! God has given no other name under heaven by which we must be saved."* [13]

More Christians die every day around the world by the hand of persecution than at any time in history. It is so commonplace that the other members of the global family hardly notice. It's hard to keep track of, it is ubiquitous. Where Christians die the most, the church grows the most. Lucifer is a loser and he can't lose any bigger than in this grim but real statistic.[14]

I would like to close with a story. As you know, I have spent time in what is known as *Garbage City*[15] on the edge of Cairo, Egypt. It is a slum filled with mountains of garbage. The city is the legacy of Islam and its treatment of Christians. The city is populated with Coptic Christians.[16] They take care of garbage for a living. In the 10th century when Islam took real power they gave Christians living in the land three options. The first was to convert to Islam. The majority took option one, why not, go along to get along? The second was to pay a tax. Most could not afford it. The third was death (usually by beheading). Many knew ahead of time that they would be confronted with this choice. Many decided to have Cop-

---

13   Humans are not kind, see the Curse in Genesis 3:1-16, Jere 17:9, John 14:6, John 8:58, Acts 4:12.

14   This is exactly what Jesus predicted and promised his disciples Matthew 10:16-23. He promised they would be 1. Arrested, 2. undergo trial, 3. jailed, 4. beaten, 5. lose their family, 6. be hated. That is why Paul was left for dead outside the city of Lystra, but when he was awakened, he went back into town, and there he met Timothy. https://www.opendoorsus.org/en-US/stories/13-christians-killed-day-average/#:~:text=On%20average%2C%20more%20than%2013,roughly%205%2C000%20people%20each%20year.

15   https://www.atlasobscura.com/places/garbage-city Please read this! Yes, it is a hard thing to know, but we must be aware of how deeply we are hated, and we must maintain the freedom of worship in our country and around the world.

16   https://en.wikipedia.org/wiki/Coptic_Orthodox_Church

tic Crosses tattooed on the hands of their children. The children knew when they grew up that their parents were martyrs.

The Coptics are Arabs, not Jews, but the Coptics were now followers of the Jew that Islam loves to hate. Jesus of Nazareth is (still) a threat to the father of lies, Lucifer. Lucifer makes sure that the hating gets done. Christians are an easy mark these days. Our insistence on the existence of absolute truth that is found only in Jesus, who is the Christ, the Messiah, ensures that the secular city will come for us. We must stand up or we will be living in our own Garbage City. We will be the broken eggs in their utopian omelet with a dash of Sharia sauce. Of course, Christ is God come to earth in the flesh, and the whole earth is offended by his presence but can't survive without it.

Moderator Hull: Thank you Larry Alex Taunton. LATs is wearing Desert Boots by Bontoni: Suede Norwegian Chukka Boots, ($1,550.00 USD). You can't get them free for wearing them like Larry, but until 5:00 PM today at Larry's lobby display, you can order a pair for only $500.00. Thank you everyone. Next up in Debate 5 we have, for a real change of tune, Don Henley, who will be speaking against the proposition as soon as he fills out the paperwork for his lawsuit against Larry & me for copywriting violations concerning *Hotel California*.

"Ciao" Chow.

THE GREAT DEBATE 5: DON HENLEY

History's Greatest Question:
Why did God become a man?

The proposition:
Jesus is God come to earth in human flesh. Yes or No?

Moderator Hull: Don Henley. I'm already star-stuck. He's only here because I secretly purchased the copywrite to the *Eagle's* entire catalog. He has his personal Satan, one Irving Azoff, who has me under surveillance. It's hard to spot Azoff coming, he is so short that I overlook him. The idea of a Jewish Devil makes sense because Lucifer's greatest rival is a Jew. Isn't it obvious that God is a Jew? All the apostles were Jews and the Bible was written by Jews. When you are in Rome and visit Christianity's most holy temple, Vatican City or plaza, among the 140 statues of saints and martyrs are plenty of Jews. In the church you see Michelangelo's *Pieta*, a Jewish Mother and the dead body of her slain Jewish son, the Son of God, therefore, God. It goes on and on, Saul of Tarsus, the Pharisee of Pharisees, AKA, the apostle Paul, after being knocked off his horse and struck blind. You don't want that guy after you. I don't think it advisable for any person or country to get after the Jews.[1] I fear for any group, nation, or even ignorant demonstrators who never have cracked a history book, who wish ill to the Jews. Young and ignorant are synonyms but their adult mentors are guilty.

Let me remind you that Don is my favorite singer. He leads my favorite band and his solo work dominates my personal playlist. He wrote the lyrics to *Hotel California*. Donald Hugh Henley is the *Desperado*, even though a Baptist one from East Texas. Don't make too much of that—if you grew up in Texas, either you were a Baptist, are a Baptist, or will be a Baptist. I did hear him muttering

---

1 See Genesis 12:1-3

something about this being the *"Last Worthless Evening"* that he would spend appearing at a debate sponsored by a guy he had never heard of. But here he is, ladies and gentlemen, *"Dirty Laundry"* and all, the man whom David Geffen called a professional malcontent—who is going to ask you for money to keep us from cutting down *Walden Woods*— Don Henley.

Henley: And I thought I was the asshole. It's true, I've got a little Baptist on and maybe in me, just enough to disgust me. I've been much more shaped by the writings of Henry David Thoreau, an American naturalist, poet, and philosopher. His formative book, *Walden*, is a reflection upon simple living in natural surroundings. His books influenced such great figures as Tolstoy, Gandhi, and Martin Luther King. That is why we started the *Walden Woods Project*—to dedicate a beautiful forest in Concord, Massachusetts where Emerson and Thoreau walked. You can donate at https://www.walden.org

Moderator Hull: Hey Don, didn't Thoreau most famously say, *"All men live lives of quiet desperation?"* Aren't we all, to one degree or another, Desperados? All that outdoor life and natural surroundings you mentioned, was pretty hard on Thoreau who died at age 44. What got you off on this humanistic path? It seems to be like one of your best ballads, *"Wasted Time."* What is the reason you have chosen a very different life of private jets and huge climate-controlled mansions than this whole naturalistic charade? Could you comment on the proposition in question? After all, that is why we are here.

Henley: Who's the pissant now? I thought it was obvious. I am speaking against it. Truth is something far too big for just one religion's ideology. The proposition is stupid, outrageous, and I dismiss it out of hand. And would you please stop using my song titles to launch your attacks on me? You are breaking so many copywrite laws, I've lost count. You owe me over a million dollars USD in royalties from just the first few minutes of this discussion. You will be hearing from my attorneys Abraham, Isaac, & Jacobs.

The proposition:
Jesus is God come to earth in human flesh. Yes or No?

This may be too much for your limited mental capacity, Mr. Hull. Truth is an enigma, a mystery, but so you can understand it, let me tell you a story about some blind men and an elephant. You may remember, Sir Hull, that line in Aaron Sorkin's *"A Few Good Men"* Jack Nicholson utters the famous line that I direct at you, *"You can't handle the truth!"* You may be as much a knucklehead as the two dim-witted soldiers who carried out the Code Red issued by the Nicholson character, Colonel Nathan R. Jessup.

But, back to my story. The blind men are representatives of the major religions/philosophies of the world—Islam, Judaism, Hindus, Buddhism, Christianity, *et al.* The elephant represents the truth. One blind man feels the trunk and says the truth is long, flexible, and very much like a tube. Another finds a leg and says it is like a tree. Yet another feels the side of the elephant and says truth is a solid wall, strong and sturdy. Another grabs the tail and makes his own observation. But none can see the whole elephant, so they all have only a part of the truth, *ipso facto*, no one has *all* the truth. The truth can only be seen by a sighted person, a person who can stand back and say, *ah ha!* now I can see it!

What is so galling about biblically based Christians is their certainty. It's arrogant. It lacks the humility of Jesus. There is, therefore, nothing Christian or enlightening about it. You abuse the memory of Jesus by making him God, and the only way to God. That is the worst possible way to stain his memory and ruin his ministry. Mr. Hull, I can't believe I'm sinking to your level here, but I look into your eyes and see *"Lyin' Eyes."* I suppose the next thing you will say is something absurd like, God causes all things, even that the soul of my dearly departed brother and colleague, Glenn Frey, is languishing in Hell. This working together for the good concept is nothing more than a cheesy cliché. I apologize, ladies and gentlemen, I'm very emotional about this. Please listen to my sentiments in the song, *"The Last Resort,"* concerning the sins of Christianity. The opening line sets the tone, *"She came from Providence, the one in Rhode Island."*

Moderator Hull: Ah, *Where Eagles Dare*—oh, that was Alistair MacLean, not Don Henley. *The Last Resort* was a masterpiece Don, it made you America's musical Poet Laureate. But I must say, a lousy theologian. I would say philosopher, but since when have philosophers been held to account for their nonsense?

Before we take a much needed break, Don, I have a question for you. It concerns the problem of the Storyteller. Who is the person who is qualified to stand back and who sees the entire elephant? The Storyteller assumes to know the truth—not spiritually blind like the rest of us. In effect, the Storyteller is saying, I'm not blind, not mortal like the rest of you. It is an astounding claim. Yet it is made with a mask of humility. How do you know Don? Are you the one who is not blind and can see the entire truth? I think you have driven yourself into a cul-de-sac. See you after the break.

Twenty-five minutes later after a ten-minute break.

Moderator Hull: Don, I'm sure you've had a chance to gather with your great team. I'm pretty sure you didn't call Joe Walsh. He recently said that he had more fun in the seventies when he was in his twenties than he is in his seventies living in the twenties. And this is a sober Joe Walsh. Thank God/or Buddha. Joe is a Buddhist. Buddha does have a weight problem—sitting under that fig tree for 49 days, with no cardio, you get chunky. Jordan Peterson seems to have been doing most of the talking, Oprah took a call, probably from Barack Hussain Obama, her spiritual mentor. What's that red dot between her eyes? Seems like Mamet spent his time doodling. Ok, Don, time to answer the question, who is the Storyteller? Who can see the entire truth?

Henley: God is telling the story. He can see all things. He knows the truth. He is the combined collective conscience of all that is true. Ultimate reality can only be known by God. I hope this will assuage your combative spirit Mr. Hull, so we can get on to some deeper truths.

Moderator Hull: Oh, you mean the deeper truths you learned during those *Cocaine Nights* of fun and frolic during the 1970s? Did you snort a couple of lines after you read *Doors of Perception* by Aldous Huxley? I know that's where the *Doors* got their name. Lead singer, Jim Morrison, was found dead in a Paris bathtub at age 27. Dead by illusion or disillusionment. Is this your *Brave New World?* Weak men die of excess in bathtubs, weak leaders are dangerous to their followers, their fecklessness is provocative, empires fall because of them.

Strong men step up, speak up, and do the hard stuff. Weak men will appease, strong men insist on victory. Jesus came through the back door of history but became the victor. He is not a king *among* kings, not a lord *among* lords, but *the* king of kings and *the* lord of lords. He is not just one of *many* judges of the human drama, he is the *only* judge. I don't get a vote, Don, you don't get a vote, the Dali Lama doesn't get a vote. Christ alone decides, he has all the power. There is no other power left, he has it all. *"... the Father judges no one, instead, he has given the Son absolute authority to judge."* [2]

Don, I would agree the great Storyteller is God. But he told his story in the Bible. Europe and Western civilization thrived for a thousand years based on the story. The punch line of his story is that Jesus of Nazareth is God. He intervened and his love is confrontative. It is love that says, "You've got to change." His love is a furious and jealous love, determined to eliminate evil. He has said, I will make it possible by sacrificing myself for you.

Don, the ultimate reality is what the Greeks called λογος, the *logic*, the design behind all things. His disciple, an eyewitness, the apostle John said, *"In the beginning was the word and the word was with God and God was the word."* Also, *"And the word became flesh and lived among us."* His life, ministry, death, and resurrection are the manifestation of God's eternal being. When you claim that one religion or person is the absolute truth, you are making a truth

---

2 John 5:24 NLT.

claim yourself. Again, how do you know? What is your source? On what basis do you make such a claim? You are being exclusive, you are being narrow minded, you are saying, my view is the right view, which is to say, no view is the right view. Don, quit resisting, do what you know deep within—get on your knees, give in, and suddenly the world will make sense. You can still sing out your questions and fears and social commentary, but let God sing through you. Check out of *The Hotel California*. God says you *can* leave it, you *can* escape it, you're not trapped!

Henley: Mr. Moderator, the most Reverend Hull, life is complicated. We are all living at the mercy of our own ideas, commitments, communities, and realities. I appreciate your sincerity. It seems you really do like my music and we could possibly be friends—or I could at least treat you with the respect of a fan— if you would drop all the drama. My quiet desperation is not, I suspect, unlike yours. There would be a high cost for either of us to change course. I would lose a lot—family, friends, my connections to the controlling elites, my political contacts, and much of my funding. I don't need money, but many causes do, and I am committed to them. I would be cancelled, even though I wouldn't starve. I would like to end my comments the way I end my concerts with the last stanza of *Desperado*. It seems fitting.

> *Desperado, why don't you come to your senses?*
> *Come down from your fences, open the gate*
> *It may be rainin' but there's a rainbow above you*
> *You better let somebody love you—let somebody love you*
> *Let somebody love you before it's too late.*

Moderator Hull: Looking back at your life and career Don, I think of the configuration of the Eagles that were the best. It was your first concert back together in 1994. You, Glenn Frey, Timothy B. Schmit, a newly sober Joe Walsh, Don Felder. Your voices were in full bloom, the harmonies were beautiful and perfect. The softness and fullness of everyone's voices were at a peak. You had been separated for fourteen years, doing your own things quite well, I might add. But as you have said and Frey has also mentioned, you could only make that magic sound when you were together, with that group of guys.

Then it happened, reconciliation, forgiveness, new relationships, healing, and it released a new power in all of you.

Now, time has passed, former members have died. New and capable singers have replaced them, but the voices have changed. You're still fantastic but, without Glenn, something just isn't right. I hope you sing until you can no longer spit out a note. When I think of you and Glenn, brothers, soul mates, what God has joined together, let no man tear asunder. When the band was torn apart, the world mourned, we all wished, some may have prayed, that you would reunite.

One band member, I think it was Don Felder, speaking of reconciliation, said that the band would get back together when *Hell Freezes Over*. Just for the record, Don, Hell does not freeze, neither does it get hot. It is a place, but not the place described in the metaphor. Hell is a state of being that, after this life, is without God. Damnation is a state of "coming apart" God is the glue that holds us together and makes us persons. When that glue is gone, when God is not present, a state of being unknown to humankind takes place. It *will* happen, justice will be done—and when it does it will be agony for the human being—separation from God. It will make all other Hells seem like practice. *The Heart of the Matter*, Don, is indeed, forgiveness. God brings reconciliation, forgiveness, joy, and harmony—you know that. Skeptics may say Don Henley will bow before Christ when Hell Freezes Over. OK, Don—you're On.

THE GREAT DEBATE 6: DR. SCOT MCKNIGHT

History's Greatest Question:
Why did God become a man?

The Proposition:
Jesus is God come to earth in human flesh. Yes or No?

Moderator Hull: *Mazel tov,* Dr. McKnight. Your book, *TOV,* means goodness—goodness versus toxic. I'm afraid you may find this debate toxic. This debate is more like the late Las Vegas Raiders owner, the slick and litigious Al, *Just Win Baby,* Davis[1] than it is about the penetrating question, did *Joan of Arc*[2] get a fair trial? Dr. McKnight comes to this debate from Chicago, a town that both asks and answers the question, "Who do I pay off?" which of course, answers the second question, "What is the right thing to do?"

Scot recently left his beloved Northern Seminary[3] which is nestled into the niche suburban colony of Lisle, Ill. Twenty-seven acres of progressive thought surrounded by thousands of acres of even more progressive thought—theological slums such as Wheaton, Naperville, Carol Stream, and the dreaded Oak Park. I must say, a missional setting that seeks to operate much differently than the Chicago machine. But have they been successful? It seems the entire place is getting a redo, one you won't be able to watch on *Fixer Upper* with Chip and Joanne. These schools discovered they had more Toxic than *TOV*. Seems like you can't erase human nature, which never improves, especially with mandates and new curriculums. What does one do when people who all believe a gospel disagree on what the gospel is?

---

1 https://en.wikipedia.org/wiki/Al_Davis

2 https://en.wikipedia.org/wiki/Joan_of_Arc

3 https://julieroys.com/professor-author-theologian-scot-mcknight-resigns-northern-seminary/

Scot is quite popular and has created a great deal of *TOV* in the world. His work has been praised, extolled, and even purchased. He is here today because he sometimes lacks good judgment. He wrote a great introduction to my book, *"Conversion and Discipleship, You Can't Have One Without the Other."* Maybe he will explain how to read Romans backward. The first question I would like to ask Dr. McKnight is how did you score 2,263 points in your four years at Grand Rapids Bible College? Was it the way you held the laces on the basketball, was it the black high tops, was anyone guarding you, did you have your own whistle-blowers? Oh, and how did you get from *Grand Rapids Bible College* to becoming an Anglican Priest? Maybe you should write an autobiography. Why do I think you already have? Scot, welcome into the belly of the beast.

McKnight: *Mazel tov* to all of you. This reminds me of a lot of things, but I was thinking of Jean Paul Sartre's[4] *Nausea*, and his play, *No Exit*. I did notice that all the exits are soldered closed. I am assuming you are all still here, the house lights are down, and the stage lights are blinding me, but your exits are closed, and we are all prisoners of our own ideas. I think Mr. Hull's characterization of the Northern Seminary's "redo," as he put it, is more a reflection of his mind than the reality. His introduction reminded me of Henri Nouwen's description of a disturbed mind as "a banana tree full of monkeys." I am not here to defend my outstanding basketball career, but to speak **for** the proposition. By the way Mr. Moderator, I scored all those points before the three-point shot and I was prohibited from using my famed step back shot—it was considered dancing.

About The proposition:
Jesus is God come to earth in human flesh. Yes or No?

Of course, Jesus is God come to earth in human flesh. The question was asked how I became an Anglican Priest. It is because I

---

4 https://en.wikipedia.org/wiki/Jean-Paul_Sartre

am a *Nicene Creed* kind of guy. It represents the collective wisdom of the church in 325 AD. Yes, Constantine, a classic opportunist, a typical politician, called the Bishops together and insisted they come up with something. He was sick and tired of the bickering in the Roman Church. They were to confront the Arian heresy named after an Alexandrian Bishop, Arius, leader of a movement that taught Jesus was not divine. Three hundred Bishops and three months later they issued a statement connected to the three hundred previous years of Christian living and dying which set a foundation for the church to build on. At the center of it stands Jesus of Nazareth, namely, God come to earth in human flesh. Please allow me to recite it for you.[5]

WE BELIEVE in one God,
the Father, the Almighty,
maker of heaven and earth,
of all that is, seen and unseen.
We believe in one Lord, Jesus Christ,
the only Son of God,
eternally begotten of the Father,
God from God, Light from Light,
true God from true God,
begotten, not made,
of one Being with the Father.
Through him all things were made.
For us and for our salvation
he came down from heaven;
by the power of the Holy Spirit
he became incarnate from the Virgin Mary,
and was made man.
For our sake he was crucified under Pontius Pilate;
he suffered death and was buried.
On the third day he rose again
in accordance with the Scriptures;

---

5   https://en.wikipedia.org/wiki/First_Council_of_Nicaea

he ascended into heaven
and is seated at the right hand of the Father.
He will come again in glory to judge the living and the dead,
and his kingdom will have no end.
We believe in the Holy Spirit, the Lord, the giver of life,
who proceeds from the Father and the Son.
With the Father and the Son he is worshiped and glorified.
He has spoken through the Prophets.
We believe in one holy catholic and apostolic Church.
We acknowledge one baptism for the forgiveness of sins.
We look for the resurrection of the dead,
and the life of the world to come. Amen.[6]

This remarkable summary of the Christian faith doesn't touch a number of other issues that separate Christians from other Christians. And Christians from non-Christians.
1. It doesn't include the Pope
2. It doesn't include the perpetual virginity of Mary
3. It doesn't include transubstantiation
4. It doesn't include who is saved and who isn't
5. It doesn't include praying to saints
6. It doesn't include statements about Hell
7. It doesn't include smoking, dancing, or sexual proclivities
8. It doesn't include social commentary or ethics
9. It doesn't include politics

It doesn't consider so many controversial debates that, frankly, won't be on the final exam. The Creed gives me a core of belief that doesn't require me to cross my fingers or to cross myself. It also admits that "I don't know" about many of life's issues. I don't get a vote on who gets in and who is out. My job is to come before God daily, submit myself, and follow Him as a disciple. This frees me to have an opinion as diverse as women in ministry or how to interpret the *Revelation of John*. I am convinced I am right about

---

6   http://anglicansonline.org/basics/nicene.html

these things but they don't touch our proposition. Mr. Moderator, I hope this wasn't too dull for you, I know how substance tends to bore you. Bill, I'm over here—did you hear me?

Mr. Moderator: Oh! Thank you, Dr. McKnight. Wow, sorry about that. Don't you think it's a bit hot in here? During the fifteen-minute break—that everybody knows is thirty minutes—please stop by Scot's *Table of TOV,* where you can buy all his books. Don't worry about the number of volumes involved, one copy of each of his hundreds of works will be available on pallets at the loading docks. We have forklift operators standing by who will slip those pallets on a DHL 18-wheeler and they should be delivered to your homes in 8-10 business days. Financing is available for those who would like to make payments or use your reverse mortgage—all purchases remain confidential so your spouse will not find out. Any pictures or autographs with or of Dr. McKnight will be $100 each, with all proceeds going to the *Me Too, Oh Woe is Me, Foundation, Lisle, IL. If that doesn't ring your bell, you may request funds be sent to "Rosie the Riveter" Foundation. Whose motto is "Quit whining and get to work." 1014 Florida Ave. Suite 212, Richmond, CA 94804.*[7]

The Break Begins Now!

Moderator Hull: Finally—forty minutes. That is a new record for a fifteen-minute break. We are glad that Dr. McKnight has made it back to the dais—he has many fans here today. I don't know how many units you sold, Scot, but I saw your staff gathered at the loading dock popping the cork on a *Dom Perignon, a Lady Gaga 2010 Vintage,* and screaming, *"Mazel TOV!"*

Settle down, everyone. You may have heard that we have some mostly peaceful protesters outside. I hope you didn't mind them burning my dummy in effigy during the break. I understand they are from the *Moody Bible Institute,* and they feel they have been left behind, marginalized, and abused for their race and gender. It's a group of young white men—they get blamed for everything. They

---

7 https://rosietheriveter.org/pages/support-us

have been declared *Oppressors* at Moody, harassing young women in the tunnels beneath the Institute. Luring them with candy, cards, flowers, and big smiles, offering to carry their backpacks. This was formerly known as flirting and/or dating. I met with their leaders in an act of solidarity. After we knelt in prayer, one young man said the dummy wasn't me, but our esteemed presenter Dr. McKnight. Scot, it looks like you're the dummy.

Stop laughing, ladies and gentlemen. Let's get on with it. Dr. McKnight, please forgive all this. When do we ever get to laugh at ourselves, or our friends, or even people we admire? Back to Jesus. Could you remind us of what you were talking about before the mayhem broke out?

McKnight: Time, decorum, and character don't permit me to react to your comments, parody, and outrageous conduct. I do somewhat feel like I'm in a *Monty Python*[8] skit or a Freudian dream sequence having to do with your sexual repression, Mr. Hull. I will reduce the proposition to what matters and what doesn't matter. A familiar Pauline passage, I Corinthians Chapter 13, is read at many weddings. But it has something to say that is core to the uniqueness of Jesus as God come to earth in the form of a man and how we can know him. Paul uses a series of ifs.

Paul describes love in 13:4-7

Patient, kind, not jealous, boastful, proud, rude, doesn't demand its own way, and it goes on listing testable character traits based on action. Agape love is actions that focus on others. Contrast this with what we extol and treasure in present society.

If I could speak in all languages, even of angels, and have not love, it is just noise, I'm nothing!

If I could understand everything, even the future, knew God's Secrets, but not love, I am nothing!

If I was the most sacrificial, the most giving, but did not have love, I am nothing!

---

8 https://en.wikipedia.org/wiki/Monty_Python

The greatest preachers, evangelists, prophets, scholars, celebrities, all honors, wealth, and power that comes with the gifts mentioned—all the above are nothing.

We don't even know what we don't know.

"Now our knowledge is partial and incomplete, and even the gift of prophecy reveals only part of the whole picture! But when the full understanding comes, these partial things will become useless ... Now we see things imperfectly as in a cloudy mirror, but then we will see everything with perfect clarity."

The perfect is the eternal state. But it is just another way of saying Jesus. For Paul says what he knows, *"All I know now is partial and incomplete, but then I will know everything completely, just as God now knows me completely."*

Paul has seen a lot. Jesus knocked him off his horse, blinded him, and restored his sight. His life was totally changed. He claimed he was taught the gospel by Jesus, himself, that he visited celestial heights, and had seen what no man had seen. But the more he knew, the greater the mystery. He pictures it like a person looking through a broken & darkened mirror. The closer he got to Jesus, the more he learned and the greater the mystery.

We live in a *but-then* world, and God exists in a *now knows* world. Jesus came to our *know-nothing* world and made it a *but-then* world. We are headed into a *now-known* world and our leader, our Rabbi, our Savior, our God, has and is now, living among us. Jesus, indeed, is God come to earth in a person. Thanks be to God! Christ has risen, He is risen indeed!

And if he hasn't, Paul would be the first to tell us to scrap the whole thing, that we of all the people on earth are the most miserable and should be pitied.[9] But where does that leave those who don't have that hope? Even worse than that. If left to humankind, what could be achieved? Longer existence? How about comedian, Mel Brooks, as the 2000-year-old man?[10] What if man could

---

9 I Corinthians 15: 14

10 https://en.wikipedia.org/wiki/2000_Year_Old_Man

achieve eternal existence? That is the very definition of Hell. That is why getting old is so hard. How much harder could it get if one had to live in decay for 2000 years? God offers eternal life, a resurrected life. The abundant life is life *with* God. Eternal existence *without* God is defined as Hell.[11] *The Great Divorce* by C.S. Lewis is a very insightful book about the twists and problems of moral life, and it is funny. An extraordinary meditation upon good and evil.

Moderator Hull: Thank you Father McKnight. May you grant priestly absolution for my sins this day. Of course, neither of us really believes in that part of it, do we? We, being fellow followers of the "middle way," aka, Anglicanism. The problem with being Anglican is that we are in the middle of the road and must dodge traffic in both directions. The middle is full of mystery, and that is the crux of it, isn't it? God come to earth in human flesh is a mystery, the greatest mystery one can wonder about.

Next up will be **Jordan Peterson**—let's see if we can get the very serious Jordan Peterson to give a big smile and a hearty laugh—what I wouldn't give to see him roll around on the floor holding his stomach in a fit of laughter!

---

11   In the Gospel of John he makes a distinction between biological life and eternal life. Biological life or existence is Bios, eternal life is Zoe. They are different in quality and origin. Bios is mere existence, Zoe is new life, resurrected life. Bios is eternal existence without God, or Hell. Zoe is life with God, or Heaven.

THE GREAT DEBATE

THE GREAT DEBATE 7: DR. JORDAN PETERSON

History's Greatest Question:
Why did God become a man?

The proposition:
Jesus is God come to earth in human flesh. Yes or No?

Moderator Hull: Welcome everyone, for those who are looking for the seminar on *Seven Habits of Highly Uptight Mormons*, Steven Covey is in the Joseph Smith Memorial Salon just at the top of the stairs. I made that announcement because we have hundreds of people trying to get into this event, *The Great Debate, on History's Greatest Question, why did God become man?*

The reason the multitudes are teeming like early boarding on Japan Airlines is the appearance of our next speaker against the proposition, **Dr.** (yes, it is a PhD), **Jordan Peterson.** Sorry, Jill Biden, who holds an online EdD from the University of Delaware which is a subsidiary of the Democrat party.

Before Dr. Peterson became a thorn in the side of the Canadian political elite, he was an extraordinary professor of Clinical Psychology at the University of Toronto. He comes to us today a star in the galaxy that is awash with celebrity. His books have sold millions, and his speaking tours in the United States and abroad are sold out. Unique for a not-Christian person, Jordon has filled auditoriums in Canada with young people, the majority of whom are young men wanting to hear three-hour lectures on the Bible.[1] Yes, you heard right, he has done what no great pastor or evangelist or Wrestle Mania event has done in his country. In a nation that has more churches than they do Christians to put in them, he has become a source of hope to his nation. What Satan has meant for evil, God has used for good.[2]

---

1 Look it up yourself, you lazy bum
2 Genesis 50:20

What did this get for Dr. Peterson and his family? Fame? Yes. Fortune? Yes, but also came illness, misery, and near-death experiences for Peterson, his wife Tammy, and his daughter, Mikhaila. We are very pleased that both Tammy and Mikhaila are present with us today. I think Jordan and his family may be added as an apocryphal addendum to the Book of Job. Look for it in the new *Jordan Peterson Jungian Archetypes Study Bible*. Jordan's wife, Tammy, has become a Christian and attends church. And guess who goes to church with her? You will hear from him in just a moment. Mikhaila has become a follower of Jesus as well. She is married to a Christian man. It seems Tammy and Mikhaila have cried out as Job, *"But as for me, I know that my Redeemer lives, and he will stand upon the earth at last. And after my body has decayed, yet in my body I will see God!"* [3] But as usual, good old hubby and dad is a holdout. He is in his last days as a NOT Christian.

So here he is, possibly, for the last time, Jordan Peterson speaking against **The proposition:** *Jesus is God come to earth in human flesh. Yes or No?*

Jordan Peterson: You don't fight fair Mr. Moderator. I wasn't about to laugh at your silliness, but my eyes were a bit moist thinking of the horrible days my family has been through. Seeing Tammy and Mikhaila sitting in the audience, I was overwhelmed with gratitude. I suppose we are here to discuss to whom or what I should be thankful. Eh.

When someone says, "What will it take for you to believe in God?" I wonder, "What in the hades are they talking about when they say God?" OK, I no longer refer to myself as an atheist. That position held by Sam Harris or Richard Dawkins is not logical, scientific, or even tenable. You can't have logic, science, or any convincing argument without having faith in the reliability of one's brain, the existence of matter, and order or design. That all requires a cause behind the effect, all of which demands a creator or beginning.

I don't think being agnostic helps much because it doesn't advance truth in a meaningful way. Anything atheistic or agnostic is

---

3 Job 19:23-26 NLT

an endorsement of God or something we call God. It just seems like a reaction—they don't want to have a boss. In that sense, I am a theist. I speak here against the proposition that God became a man because that is a big leap. This sounds weird, but the first part of faith is *thinking*. I need to do more thinking to get to the point where I can step across that chasm into the land of faith. It requires more than I can presently give to take on board that Jesus is God.

Moderator Hull: Jordan, what do you mean by God? We want to know what pieces to the puzzle are missing and if you are confused. Follow rule 10 from your mega bestseller, *12 Rules for Life. An Antidote to Chaos.*[4] Rule 10 is "Be precise in your speech." How do you get out of your chaos? I don't mean Canada, which is run by Justin "Blackface" Trudeau. I'm talking about your mind. By the way, what are your personal pronouns?

Jordan Peterson: Ha! Ha! Eh. Ah—memories from my claim to fame or infamy—my challenge to the insane Orwellian Canadian Commission that attempted to force me to address my students at University by their preferred pronouns. I didn't object to granting students such courtesy upon request, but I would not, based upon their governmental decree. That would violate my conscience and freedom of speech. My personal pronouns are he, she, Shemp, Moe, Larry, and Curly.[5]

Moderator Hull: Could we get back to God?

Jordan Peterson: As you may know, I am a Jungian.

Moderator Hull: You say tomayto, I say tomahto. You say Yungian, I say Jengian. Do you mean as in Carl Jung, the colleague of Freud, or as in Jenga, the board game? You know, where the player develops a construct and builds a tower and tries to keep the center of gravity to keep the tower upright. Pieces are moved around carefully and strategically, if not, the entire tower collapses. Isn't psychoanalysis somewhat the same? The ID, Superego, and Ego, are moved

---

4   12 Rules for Life; Random House Canada.

5   Shemp, Moe, Larry and Curly, aka, the Three Stooges even though there were four.

around with a Jungian dash of mysticism, a bit of witch's brew, a mistress here and there, while trying to keep the entire thing from collapsing? And the winner gets his Oedipus wish granted.

Jordan Peterson: Nice, what's your name again Mr. Moderator? I'm with Andrew Klavan on this—do you exist, do I exist? Does this stupid debate exist? As Heidegger asked, "Why does anything exist?" I must start with René Descartes, that 17th century Priest's dictum, "I think therefore I am." But I want to go deeper, more primitive, "I breathe, therefore I am, or even, I am conscious, therefore I am." Descartes was trying to get at what could be proven by logic, by reason, by Aquinas' five arguments for the existence of God which, of course, was the popularization of Aristotle's logic. This, then, became the dogma of the Roman Catholic Church. Then we must go right for the biblical jugular. God declared to Moses in and around the burning bush episode, "Tell the Pharaohs, tell the Jewish slaves, I AM sent you!"[6] Then next we must consider what Jesus' beloved disciple, the Apostle John, wrote in his gospel when Jesus repeated God's statement to Jerusalem's elite theological class, "Before Abraham was, I AM." John highlights other instances, as well, when Jesus claimed to be God. *I am the light of the world, I am the bread of life, I am the good shepherd, I am the resurrection and the life, I am the way, the truth, and the life, I am the vine.*

Mr. Moderator, may I go deeper?

Moderator Hull: Keep boring—you may hit a real gusher soon. This seems like that movie I took my wife to on our first date. It was the 1966 film, *Fantastic Voyage,* with Raquel Welch where a pellet was shot into a person's bloodstream and Raquel, Stephen Boyd, and some other actors went through the human body in a capsule. Wherever Raquel went, count me in. She was Kim Kardashian with talent, a 180+ IQ, and smaller caboose. This seems like the same thing, but into the incomprehensible mind of Jordan Peterson. But that's cool because that is why we are here, that is why the place is packed. Whenever you come back to us Jordan, we will give you a standing ovation.

---

6   Exodus 3:14

Jordan Peterson: We must deal with the Apostle John's primary claim. He starts his gospel off with a very Big Bang! He introduces Jesus as the central figure of history, in fact, as God himself. *"In the beginning the Word already existed. The Word was with God, and the Word was God. He existed in the beginning with God. God created everything through him, and nothing was created except through him. The Word gave life to everything that was created, and his life brought light to everyone ... So the Word became human and made his home among us."* [7]

This is an extraordinary claim. John believed it, Jesus proclaimed it, and billions have believed, or at least grew up, under its influence. It actually is saying in the "I AM" claim that God has never not existed. God, the first cause, the Alpha, didn't start anything from scratch because he always existed, but he did create matter, the solar system, everything that exists. As Saint Augustine said in his *Confessions*,[8] God invented time itself. And then space so we would have a place to live. Then he created us in his image so we could understand personality, so we could relate to him. We live and we die, and then enter into this severe mercy called death to end the curse and then start again in a new place with a new beginning. In the meantime, God writes himself into the human drama, feels somewhat responsible for the mess—so unlike any other divine offering, he decides to die in order to pay the debt owed him. It's all so very confusing and mysterious. But as the Apostle Peter said to Christ when many disciples were leaving Jesus, *"Lord, to whom would we Go? You have the words that give eternal life. We believe, and we know you are the Holy One of God."* [9]

We humans don't have many options, we all seem to choke on the ones we have. I am not likely to admit I'm broken, I can't handle it, I'm a sinner, I'm not good enough. God offers us eternal

---

7   John 1:1-4 & 14

8   Augustine's Confessions is considered the first real autobiography written in the 400s AD when he was Bishop of Hippo. Found in Confessions 263

9   John 6:66-69 NLT

life with him rather than a mere hellish eternal existence without God. It is, indeed, the greatest story ever told. But I can't get there, I can't bring myself to believe it. I can't but think about *Michelangelo's Sistine Chapel*[10] ceiling. The finger of God is reaching out to man. That is me, that is us, we are reaching out to God. I can see my hand reaching out to God, but I can't quite get there no matter how hard I try, I can't seem to touch the tip of his finger.

My only hope is that one day his hand will reach out and touch mine. The finger of God, that is what I am waiting for, that's the one thing I want, it is the one thing I don't have. Jesus told his disciples, I have chosen you, but one of you is a devil. I can't help but think that devil is me.[11]

Moderator Hull: A fantastic voyage indeed. Thank you, Jordan Peterson. I know you have the reputation for a fantastic mind, a deep thinker, and I'd say you went too deep for a mere snorkel—you were in full scuba gear mode. Some may be confused concerning your journey, but I'm wondering whether your argument was for or against the proposition. Officially you were against, but it seemed like you were rooting for the *yes* side. I know that your wife and daughter were laughing, crying, and waved their *pom poms*[12] several times when you made points that were favorable to the *yes* side.

I would suggest you make up your mind before you do this again. And I think, Dr. Peterson, we all know what you are going to do. I'm sure your decision will not make everyone happy. Especially the dyed-in-the-pickle-juice doctrinaire Christians. Not the militant atheists, agnostics, and other egotists who think they know better. For the fool has said in his heart, there is no God. But I can think of two people sitting on the front row, who will never get over it. May the finger of God be with you.

---

10   https://www.history.com/news/7-things-you-may-not-know-about-the-sistine-chapel

11   John 6:70, 71. He named Judas, but who among us has pure motives? That is part of it, admitting that even our motives are impure, tainted, and not worthy.

12   Sorry, I can't really describe a pom pom—please consult a cheerleader website.

Ladies and Gentlemen. Please remain seated as Dr. Peterson and his party are escorted into the lobby by our lovely guest security force from *Chip and Dales*. The Peterson's will be available for autographs and photos, but not Jordan Peterson. Jordan, a renowned clinical psychologist will hear your confession for a small fortune. He will be seated behind a special screen for sake of privacy. Please begin all confessions with the phrase, "Bless me Jordan, for I am possibly a sinner." Expect then to receive a thorough diagnosis and exegesis of your soul which will convince you that are no better than a Nazi. You will love it—you'll think you are being roasted by Don Rickles.

Next Session will be with Dr. Nancy Pearcey speaking for the proposition. Please, when she brings up her book, *"Love Thy Body,"* it is not a proposition.

THE GREAT DEBATE 8: DR. NANCY PEARCY

History's Greatest Question:
Why did God become a man?

The proposition:
Jesus is God come to earth in human flesh. Yes or No?

Moderator Hull: Nancy Pearcy, I must begin with an apology. You are so nice, so thoughtful, you are properly attired, buttoned up in every way. You are truly a class act. Your presentations are faultless, decorum is your nature, and your books are creative, ground-breaking, and are the arithmetic of the soul. I am so sorry to drag you into the morass of my troubled mind. For those who don't know, Nancy is not a typical scholar who wrote a PhD thesis on *Climate Change and Allen Ginsburg's Howl*,[1] then demands that you take cold showers to save the earth.

She's the best kind. She earned her knowledge the old-fashioned way. And I'm not talking about Kamala Harris' trek through the corridors of power. Nancy has always been smarter, more hard-working, and better than most of those around her. She was and remains independent. She walked away from her Lutheran upbringing when she was 16 and she thought her way into agnosticism. She excelled in the classroom, but God intervened and caught up with her in the mountains of Switzerland at *L'Abri*, founded by Francis and Edith Schaeffer. I can promise you, Nancy, this is not Switzerland, but you may yodel[2] before I finish. Nancy has written many award-winning books—such gripping mysteries as *Love Thy Body, (an ode to Ozempic?), Saving Leonardo (DiCaprio?), Finding Truth, Total Truth, You Can't Handle the Truth (with Jack Nicholson?), and most recently, The Toxic war on Masculinity, (why girls don't want*

---

1 https://www.poetryfoundation.org/poems/49303/howl
2 #

loser boys in the cheerleader locker rooms). Please see Nancy's many achievements and awards on her Faculty page at *Houston Christian University*.[3] She heads the *School of Christian Thought & Apologetics*. She has achieved all this without an earned Doctorate. She joins Karl Barth, Fredrich Nietzsche, Eugene Peterson, Reinhold Niebuhr, Soren Kierkegaard, John Stott, and Jimmy Swaggart as those who have distinguished themselves in real life by producing results. So, ladies and gentlemen, speaking for the proposition, I give you Dr. Nancy Pearcy.

Nancy Pearcey: Thank you, Bill, you are up to your usual tricks. I'm here today because I thought this debate was real, that the presenters were really here. Right now, I'm not sure where I am or why. But since I am here, as René Descartes said, "I'm here, therefore I am." Or was it Hannah Arendt's boyfriend, that adulterer Nazi-loving Martin (I have an earned Doctorate, snob), Heidegger, who in his famous work, *"Being and Time"* in 1927 asks the question, "Why does anything exist at all?" Whew! I feel flushed—but I must say that sure felt good. I'm getting out my angst, a lot of Freudian repression gibbering about in my subconscious. I think I am experiencing a mind meld with you, Bill, which is all very troubling but intoxicating.

Moderator Hull: Hey Siri, I mean Nancy, on the count of three, I want you to return to your normal state, you're not Martin Heidegger's betrayed wife, Elfride Petri, with a jagged knife in her hand ready to stab his mistress, Hannah Arendt, or even Martin, nor are you Mary Queen of Scots or Joan of Arc—you are writer, scholar, and holder of an honorary doctorate from *Cairn University*,[4] wherever that is. Ok, exhale the fantasy and inhale reality on the count of three—1, 2, 3.

Nancy Pearcy: Thank you Bill, it's so nice to be with you again.

The proposition: *Jesus is God come to earth in human flesh. Yes or No?*

---

3   https://hc.edu/contact/nancy-pearcey/
4   https://cairn.edu

Concerning the proposition, allow me to approach the question like I would any subject. First, I must define the problem and then offer a solution. If I can't define the problem and offer a solution there is no need for a presentation, or to write a book, or to have a conversation.

The Problem: God had a problem. In Paradise Garden, Adam, a man as real as you want him to be, lost his focus—he wasn't meeting Eve's deepest need and she wandered away and got sweet-talked by a crafty gigolo. God went looking for Adam and found him crouched behind a bush, blushing because he realized he was naked. It went downhill from there. God cursed them, their paradise, and threw them out, never to return.

God then decided to gradually reveal himself to humans because the most cursed thing about them is their minds, their inner persons, and how they are disinclined to give up this newfound freedom of running their own lives—even though it is ruining them, bringing death, disease, and one disaster after another. There was now a separation between God and his creation, between his holiness and their rebellion. It was like a debt that humans owed to God, but wouldn't pay it, couldn't pay it. They didn't even understand it.

The Solution: The situation was very much like *Michelangelo's Sistine Chapel* ceiling. Rather than offering his fist, God offers his finger. Man reaches for the finger of God. No matter how much man strains, he can't touch the finger of God. God makes a decision. He must reach out, bridge the gap, and touch man's finger. That finger reaching out is God in human form becoming a man. What the church calls incarnation, what the Greeks called logos, what the Jews called Messiah—a form of communication so powerful, so vivid—God living among us, Immanuel. I say yes, yes, indeed to the proposition.

Moderator Hull: Ah, that's the Nancy Pearcy we all know and love. I can see Oprah is smiling and amening your presentation, Dr. Pearcy. Frankly, when Oprah is pleased, I get worried. I think she is ok when you speak in such general terms. Nancy, I think the *total truth*, might take that smile right off of Oprah's face and she may go gonzo[5] on you and buy *Houston Christian University* and turn it into a theme park.

I think we should take a short break. How about twenty minutes? That should be long enough for your husband to sell your wares and for Oprah to call her attorneys. When we come back, and I know you will come back. We will be closing the soft serve ice cream dispenser so, everyone, take a comfort break, get a drink, and get ready for—I wouldn't call it mud wrestling, but I would call it muckraking.[6]

Moderator Hull: Wow, it's only been 35 minutes and you're back. Even Oprah is back, her face is very much at rest and business-like. I think it is safe to say, *Houston Christian University*, you have a problem! You can see total truth's Murderer's Row over there, Mamet, Henley, Peterson, Winfrey, I'm sure the idea of *total truth*, the existence of one absolute truth, gives them all a *Mylanta*[7] moment. Then, however, comes Jesus' claim, *"I am the way, the truth, and the life, no one comes to the Father but through me."*[8]

The very idea of God becoming a human being requires total truth. This is the essence of the proposition and the world hangs in the balance. Nancy, why does this proposition exist, incarnation, God with us, why is there no other option? Make your case.

Nancy Pearcy: Discipline for me is difficult right now, as there is so much to say. But I must stick to the point. Jesus is God's only begotten son, not just one of them. He is a member of the Triune God, not just a noble character in *Lord of the Rings*. He is God/man united in one person. God wrote himself into the drama of humankind and in that act decided to save the world from itself. Jesus' claims are so dramatic, so cosmic in nature, that they can

---

5 https://en.wikipedia.org/wiki/Gonzo_journalism
6 https://en.wikipedia.org/wiki/Muckraker#Origin_of_the_term,_Theodore_Roosevelt
7 A common antacid.
8 John 14:6

only be believed or thrown on the ash heap of history. Total truth is not accessible by reason alone or by faith alone. total truth is a *person*, total truth satisfies both reason and spiritual yearning. As C. S. Lewis said, "Christ's resurrection was a myth that became fact. It had all the wonder and beauty of myth, answering to human history's deepest needs for contact with the transcendent realm. And yet—wonder of wonders! — it had actually happened in time and space and history."[9]

Jesus' declaration of I am the way, I am the source of life, and finally, I'm the only option because I am the only source of life, I am God, therefore, you must decide and deal with me, is what total truth is about. Now, who gets in and who is left out or behind is a separate conversation. You can believe, for instance, in the total truth of Jesus, and that no one is saved, or receives eternal life apart from him, and still allow for God's judgment to be just and fair. It is possible to know God, but not know his proper name. Most of the world's population, past and future, find themselves in a rather primitive position, informationally, about who Jesus was and what his life and teachings meant. It is entirely possible for people to worship what they don't know. The Samaritans did it, Islamists do it, agnostics do it, ignorant students do it, and Baptists do it. total truth is revealed truth, just as the Samaritan woman's eyes were opened and she bowed the knee. Jesus is the only way, but there is so much we don't know. Don't be so sure that Jesus, the judge, won't turn to you one day and say, "Depart from me, for I never knew you."

Moderator Hull: Ah, Murderer's Row doesn't know whether to laugh, cry, stand and applaud, or invite you to coffee. Oprah's back on the phone calling off the lawfare. You've left them in Nobel Prize winner T.S. Eliot's *The Waste Land*.[10] The audience is stunned. Thank you, Nancy, for letting your hair down and allowing us to

---

9   Taken from Total Truth, Nancy Pearcy, page 120 These are Nancy's words, summarizing Lewis's conclusions. Total Truth, 2004, Crossway Books, Wheaton, Ill

10   https://en.wikipedia.org/wiki/The_Waste_Land

enter into the mystery of total truth. Ladies and Gentlemen, you might want to stay, because Oprah is next and everyone in attendance will get a new car. It will be electric—it's the Obama Edition with his autograph branded into the leather seats. It only goes about 150 miles before recharging. But don't worry, the stations for recharging are usually only 200 miles apart and the lines are only a few hours. Usually, motels are nearby. Try not to climb mountains, cross deserts, or forge rivers. If you enter a river and the car begins to sink, you have 1 minute before the car doors lock and you will drown. On the upside, parking has gotten easier because of all the unused electric parking stalls. Please pick up your car after the debate. I hear Elon Musk will be out front to provide a different option. He is *persona non grata* with the Oprah/Obama crowd since he bought Twitter, now **X**, and restored freedom of speech to the planet Earth.

THE GREAT DEBATE

THE GREAT DEBATE 9: OPRAH WINFREY

History's Greatest Question:
Why did God become a man?

The proposition:
Jesus is God come to earth in human flesh. Yes or No?

Moderator Hull: Welcome ladies and gentleman. I use the singular, gentleman because apart from me, there is only one other man in the audience. There may be some men out there who are pretending to be women. Hey boys, the women's locker room is just out the door and to the right. But I am using the normal criterion for "what is a woman?" which is an adult female. Ladies, you have taken every seat. You might remember just a couple of years ago there was much confusion in the culture when a certain genre of Supreme Court nominees, politicians, women, and activists, suddenly got stupid and couldn't answer the question, "What is a woman?"

Ladies, and the guy in the third row in the floral dress and a clean shave, you're present to hear from the 3.5 billion-dollar woman, Oprah Winfrey (after a two-minute standing ovation). What can be said about this woman that she hasn't already said? She's beautiful, she's rich, she's famous, she's grown right in front of us. She has lost more weight on national TV than she weighs now. She is an Academy Award winner for her role in *The Color Purple*, a gripping story of her quest to turn every red state to purple. Oh, I'm being waved off by the producer. I didn't know we had a producer, but she is waving me off. Apparently, I got that mixed up with a real movie by the same name which I haven't seen. I am being told she won the Oscar for a 1985 film, *The Color Purple*.

Oprah has been feted by such greats as Barack Hussein Obama, and other Chicagoland greats such as Dr. Jeremiah G.D. America Wright, Jesse Jackson, and Saul Alinsky. She has received every award and honor that America grants. Well, except the National

Rifle Association's Merit of Honor. Oprah is a Christian—she says Christ is the only savior. But she also says, "I am my own salvation … Heaven is not a location" (April 24, 2008). I suppose Hell is not a location either. So, it seems there is no use in telling anyone to go there. She says there is no sin, she says that her church is the historic T.V. show she built. Today we are going to find out what kind of Christian she is. I suppose we should start with a question for you, Ms. Winfrey, What kind of Christian speaks against God becoming a man? Is it the man part? Is it the God part, and for you, is the position already filled? I would like to remind all of us in the room today of the proposition in the form of a question.

The proposition: *Jesus is God come to earth in human flesh. Yes or No?*

Oprah, why have you chosen to say no?

Oprah: I would like to introduce my lifetime partner, Steadman Graham, in the third row in a beautiful floral dress. Hi Honey, glad you could get in today. So much truth can be found in the minds of the great poets, Mr. Moderator, in the words of my departed friend, John Lennon, *"Imagine there's no heaven, It's easy if you try. No hell below us Above us, only sky."* I am that I am and I'm here, wherever here means, so I am happy to be here.

Moderator Hull: Thank you, Oprah, that is the kind of clarity we are looking for. You have said that your "gospel" is to be strong, and have self-worth, a deep purpose, deeply trust in yourself, and connect to nature. At the same time, you seem to think "Jesus is just alright with you." Ms. Winfrey, excuse me, but this is not a *Doobie Brothers Concert*, are you really alright with the Jesus who said, "I am the way the truth and the life, and no one comes to the Father but through me."[1]

Oprah: I'm not a theologian, but I know how to connect with

---

1 *Doobie Brothers* is a Rock and Roll Hall of Fame singing group founded in the 1970s. They have a famous song, *Jesus is Just Alright*. "Doobie" is slang for marijuana cigarette which was illegal in the 1970s. The idea is that Oprah is a bit *high* with her theological, have-it-her-way, meanderings.

the divine. When I walk about in nature, I hear her voice in the rustle of wind in the trees, the singing of birds, the patter of rain, rays of sunshine. These are the moments I most often want to bow my head and think of the Jesus I love.

Moderator Hull: Excuse my impertinence Ms. Winfrey, but you have your own television network, a magazine, and many homes and properties around the world. You are like the once great British Empire—the sun never sets on your real estate kingdom. Your life is cluttered with fame, fortune, and awards. You are loved and wanted everywhere on the globe. I suppose you need these moments of silence and solitude. I think the hardest thing for you to purchase, possibly a treasure out of your reach, is to find someone to tell you the truth, to say, "Hey lady, you're full of it," and that you would hear it! Are you alright with that kind of Jesus?

Oprah: Jesus is a gentleman. He has never spoken to me with that tone. When I speak against the proposition, I am speaking against what you and what others have done to my Jesus. I speak against the exclusivity of it. I speak against the idea that there is only one metaphysical truth, only one way to know God. I am speaking for billions of those that Christianity, as a religion, has left out, persecuted, killed, ostracized—and that includes women. I am thinking about non-egalitarian abuse, priests' sexual abuse of acolytes, and the church covering it up. Look what you have done to my Jesus who would never do any of that.

How could I be for such a doctrine, that God is man, became a man, and started a church that is run by men for the sake of men? That is why I say NO, Jesus isn't God turned into a man. Jesus is God's lovely and sensitive soul son of God. The Bible was written in a time of primitive patriarchy, but my Lord and my God, I think is androgynous, one who transcends human sexual identity. In some way, God spoke through the man Jesus, but I believe God speaks through many means just as powerfully. There is one thing I know for sure—God is much greater than some silly idea that he was born of a virgin. She was only fourteen, and that is illegal in all fifty states.

Moderator Hull: You are absolutely sure that there is no absolute truth?

Oprah: Yes, I am!

Moderator Hull: That's interesting. You realize that being absolute about the non-existence of an absolute is self-contradictory? I think you might want to look up the difference between special revelation and general revelation. You speak about nature and the heavens, which both declare the glory of God. You can choose either the telescope or the microscope—look into those worlds and they speak powerfully of God. The telescope shows you the macrocosm, the big world and beyond. The microscope shows you the microcosm, or the small world, the secret to life itself in the genome code of the DNA. But special revelation is specific, and it is received. It contains information no one can figure out or that would even enter a human mind.

The special revelation is found in the first sentence in the Bible: "In the beginning God created the heavens and the earth." The genesis of all things is revealed in the biblical story. The idea that God would visit us, live among us, and die for us, is a thought that would never have entered a human mind on its own. It is a special, received, revealing of God's mind and nature. You can't feel your way into it, meditate your way into it, or receive it by any human means such as chanting, walking naked in the woods, or puffing on a special pipe full of chemicals—none of it will reveal such a story. So, Ms. Winfrey, this is a matter of answering a question. What is your highest authority? Is it you and your perceptions, desires, and feelings? Is it what it has been for most of us at one time or another, our yearning for self-sovereignty? Or is it God's living word, starting with the living Jesus Christ—Jesus' disciple John wrote:

"We proclaim to you the one who existed from the beginning, whom we have heard and seen. We saw him with our own eyes and touched him with our own hands. He is the Word of Life. This one who is life itself was revealed to us and we have seen him. And now we testify and proclaim to you that he is the one who is eternal life, He was with the Father, and then he was revealed to us. We proclaim to you what we ourselves have

actually seen and heard so that you may have fellowship with us. And our fellowship is with the Father and with his Son, Jesus Christ. We are writing these things so that you may fully share our joy." [2]

Moderator Hull: Oprah, based on your comments here today, I would say the incarnate God, Jesus of Nazareth, is a perfect cup of tea for you. He is someone you can see, hear, touch and with whom you could have a personal relationship. He checks all your boxes because he has not come to be served, but to give himself as an offering for others. But he demands from you what you have not yet been willing to give—your relinquishing of self-sovereignty. He wants you exclusively. There can be no rivals, no other gurus, options, or gods, and you can't play nice with those who would threaten his preeminence in your life. When you check the YES box, *I believe Jesus is God come to earth in human flesh* you can then bow before him and say with Thomas, "My Lord, and My God."

---

2 I John 1:1-4 New Living Translation

THE GREAT DEBATE 10: DR. HANNAH ARENDT

History's Greatest Question:
Why did God become a man?

The proposition:
Jesus is God come to earth in human flesh. Yes or No?

Moderator Hull: Welcome Ladies and Gentlemen to a rare opportunity. Hannah Arendt hasn't appeared or given a speech since December 4, 1975. Nearly fifty years. Her whereabouts have been a tightly held secret, even to her. For a woman of a certain age, 118 years old, I must say Dr. Arendt, you look marvelous. What is even more amazing is you have been chain smoking *Chesterfields* the entire time.[1]

Dr. Arendt was born in 1906 near Hanover, Germany. Early on her mother noticed a keen intellectual capacity and a love for books. Hannah's capacities were extraordinary, and she entered into intellectual life very early by being chosen to study with one of Europe's greatest 20th-century philosophers and Nazi weasel, Martin Heidegger. He was notoriously ambitious and unprincipled for his mistreatment of his mentor, the Jewish father of phenomenology, Edmund Husserl. After benefiting from Husserl, he shut out his mentor from further academic appointments because Husserl was Jewish. Heidegger's ascendance to the rector of Freiburg University speaks to his influence. His book, *Being and Time* (1927), was famous. In it he asked the question, "Why does anything exist?" The answer, I might add, is simple if you believe in God, but quite vexing if you don't. His appetites were many and they manifested themselves in his academic career, but also in his choice of students. This is where the young Hannah Arendt came into view. She was brilliant and beautiful. Dr. Arendt became both Heidegger's

---

1 Seems that Dr. Arendt liked Chesterfields, Lucky Strikes, and Camels.

protege and mistress. It seems Heidegger's anti-semitic pro-Nazi bent went just so far—he had taken a Jewish mistress. But so had Adolf Eichmann.

In due course, Hannah left Heidegger behind and went to study with Karl Jaspers for her PhD. Interestingly, she wrote her thesis on *Love and Saint Augustine*. Dr. Arendt is fully conversant with Christian theology, its history, and its content. She is best known, however, for more current events. She was a survivor of the Nazi effort to exterminate the Jews and was able to escape to America via France in 1941. Her most famous or infamous works are *Eichmann in Jerusalem*, covering Eichmann's trial in 1961, and *The Origins of Totalitarianism* published in 1951. In the Eichmann case, she was writing articles for the *New Yorker Magazine*, associated with the *New York Times*, a former newspaper.

Well, I could go on, and probably would if not compelled by Dr. Arendt's continual glances at her watch. That must be some watch—it's been buried with you since 1975 and it keeps on ticking—must be a *Timex*.[2] I'm not sure what you are in a hurry about, Hannah, as it's back to the crypt until the judgment. Jesus said everyone will be there and he meant everyone. Jaspers, Heidegger, Kant, Hegel, Augustine, Saint Paul, Athanasius, Charlie Chaplin, Babe Ruth, Dietrich Bonhoeffer, even Nietzsche—and final justice will be sorted out. What's the over-under on Hitler, Mao, Marx, Freud, *et al?*

Only one judge, only one opinion counts, that of the Jewish carpenter from Nazareth. I like your chances. I hope at least by then with all these intervening years to, as you Germans say, *denken* which sounds to the American ear as "thiNGk," meaning in English, think about it. You said Eichmann was banal[3] because he

---

2   Timex was an inexpensive watch advertised on 1950s American Television by a spokesman John Cameron Swayze. The tag line about the Timex watch, " It takes a licking, but keeps on ticking."

3   Banality: the lack of originality, freshness, or novelty. Similarly, triteness, pedestrian, conventional

lost his ability to *denken* clearly as an individual, and because of that, he committed the crimes he did.[4] I hope you will join our side and be able to speak in the affirmative, that indeed, Jesus is God come to earth in human flesh. After all, Dr. Arendt, he was a Jew killed by the state. But he was also God who voluntarily sacrificed himself in order to break the curse and close the distance between himself and his creation. Nothing banal about that.

The proposition: *Jesus is God come to earth in human flesh. Yes or No?*

Dr. Arendt: Herr Hull, I'm no philosopher just as you are no theologian. We've both had the training, but it didn't stick. As one of my New York friends, very much a catholic, William F. Buckley, said when asked why he was a conservative when most of his friends were liberals, "I'm a conservative by conviction, but I'm not of the breed." Meaning he was trained that way and thought that way, but he never felt culturally at home with them. I think, Mr. Moderator, that Buckley, myself, and you, are living proof of life in philosophical exile.

First, I was exiled by the Nazis from my country and its great literary heritage. Then I was exiled from Europe to life in New York City and finally, exiled from the Jewish community around the world after my articles appeared in the *New Yorker* concerning the banality of Adolf Eichmann. Arius, Athanasius, Daniel, Jeremiah, the Apostle John on Patmos, Martin Luther in Wartburg Castle, even Napoleon on Elba—many greats were exiled. But exile has its benefits, usually time alone to think about what is true. In Luther's case to create the *German Bible,* or John, the *Revelation of Jesus Christ.* As you might suppose I've had many years to consider the

---

4 John 5:16-30 "Don't be so surprised! Indeed, the time is coming when all the dead in their graves will hear the voice of God's Son. And they will rise again. Those who have done good will rise to experience eternal life and those who have continued in evil will rise to experience judgment."

nature of Christ. Since so many have already opined on his nature, his mission, his death and proposed resurrection, I would like to thiNGk for a moment whether Jesus, like Eichmann, was just following orders.

It is immediately clear that Jesus was not banal. He was original and outrageous in his claims to be the "Son of God." His ideas were fresh and revolutionary, and he was unthreatened, even though he was about to be executed by tyrants. He even told Pilate, *"You would have no power over me if it were not given to you from above."* It seems Jesus was taking orders, in fact, it is clear that he was doing the will of his Father. He was reporting in prayer to his Holy Father. I have concluded that Jesus is God's Son on a mission, and a wonderful and good Son he was. But he is not God himself.

Regardless, one only needs a few days reviewing the piles of bodies in mass graves from Auschwitz to Dachau, the horrors of history at the hand of Lenin, Stalin, Mao—or even the millions of Biafran children who starved to death because of corrupt governments—to see cause enough for any real God to wretch. It seems whoever is in control, God the Father, God the Son, or God the Holy Spirit, this triune combo platter of deities has failed miserably to take care of their world, their people, and I see no reason to be hopeful.

Moderator Hull: Thank you Dr. Arendt. I must say a rather dark view. You found so many friends in New York in the *New School*. I am afraid their philosophical ground is very old school. There is no virtue in being sure that you don't know anything for sure and no one can know anything except what is experienced through the senses. It is a failed philosophy, fascism with a smile rather than a Jackboot. I'm not sure how you could arrange this, but you should get a tour of New York City before you return to *Bard College Cemetery* so you can see how the new left has destroyed your beloved city. A lot has changed—I think it is called decadence—since you left in 1975. And I must warn you, watch your step.

You may also want to take Augustine's advice since you wrote your PhD dissertation on his teaching. You may recall his conversion. He was a brilliant product of the classical world, a professor of rhetoric in 384 at the *Imperial University* in Milan. He was in a garden, there was the Bible on a table, probably not the New Living Translation. He heard a child's voice singing a repeated lyric, *"tole lege, tole lege, tole lege."* Pick it up and read it, pick it up and read it! He picked it up and read it. That was the point when he coined the phrase, *"Credo ut intelligam,"* I believe in order to understand. He realized that in order to understand the world, and for it all to make sense, he must start with belief.[5]

This is where, Hannah, your brilliance is the enemy of belief and blocks you from understanding. Doubt is not higher or smarter than belief. Doubt is the rebar inside the pillar of faith. Pick it up and read it Dr. Arendt—the revealed truth is what you can never figure out. This is why the Apostle Paul so rightly said, *"This foolish plan of God is wiser than the wisest of human plans, and God's weakness is stronger than the greatest of human strength."* [6] As the great Saint Francis of Assisi said, he would need to stand on his head to see the world aright.

Time for a short break. Dr. Arendt, you have many books. They are still selling quite nicely and those named in your will are enjoying the royalties. Dr. Arendt doesn't need any food or drink, just more Chesterfields, please. See you back here in a few minutes—decomposition could be a problem.

Moderator Hull: Welcome back—only twenty minutes—very good. No pictures, no autographs, and no personality booth for Dr. Arendt saved us a lot of time. Hannah let me know she now values time more or less. More, in that she would like some of it back, less, in the fact that there is an afterlife in which she is con-

---

5   Entire story found in various stories. This is a summation taken from Leslie Newbigin's talk, Nihilism, to be found on YouTube

6   I Corinthians 1:25 NLT. The entire passage, however, is needed to get the full impact (1:17-31).

scious. She confided in me that she wonders if there is a last judgment as she will want to review her options.

Dr. Arendt, have you considered not smoking? You have not smoked for nearly fifty years, so why would you start again today? And could we hear your conclusions considering some of the points I made just prior to the break?

Dr. Arendt: You are right Reverend Hull, I haven't smoked since 1975, but since I am already a pile of ashes, it seems redundant, and reductive. But today I am making an exception, this might be reincarnation, but I wouldn't call it Nirvana. It is somewhat nerve-racking. I'm out of practice, one can get rusty.

Regarding the proposition, **Jesus is God come to earth in human flesh.** I would make one observation. On the more positive side, Jesus was quite human in the garden of Gethsemane. He cried that he wanted out! That bolsters my belief that he was very human, that Jesus was an honest broker. His statements on the cross, *"My Lord, My Lord, why have you forsaken me?" "Father, forgive them, they don't know what they are doing."* His dialogue and promise to the thief on the cross and *"Into your hands I commit my spirit."* Finally, *"It is finished."* This makes it difficult to categorize his mental and emotional state. Was he delusional? Was he just playing a role, and if he was, then truly he was insane. It seems however, his disciples fell asleep not far away from his agony. They were afraid, bored, but truly believed he was sane, and a true miracle worker. Wonderful fodder for a late night and a great Scotch.

I would, however, not be able to throw in with you, Mr. Moderator. The jury is out and the jury is in so to speak. In this case, the Judge must give a directed verdict because he knows what no one else knows. It's all part of *Heilsgeschichte,*[7] [7]dear Moderator.

Moderator Hull: Thank you, Hannah Arendt. Your car is waiting, and I've instructed them to drive you through NYC, the full tour. There is this man who happens to be stuck in Manhattan right now and he will be your host. Look for him—he has golden

---

7 Heilsgeschichte is the German for Salvation History.

hair, an orange tan, blue suit, red tie, and he tends to exaggerate, but he can fill you in on the way things are going.

We are looking for our next speaker, Mr. G.K. Chesterton. He tends to get lost and his wife has just put out a *"Silver Alert."*[8] We should find him soon.

---

8   Silver Alert is a warning issued in a region for an older person who has gone missing.

THE GREAT DEBATE 11: G.K. CHESTERTON

History's Greatest Question:
Why did God become a man?

The proposition:
Jesus is God come to earth in human flesh. Yes or No?

Moderator Hull: Ladies and Gentlemen, we've saved the best for last. Mr. G.K. Chesterton is our final presenter. Possibly the greatest presenter of his age, and his book, *The Everlasting Man,* the finest apologetic for Christ in the English-speaking world. Known for his quips and quotes, he was extremely entertaining and along with H.G. Wells, provided the United Kingdom with its most brilliant nights of philosophic entertainment. *Everlasting Man* was a response to Well's *An Outline of History.* What makes Mr. Chesterton's appearance here today quite miraculous is that just a few years ago I visited his grave.

Even though I am somewhat suspicious that he was actually there, it's located in the little town of Beaconsfield, England a short distance off the M40. He lies beside his wife, Frances, in an unpretentious Catholic graveyard tucked behind a small parish church. Much like standing before Churchill's grave, or C.S. Lewis' or Wesley's, the grave emits humility, even though greatness somehow rises up and penetrates your soul. Yet, here we are and here he is. Gilbert Keith Chesterton is 150 years old. He has spent the last 88 years in Beaconsfield behind the church in a simple grave.

Mr. Chesterton, you could break some big news here today if you could tell us that possibly you have been in another location and in a full state of consciousness. Have you been in Purgatory, and if you have, haven't your book royalties been enough for the Roman Church to get you out? We know Luther wouldn't be pleased with that, but you probably are not a fan of that big gaseous beer-guzzling windbag. I know you believe the Reformation is nothing but a pale shadow of the true Church.

Sir, you do look a bit rumpled, but as I understand it, that is the norm. It appears you have lost a bit of weight. What, you are around 21 stone now, height about 6-4? Apparently, no pubs in purgatory. You should have stayed Anglican, skipped purgatory and all that other made-up nonsense, and you would be in heaven by now. Possibly you didn't think that Purgatory included appearances in events such as these. Ladies and Gentlemen, the creator of the famous *Father Brown Mystery Series*, both in book and television—and the man who said, "You can turn back the clock, we do it every year." A journalist, an art critic, and a newspaper man, Gilbert Keith Chesterton.

G.K. Chesterton: Mr. Moderator, it is unusual for me to meet someone taller than myself. With a name like Hull, it is obvious you are well-bred and of Anglo-Saxon lineage. Apart from that, I am a bit woozy—I could use a pint to clear my head. My appearance here today confirms the Everlasting Man's statement, "I am the resurrection and the life, anyone who believes in me, even though they die, they shall live."[1] But like the Apostle Paul has said before, I am not permitted to speak of everything I have seen in the presence of God.[2] I am not at liberty to tell you everything I know, but I will tell you what you need to know.

The proposition: *Jesus is God come to earth in human flesh. Yes or No?*

I will begin by telling you what I considered naming my work other than *The Everlasting Man*. It could have aptly been titled, *The Man Who Made the World*. God entered the world filled with demons and he cast them out. He came to a world of many gods and split history in two. God entered a drama already in progress, he

---

1 John 11:25. My paraphrase

2 2 Corinthians 12:1-4. Paul was caught up into the third heaven, into paradise and heard things so astounding that they cannot be expressed in words, things no human is allowed to tell.

presented what God is like and Who God is, and then that God sacrificed himself for the creatures and the creation by washing away their sin and separation in his own blood.

But there is a great back story. The Everlasting man did make the world. Before time existed he created the world.[3] He created man, breathed into him the breath of life, cursed man, and sentenced him to a life of separation, difficulty, suffering, and much futility. Paradise, as Milton wrote, was lost indeed.[4] He appeared as the Angel of the Lord in his pre-incarnate form.[5] He suffered as a man in this world.[6] Christ was a teacher, but his primary mission was not to teach. It was to suffer and die. Allow me to quote myself,

"When the world shook and the sun was wiped out of heaven, it was not at the crucifixion, but at the cry from the cross: the cry which confessed that God was forsaken of God. And now let the revolutionists choose a creed from all the creeds and a god from all the gods of the world, carefully weighing all the gods of inevitable recurrence and of unalterable power. They will not find another god who has himself been in revolt. Nay, the matter grows too difficult for human speech. But let the atheists themselves choose a god. They will find only one divinity who ever uttered their isolation: only one religion in which God seemed for an instant to be an atheist."[7]

There is more however, one can return to Plato's Cave, a cave that became a grave, then an empty grave, and Paradise born anew. If you don't mind, Mr. Moderator, I need a break—I'll take that pint now.

Moderator Hull: Thank you Mr. Chesterton, I want to call you Dr. Chesterton, but you traffic in a world where productivity and competence rule the day. I want to speak for the many people in our

---

3   Colossians 1:15-20
4   Genesis 1:26-28, 2:7, 3:1-16.
5   Genesis 16:10, 16:13, 18:1,22:15, 34:11,48:16, Exodus 3:6, Isaiah 42:8
6   Philippians 2:1-16
7   GKC, "The Eternal Revolution" from the book, Orthodoxy.

auditorium. I think the composition of those in attendance would be much like the vast crowds before which you and H.G. Wells debated or performed. They would find The Everlasting Man to be the everlasting read that created in them the everlasting question, "What is this book really about, please explain it to me." One vast difference in the crowds, however, is this audience lives in 2024, not 1914. They live in a world of likes, dislikes, click bait, funny little masks, and most have not read a book through in years. Their schools have dropped requirements for entrance, and people are granted degrees based on being in political agreement with faculty members. They do not possess the literary background, or frankly, level of education to grasp your meaning. I'm not suggesting they read the Cliff Notes for the book, but I am going to suggest Dale Ahlquist's excellent Guide to The Everlasting Man.[8]

G.K. Chesterton: Quite ghastly Mr. Hull, Sorry I woke up! Who is Dale Ahlquist?

Moderator Hull: American's greatest authority on you and your work, Mr. Chesterton. He is with us today and I will introduce you right after the debate.

Alright everyone, the usual fifteen-minute break, I will see you in thirty minutes. Again, as with Hannah Arendt, do not approach Mr. Chesterton during the break. Our crack protection detail from *Chip and Dales* will establish a perimeter around our guests. Just got a note from G.K. It reads, "Who is Hannah Arendt?" Mr. Chesterton's books will be for sale in the lobby.

Moderator Hull: (35 minutes later) Welcome back. Mr. Chesterton has now met Dale Ahlquist and has been versed on Hannah Arendt. I must say the most shocking revelations to G.K. are the casual clothes, the bare skin, the many tattoos, and all the clicking and beeping coming from your pockets and purses—and so many straight white teeth! He mentioned something about programmed zombies. It is time for the concluding remarks from our guest, the kill shot, if you like. Mr. Chesterton, you have the floor.

---

8   The Everlasting Man: A Guide to G.K. Chesterton's Masterpiece. Introduction, Notes, and Commentary by Dale Ahlquist.

G.K. Chesterton: Thank you Mr. Moderator, you have been a wonderful host. As I review the august panel of presenters on the dais today, I can't help but think of ourselves as a collective of humanity, past and present, a *Ship of Fools*. We have a choice to make. We can be fools or we can be fools for Christ's sake. A fool is someone who has declared, "There is no God."[9] Or one who is even more ignorant saying, there may be a God, but his existence is only moderately important. A fool for Christ's sake is what the Apostle Paul said that his dedication to Christ made him look like. But he concluded that "the foolishness of God is wiser than the wisdom of man."[10] It is very much like H.G. Wells', *An Outline in History*, where he left out the main character. *The Everlasting Man* puts Jesus, the Christ, onto center stage. I might call it *A Short History of Mankind*. What strikes me most about this world to which I have awakened is how much it is akin to what I predicted one hundred years ago—A New Dark Age. I just didn't think of it as illuminated by so much artificial light. People are walking around in spiritual darkness while squinting because of the brightness of the Angel of light.[11]

I conclude with my summary of the *Everlasting Man* in my book, Orthodoxy. *"Once Heaven came upon the earth with a power or seal called the image of God, whereby man took command of nature; and once again (when, in empire after empire, men had been found wanting) Heaven came to save mankind in the awful shape of a man."*[12]

Moderator Hull: It is great comfort to us, Mr. Chesterton, that we can take refuge in your words, and in one of your most famous quips, *"When the world goes wrong, it proves rather that the Church is right."* I suppose you must now take your leave. We will miss listening to you because we want to know more. But I would suspect

---

9   Proverbs 14:1

10 I Corinthians 4:10, I Corinthians 1:25.

11 2 Corinthians 11:14, Satan disguises himself as an angel of light

12 The Everlasting Man: A Guide to G.K. Chesterton's Masterpiece. Introduction, Notes, and Commentary by Dale Ahlquist.

that your wisdom would refer us to Paul's famous words, "We now look through a mirror darkly." And one thing we see clearly is the man from Galilee. He is above all things, and in him, all things hold together. He was there in the beginning. He will also be there in the end. Many blessings good friend, see you soon enough.

Ladies and Gentlemen, thank you for your attendance at our debate. You can now retreat to the giant Book Fair and please clean up around your seat. Good night.

THE GREAT DEBATE

04

SEVEN DEADLY SINS

1. PRIDE

For 1500 years the Catholic Church was the only show in town. They were the cultural authorities on what it meant to be a good person and how to live a good life. There was no daylight between your local priest, cultural norms, and the time of day. Church bells would call citizens to daily worship, the city calendar was the church calendar, and the seasons were Advent, Epiphany, Ash Wednesday, Lent, Easter, Ascension, etc. The Eucharist had so much magical power that farmers would sneak a bit of the "Host" home to give to their sick animals. It was in this milieu that they named Seven Deadly Sins that could ruin your life. It is not lost on me that the Seven Deadly Sins: Pride, Envy, Wrath, Lust, Greed, Sloth, and Gluttony are the darlings of today's progressive elites. **Pride** is the ambition to win at all costs. **Envy** is resenting the successful. **Wrath** is outrage and grievance. **Lust** is sexual freedom without consequences. **Greed** is wanting what others have earned. **Sloth** is deeming hard work optional, even racist. **Gluttony** is being body-positive about obesity and diabetes and spilling out of your bathing suit.

All humans are naturally tempted to indulge in the seven deadlies, the difference is that most of us know they are bad for us. Those buffered by wealth, privilege, private jet aircraft, valet medical care, and the best rehab facilities in the world champion them. Yes, we are all hypocrites, we are inconsistent and fail in our efforts to be better, but we aspire to something higher and more noble. That is why we go to church and pretend for a few minutes to be better, more glorious than we actually are. We fall short, but not for want of trying—sing about something better, pray for something better, behave better— think more lofty thoughts. Let's get started: the first among the deadlies is Pride.

Pride

Pride is chief among sins. My favorite way to think of it was penned by C.S. Lewis:
"Pride gets no pleasure out of having something, only out of having more of it than the next man. We say that people are proud of being rich, or clever, or good-looking, but they are not. They are proud of being richer, or cleverer, or better-looking than others." [1]

Pride is chief because when it comes to God, it is to become God's rival. Pride provides some hints as to the origin of evil. Lucifer is its progenitor, but not entirely its creator, for he, himself, is a created being. We are left with the issue of something—evil—coming from nothing. At least nothing if God didn't create it. I think of it as more of God creating a recipe for humans that had the possibility of the choice to create rebellion. And at the root of rebellion and rivalry is pride. Isaiah the prophet treaded on this revelatory ground. God told him that no one would listen to him anyway, so he was unafraid of any response to his revelations.[2]

Lucifer, you might recall was and remains, dedicated to destroying God's reputation and dethroning him. He was thrown out of Heaven by Michael the Archangel long ago. He is the falling star in Revelation chapter twelve.[3] He got his start in his failed coup:

'How you are fallen from heaven, O shining star, son of the morning! You have been thrown down to the earth, you who destroyed the nations of the world. For you said to yourself, "I will ascend to heaven and set my throne above God's stars. I will preside on the mountain of the gods far away in the north. I will climb to the highest heavens and be like the Most High." Instead, you will be brought down to the place of the dead, down to its lowest depths. Everyone there will stare at you and ask, can this be the one who shook the earth and made the kingdoms of the world tremble? Is this the one who destroyed the world and

---

1 Mere Christianity, C.S. Lewis, Chapter 8, " The Great Sin"
2 Isaiah 6:9-13
3 Revelation 12:7-9

made it into a wasteland? Is this the king who demolished the world's greatest cities and had no mercy on his prisoners?' [4]

The pretense of Lucifer is astounding! The destruction he left should send chills through the body of any 21st-century reader. He approached Jesus in the wilderness as though he had power over him. There he was, proud, deluded, without a clue, but with enough permission and power to destroy all those who would follow him.[5] Lucifer is full of pride, but once he gets into power, he destroys because pride is a lie, pride is fake. It promises prestige and glory, but it always brings misery because the pot at the end of this rainbow is full of shit.

One only needs to reflect on the daily helping of death, destruction, and despair of cable news. It is the work of Lucifer around the entire globe. It can be overwhelming, particularly if you have no real reason to hope for something better. Pride is a lie because no one is really proud of who they are. As Isaiah so graphically stated it:

"We are constant sinners; how can people like us be saved? We are infected and impure with sin. When we display our righteous deeds, they are nothing but filthy rags." [6]

None of us are proud of who we are. And if we are, we have been deceived by the schemes of the evil one. We are mistaken about who we are, and what we are, and we must, as soon as possible, get our lives into alignment with God. Any delay in this will make us a tool in the hands of the evil one and a participant in our own destruction. Lucifer destroys lives, he cheats, he steals, and he never delivers.

Pride is always a lie. One cannot address this issue without thinking about the gay community and its obsession with pride.

The reason they take an entire month with parades, rainbow flags, and much more to proclaim themselves proud—is precisely because they are not proud. This is rooted in the rejection that the

---

4 Isaiah 14:12-17 NLT
5 Matthew 4:1-11
6 Isaiah 64:5c-6. NLT.

community has experienced, and the pain of not being considered normal. One can understand why there are so many celebrations. It is a lot to overcome. Not only do the members of modern Western culture pretend that it is normal, we do so under the threat of penalty. This is where pride turns into malice because pride not only wants equality, but as stated earlier by C.S. Lewis, pride insists on being better, having more, and ousting everyone who doesn't agree.

And that includes thought crimes. When we see gay men dancing down a street in a parade with their butts hanging out and sometimes even more, gay pride seems more like hate or daring anyone to object publicly. They seem to want to gross out their fellow citizens, particularly the Christian community. Recently a group supporting the gay community marched through the streets of cities chanting, "We're here, we're queer, we are coming for your children." I believe they will regret such a chant. They have crossed many lines, but this is one they dare not cross. That is why gay popularity in polls has declined 20% in the last year.

Because of the obsession with pride, Satan always destroys, and he never delivers. Pride does go before the fall. Lord Acton's famous statement, "Power corrupts, and absolute power corrupts absolutely," is true. The more power the gay lobby has, the more they will insist on taking over, getting their way, and punishing the opposition. In doing so, their quest for pride and power will destroy them and their movement. I think gay Americans should accept the equality they have achieved and go on about their lives.

They are attempting to convert us and destroy anyone who disagrees. A very odd effort indeed, for a group whose main argument used to be, "We were born this way, you don't learn to be gay." Isn't this interesting that 53.7% of the student body at *Brown University* considers themselves LGBTQ+?[7] How can we take such polling seriously considering how impressionable, vacuous, and naïve college students can be? It impresses one as a thought pandemic ad-

---

7 https://khqa.com/news/nation-world/nearly-40-of-students-at-brown-identify-as-lgbtq-university-newspaper-reports

vocated by a community that sought not to covert anyone. How is this different from the *Inquisition*, the *Crusades*, and the many holy wars waged in history? 90% of gays are positive in the communities where they live, work, and play. As citizens of the United States, they should have equal rights. But it should end there, no *special* rights and no Orwellian equity enforced by "Big Brother" whom they have bullied into compliance.

The larger point is that this is a horrible way to live. Choosing to be a victim and at the same time, be proud of being a victim, is a formula for failure. If you are always complaining about others beating you and having privileges you don't have, you will waste your life. It will make you a twisted and bitter person. This is Lucifer's goal—to lie to you, to get you to be a bitter rival of God's plan for you, and then he will destroy you—mission completed. The better way is humility.

John the Baptist and his humility

Few religious figures have been as successful as the cousin of Jesus, John the Baptist. John couldn't see his own greatness. Many thought he was the Messiah, yet he was very clear and denied any talk that he was the promised one. Others thought he might be the promised Elijah figure to help the anointed one free Israel from the Roman yoke. John even denied that he was a prophet. He proclaimed himself simply "a voice, a voice crying out in the wilderness." John wasn't promoting himself—he said about Jesus, that he was preparing the way for the promised deliverer, and he was not worthy to even untie his sandals. Even slaves were not asked to take the dirty, dusty, smelly sandals off their master's feet at the end of the day. Yet, John didn't think himself worthy of such a lowly task for his coming King. John was courageous, he was straight forward, he called upon all people to cleanse themselves, to repent of their sins and to be baptized. John was human and he was tempted to indulge his ego in pride. His disciples were even more eager to not give up ground to anyone that they, themselves, had earned. This all came to a head when John's disciples complained to him of Jesus and his disciples baptizing more people than John.

"A debate broke out between John's disciples and a certain Jew over ceremonial cleansing. So John's disciples came to him and said, Rabbi, the man you met on the other side of the Jordan River, the one you identified as the Messiah, is also baptizing people. And everybody is going to him instead of coming to us." [8]

This was John's chance to play on the emotions, even the anger and envy of his disciples. Who could blame him—his numbers were going down. He was in decline. But he surprised his disciples and showed us spiritual greatness in his humility.

John replied, "No one can receive anything unless God gives it from heaven. You yourselves know how plainly I told you, 'I am not the Messiah. I am only here to prepare the way for him. It is the bridegroom who marries the bride and the best man is simply glad to stand with him and hear his vows. Therefore, I am filled with joy at his success. He must become greater and greater, and I must become less and less." [9]

If you are not impressed, you should be. Pride is attempting to oppose God's plan, but humility is submitting to it. Pride is taking a good thing, for John, the success he had enjoyed, and trying to himself a rival of Jesus. Or at least consider himself a victim. John ended up in Herod's jail and beheaded for calling on Herod to repent. Herod had stolen his brother's wife and was living in a sinful relationship. John confronted him and his head was placed on a plate and presented to the wife and daughter of Herod. John lived out his calling by his teaching and by his life. He gave himself to God and God's plan just as his younger cousin Jesus would do. It is a superior way to live—in humility rather than as a slave to your pride. Pride will destroy you, but humility will enrich you and make you a joyful complete person in alignment with God and his creation.

---

8   John 3:25,26 NLT.
9   John 3:27-30 NLT.

SEVEN DEADLY SINS

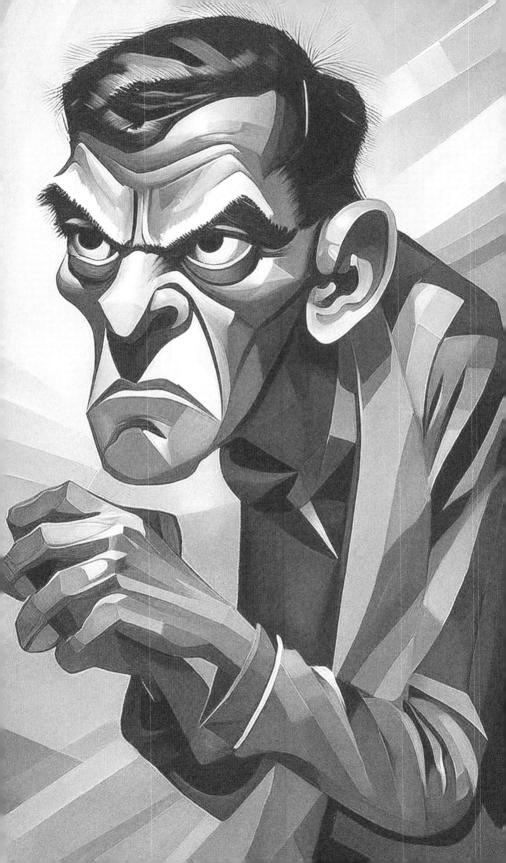

2. ENVY

"Here in Washington D.C., ruining people's reputation's is a sport."
—Vince Foster, suicide note.

But as for me, I almost lost my footing. My feet were slipping, and I was almost gone. For I envied the proud when I saw them prosper despite their wickedness.[1]

Envy takes away our ability to enjoy the life we've got. Nothing is good enough. It makes us prisoners of grievance and we serve its bitterness. But when we find ourselves going down that dark road of comparison and want, like the Psalmist, we can catch ourselves. This particular sin, like its destructive colleagues, will destroy your happiness. It's a lousy way to live. You are not happy, and no one close to you is happy.

What is envy anyway? First, it is included in most catalogs of sin found in the New Testament. Its traveling companions are "hurtful desires, jealousy, slander, greed, hate, murder, drunkenness, wild parties, liars, and officially, according to the church, pride, anger, greed, sloth, gluttony, et al.[2]

Envy, at its core, is wanting or resenting someone else's life. By default, it is a rejection of God's creation and cultivation of you as a person. You don't rejoice with another's success. It makes you sad, sometimes even angry. When those who have it better than you and have more than you, fail or suffer, it comforts you and you secretly enjoy it—you feel justified. I recall the actor, Richard Dryfuss, saying, "Other people's problems cheer me up." The Shakespearian actor, John Gielgud, along with Ralph Richardson and Laurence Olivier, was one of the trinity of actors who dominated the British stage in the 20th century, Gielgud admitted, "When Olivier played Hamlet and the critics raved, I wept."

---

1 Psalm 73:2,3 New Living Translation
2 Mark 7:22, Romans 1:29, Galatians 5:21, Titus 3:3, James 4:5,

Envy likes to hide

Envy is very dangerous to the human soul. Bonhoeffer said, "Your sin wants to be alone with you." Indeed, sin loves hiddenness. Envy is especially good at staying behind the scenes. Greed, for example, exists and thrives in denial, denial that you are greedy. Greedy people are other people who have more than you do. Envy hides in the murky waters of "It's no big deal." What's so bad about feeling a little joy when some pompous rich ass falls from grace? That is what most people call irony, karma, or justice, in the sense that there is wide agreement that the person is a pompous ass. Someone who ridiculed others for something he or she did themselves, got caught. But still, it is not a long-lived or deep comfort you feel because you didn't resent or desire their life or success before or after that incident.

A culture of grievance

It is sad but true that American culture is saturated with disappointment and grievance. The progressive ideology has made millions of new disciples—the mark of these disciples is victimhood. They would claim that It is someone else's fault that they can't get a better apartment, get into the college of their choice, make more money, have respect. Behind all of this is envy. Someone else is living the life I want and that is because they have some sort of privilege or advantage—it's not fair, and I want everything to be equal. This is called equity, equality of result. Equality of result can only be achieved by crushing the will and nature of the people and by the state enforcing the result. It is called soft totalitarianism. It is Orwellian practices behind the facade of a democracy.

The primary difference is that, for most of America's history, its citizens didn't ask the government to provide much for them. They valued freedom and opportunity. They wanted the government to provide for a national defense against all enemies, foreign and domestic, and carry out governance in accordance with the will of the people—and leave them alone. The issue for our focus here is that progressive disciples think they are victims who are owed something—and that something is a Pandora's box of freebies. That is a political argument and not for this space.

The issue before us is a creation of a culture of envy, essentially, "You have something I want, in fact, something I deserve, and I demand you give it to me!" That is what is behind the trashing of a local market or the rampant shoplifting seen on the news every day. The rule of law does not apply. That is cultural envy, a societal envy, and it will destroy the soul of a nation as surely as it will destroy the soul of a person.

The slipping of the soul

'Truly God is good to Israel, to those whose hearts are pure. But as for me, I almost lost my footing. My feet were slipping, and I was almost gone. For I envied the proud when I saw them prosper despite their wickedness. They seem to live such painless lives; their bodies are so healthy and strong. They don't have trouble like other people; they're not plagued with problems like everyone else." [3]

The psalmist goes on to describe the riches and their vast consumption of everything they want. They scoff at the unwashed, the general population. They even boast against God, their words strut through the earth. They are wicked and they are living a life of ease. His heart is dripping with envy, he even questions his faithfulness to God. He laments that he has tried to understand the prosperity of the wicked, but he was completely taken over by it.

Envy is insidious, we don't want to believe that it is part of our soul, our personality. It is easier to think of oneself as angry, proud, or lustful, but envy is so petty and small-minded. It is filled with self-pity, and weakness, and is pathetic—the *Fatal Attraction*[4] syndrome. Namely, you love what someone else has, and it likes you,

---

3   Psalm 73:1-5 NLT
4   Fatal Attraction, 1987 film with Michael Douglass, Glenn Close

but in the end, when you discover that you can't have it, you are willing to destroy everything to get what you want. Most of our envy is not extreme, but when you witness extreme and the violence that people are willing to engage in, be sure envy is behind it.

Christian envy

Not that envy is Christian, but there is an envy that many Christians have, and it seems ordinary and even acceptable. It is the holding of grudges against people we know who don't necessarily have more money, fame, health, or prestige. In fact, they may not even qualify as wicked. Actually, they have many good qualities. It is someone who works out more than you, and who looks better because of it. People who have invested their incomes in a disciplined way and now are cruising the world. They even retired early—and they were just school teachers. Friends who seem to have more fun, whose spouses are more adventurous, whose sex lives are more spicy. They have a better BBQ grill, patio, and pool, therefore, they have lots of friends. I think it was Soren Kierkegaard who said,

"Learn what you envy and you will know who you are living before."

His meaning was to be honest about what you really want in life and who or what you serve. Paul said, "For me to live is Christ, to die is gain." When we face those moments when we think that our time is short on this earth and we will be with God sooner rather than later, do we long for God or to spend a few more years around the pool in our chase lounge?

How to put envy in its place

I purposefully didn't ask a grandiose question like, "How can a person win over envy or eliminate envy?" I don't think that is the human condition's reality. Anxiety, for example, is a condition of being human; you don't eliminate it, you manage it. Or as stated here, you put it in its place. You park it somewhere in your personality with limits and conditions enforced by the power of the human will, a new perspective, and the Holy Spirit. Is there any place you can go to get it fixed, to get it out of your frontal lobe? Yes, indeed there is, and the Psalmist tells us of his experience.

It's going to seem trite, too simple, even cliché, but here it is:

"So, I tried to understand why the wicked prosper. But what a difficult task it is!" [5]

He struggled to figure it out. He is about to recognize that, at the base of all knowledge, is the insight that the deepest realms of knowledge are spiritual and not accessible by reason alone.

"Then I went into your sanctuary, O God, and I finally understood the destiny of the wicked. Truly, you put them on a slippery path and send them sliding over the cliff to destruction. In an instant they are destroyed, completely swept away by terrors. When you arise, O Lord, you will laugh at their silly ideas as a person laughs at dreams in the morning. Then I realized my heart was bitter, and I was all torn up inside. I was so foolish and ignorant—I must have seemed like a senseless animal to you." [6]

He went to church, the sanctuary, the presence of God. Often, the answer is to get into the right place as quickly as possible, with the right people. The temple, with its sanctified worship paraphernalia, the priests in their holy costumes, the rites and rituals, is all about bridging the gap between the *holy other*, and those of us who are human and flawed. He got there, and he realized how foolish he had been, how wrong he was thinking, how deep was his sin, and he confessed and worshiped.

He left different. Not totally transformed, just changed enough to get on with his day, maybe even a few days, before he would need to do it over again. That is the way it works, these sins are deadly because they don't just leave us—they tempt us, they hound us, they creep into our thoughts. As the Psalmist concluded,

---

5   Psalms 73:16
6   Psalms 73:17-22 NLT

"But as for me, how good it is to be near God! I have made the Sovereign LORD my shelter, and I will tell everyone about the wonderful things you do." [7]

This is the point concerning the seven deadlies. It is that they ruin our life. They turn life into a pile of substance known in polite company as manure. Envy is a life of self-righteous self-justification. It makes us hard to live with, it makes it even harder for us to live with joy. So, when we sense it coming on, or other's failures are making us too happy, we must get to church, get on our knees, confess our sin, and then tell everyone what a wonderful God we serve. **Ah, a miracle ensues.**

---

7 Psalms 73:27,28

SEVEN DEADLY SINS

3. ANGER

A people with understanding control their anger, a hot temper shows great foolishness.
—Proverbs 14:29 NLT.

Outrage is the devil's cocaine

"I'm outraged!" Outrage makes us feel righteous, usually self-righteous. Outrage has its place, as does anger, but both are out of control at present. One of the worst things you can say to a person is "You're a racist." Yet, especially in the political realm, it is the accusation that we hear the most. Attacking another person makes the accusers feel good about themselves. Normally, the accuser follows the accusation by throwing an object or substance at the despicable victim of their ire. It is hard to forget the scene of a crowd of partisans calling California Gubernatorial candidate, Larry Elder, who is an African American, "the black face of white supremacy" then throwing raw eggs on his head. When you yell rapist, pervert, abuser, you are, in effect saying, "I'm the nice guy, I'm not dirty like you, I will gladly cast the first stone."

Outrage is the devil's cocaine because it makes a person feel high, superior, strong, empowered, and victorious. Then there is a need to stay mad because it allows continuing the destructive rise to personal power—it is addictive. It is now out of control in our culture because two generations of therapists have told repressed and troubled people who could afford to tell their troubles to a paid professional, "express your feelings, let it go, don't repress, don't hold it in, don't try to control it." It is what the late scholar, Philip Rieff, called *The Triumph of the Therapeutic.* The Freudian revolution is complete. Hardly anyone can control their emotions anymore. Repression is heinous. Expressive individualism is the flavor of our generation. At first, we just watched the ridiculous *Jerry Springer Show* where people spewed their disgusting pathologies, so disgusting that we couldn't look away. It has had its effect. Jerry's show is no more, but his disciples and their devils have filled the streets.

Anger as a selective strategy

Typically, a person gets angry when something important to them is denied. I couldn't help but think of the NBA, the National Basketball League, and its reaction to world events. 86% of NBA players are African Americans or of non-white nationality. This is the reason they reacted so strongly to the death of George Floyd in 2020.[1] Another reason is the press proposed a false progressive narrative. That was the year of the "bubble." Because of Covid 19 the NBA decided to hold the playoffs in a closed environment. They decided to place *Black Lives Matter*[2] on the playing surface and many teams and players refused to stand for the *National Anthem*. Needless to say, it was a controversial time for our nation.

---

1   The reaction to George Floyd led to irrational chaos, such as defunding the police, to ironic, even psychotic acts like tearing down statues of heroes like Theodore Roosevelt, and George Washington and building ones to convicted felons like George Floyd. Virtually every city that defunded the police suffered—and reversed its policy. Once again, appeasement, socialistic theory, chaos, and crime always fail.
2   In the defense of the NBA, Black Lives Matter, at that time, was more of a sentiment than a reference to the organization. The organization has proved to be corrupt, based on Marxist ideology, and now is largely considered to be defunct, without cultural cachet. For the record, Marxist ideology can be simply understood as Philosopher Fredrich Hegel's dialectic: thesis, anthesis, and synthesis. Hegel's dialectic, then, is applied to economic theory and you have Marxism. Marxism has failed the test again and again, but it does call for a dialectic or debate, an argument over economic issues, to be taken to the streets. The thesis might be, white people built and control the major institutions of Western Civilization. The antithesis would be, to tear it all down and rebuild it and put the working class in charge. After a debate that could include violence, riots, looting, shootings, killings, and tearing down symbols of the power structures, then you settle for the progress of synthesis—socialistic policies within the present structure. You take the win and wait and work for the next battle. Chaos is conversation in the dialectic, that is how progress is made.

It is well known however, that other injustices did not seem to trouble the NBA. The thousands of protesters in the streets of Hong Kong were being beaten, jailed, and some even killed. These were citizens fighting for their freedom of speech, for basic rights that were being taken away by the Chinese Government. A lone General Manager of the *Houston Rockets*, Darrell Morey, spoke up in defense of the protests and was promptly silenced by the NBA. Morey was required to delete his Tweet and issue an apology. The Chinese threatened to cancel a 1.5 billion television contract with the NBA. The *Houston Rockets* distanced themselves from their General Manager's statement.

Enes Kanter, the outspoken former *Boston Celtic*, was run out of the NBA because he stood strong against human rights abuses by the Chinese Government. In particular, he highlighted his fellow Muslims being placed in concentration camps. The NBA disavows any manipulation or "blackballing" of Kanter, but the NBA's behavior regarding Kanter and its silence regarding China's human rights abuses is strong evidence of selective outrage. They weren't outraged as in the George Floyd riots, because that outrage cost them nothing. But outrage was not an option at much worse human rights abuse in China because it was bad for business. Anger can be used as a strategy and has become harder and harder to control. Anger is a form of power that the media and major industries use for their advantage—and so do individuals.

It is time to leave the realm of human manipulation of anger and enter into the sanctuary of God's purpose and use of anger.

God Gets Angry

God gets angry and I am so glad he does. It means he cares, it means he is interested because the opposite of love is not hate, it is detachment. It means God has *feelings*, and those *feelings*[3] get hurt.

---

3 God has "feelings" I put it in quotes because to describe God's inner life as "feelings" is both trite and cliché. I do so only to mean he can get hurt, sort of like us, we are made in his image, but we are not him—get it?

He takes slights personally and sometimes gets so mad that he is willing to rid the earth of us. And you know what? It's his right to do so even though millions of pretenders to His Throne would object. But then, they are *pretenders to His Throne*.

There are many cases in history of God becoming angry. There are several occasions where he decides to punish a people, usually his own people, Israel. One only needs to read the major prophets, Isaiah, Jeremiah, and Ezekiel, to see His anger. But, also, it is quite noticeable that he is *slow* to anger. He also can be talked out of some of his actions as with Moses on more than one occasion.[4] His first extended conversation with Moses is found in Exodus when Moses gives God five reasons he can't do what God is asking. Toward the end of the conversation, you can imagine the smoke coming out of God's ears, if such a scene is possible. After *five excuses* it says, *"Then the Lord became angry with Moses."*[5]

Anger in and of itself is not sinful. It is necessary. In fact, the only reason we get angry is that we are made in God's image. We get angry because we need to. Indeed, it is a big part of the way we love those around us and protect them. Anger is from the Greek word οργη, meaning a rush of passion, energy, and resolve. The Hebrew word is פנ meaning face, the nostrils, the idea that God is not stony-faced. True love always gets angry. In fact, the people you love the most have been the targets of your greatest anger. And if not directed at them, it has been toward those who threaten those you love the most.

We get angry

During the teen years one of our sons was listening to what was called "punk" and other deviant music. It was music that represent-

---

4 Numbers 11 is one of many times God becomes angry with his own people. He is angry in the Garden of Eden as well when he confronts Adam and Eve hiding from him. But God is angry and does not sin, for you can't truly love someone without becoming angry with them.

5 Exodus 4:14 NLT

ed rebellion and attracted struggling and vulnerable youth. It had endangered our son, our family, and our future together. Increasingly, our efforts to deter our son's rebellious direction raised the intensity of our confrontations with him. On one occasion we were arguing with him and he was being quite disrespectful. While I was attempting to speak with him, I heard some hammering. It was my wife hammering into pieces our son's music collection. I recall one group called *GBH, Grievous Bodily Harm*. Jane was out on the patio, breaking it all to bits, she was very angry. She was as angry as I had ever seen her. Yes, she hated the music, yes, she was angry with her son. The depths of her anger revealed the depths of her love for her son. His life was being threatened by the evil one, and she was ready to fight to the death to save him. She was in control, she didn't take the hammer to her son's head, she didn't start breaking out windows, she didn't throw the hammer at me because I was part of the problem, she didn't scream and then hammer herself in the head with it—no, it was a surgical strike. She was attacking the problem, rather than the person.

How to be angry and not ruin your life

"And don't sin by letting anger control you. Don't let the sun go down while you are still angry, for anger gives a foothold to the devil." [6]

"He who is slow to anger is better and more honorable than a mighty soldier. And he who rules and controls his own spirit, than he who captures a city." [7]

The *seven deadlies* are deadly because they take a good thing and make it an ultimate thing—idolatry. Sometimes we give in to our anger and allow ourselves to become quick-tempered. It will destroy our personality, wound our friends, and we will not be able to think straight when it counts to think straight. But when anger is under control we can say true love always gets angry. When we

---

6   Ephesians 4:26,27 New Living Translation
7   Proverbs 16:32 Amplified Bible

say God is a jealous God, it usually means he is stomping about ready to do in anyone who is harming those he loves. Jealousy is lovely, one of life's most beautiful traits, but only when it leads to protecting a person or improving a relationship. The other guy asks your girl out, Godly jealousy means you up your game and show her how much you care. It doesn't mean to slash and burn through the competition.

Paul wrote Ephesians to be read when the church gathered. It was a circular letter to be read to all the churches in that part of Asia. His advice was, and is, to not inflame our conversation and relationships with unresolved anger. The temptation is to "clam up" or "blow up." When we clam up, we will eventually blow. We will attack and carpet-bomb everyone around us. If we blow up, we say explosive words that can't be unsaid and wound deeply.

I had a wise woman tell me, "If a person hurts you, they can never be right about anything again." You are wounded. You shut them out, you turn them off, you no longer trust their word. And when you forgive them, it costs you something. Forgiveness does not come free of charge. When you forgive, you pay the debt, you take the blame, you even cause some to believe the original statement that wounded you was true. Someone will always read forgiveness and reconciliation as admission of guilt. When you forgive, it will cost you something. Of course, this is what Jesus did. *He* took the blame, *he* paid the debt, *he* instead of us. We were wrong, we sinned, but the forgiveness of God didn't come free, Jesus paid that debt.

I have heard it said, and I have thought it myself, even though I never had the courage to say so—"I didn't ask to be born, I didn't create and cultivate this beautiful and ugly, fallen world—not my idea. Now I'm supposed to plead guilty? I'm the sinner? It's my fault? That doesn't make any sense to me."

Then it occurred to me, Adam was my representative—being the first man, he was created a perfect man. Yes, he was created perfect, and he messed up, he disobeyed, he sinned, he fell, he was cursed, and now so am I. My protest is based on the proposition that if I had been there instead of Adam, I wouldn't have screwed up!" It is tantamount to me saying, "If the human race were like me, we wouldn't have this problem." Frankly, I'm sort of mad about the whole thing, the fact that we humans must suffer and then die. It doesn't seem right. Not many of us would admit that we are angry with God. But don't you see? There is something in us that wants us to straighten God out and correct him—*I could have done better!*

Has it ever occurred to you that the proof that we are mad at God is that when he became a human, when he limited himself, and became a man, as soon as we could get our hands on him, we killed him? After all, when Adam and Eve, the perfect us screwed up, God scolded them, cursed them, threw them out of paradise, and made it impossible for them to return. Until Christ came, that is. Now there is a way back. Hey Christians, get unmad at God! Trust him, follow him, enjoy him! He has come that we can have life and live it to the full.[8]

Accept that anger is something helpful and useful when we are not mad at God anymore. There is no reason to be an angry person. When he was on the cross he said, "Father forgive them, they don't know what they are doing." That is what we should be thinking about those around us who would oppose us, hurt us, deny us, or seek to destroy us. But, remember that those who don't believe, those who work against God and his kingdom, are victims of the enemy. They need help, "Father forgive them, they don't understand what they are doing." You just can't be an angry person and understand the gospel.

---

8 John 10:10

4. LUST

"...anyone who even looks at a woman with lust has already committed adultery with her in his heart."

I hear that the sexual revolution was fun. I spent the 1960s in school starting at home and ending with college graduation in 1969. I watched it on television, read about it in magazines, but it didn't penetrate my world in any meaningful way. Over that turbulent and highly romanticized decade I was able to establish an interest in the opposite sex, go on dates, find a mate and get married. I can't imagine needing any help from the progressive left to enhance my already fully operational lust.

But I do know that over the last fifty years that the sexual revolution has been successful. At least In that thin slice of Americana called the cultural elites, the educated class. They don't like trickle-down economics but, do believe in trickle-down decadence. Remarkably, the elite culture of America is still largely conventional. They get married, have children, and continue to operate in a protected bubble provided by their wealth and cultural power. They fly private, live in communities with private security, and operate a very segregated life into which you may only enter by having the proper funding or ideology but there are many hidden traps. Much like the Climate Change Religious Cult, progressive elites live as though there is abundant evidence to support their orthodoxy, though their computer models and predictions have formed a vast graveyard of wrong prophetic mistakes. If their scientists were Old Testament prophets, they all would need to be stoned.

One can pretend that the sexual revolution and a life of unchecked lust works and helps people, but the opposite has happened. The middle class is under siege, and the racially diverse underclass is suffering from the elite's philosophies that have created unworkable policies and crime-ridden cities from which people are fleeing. Being a rich and well-connected Marxist is only possible in a wealthy capitalistic society. It creates the worst kind of self-righteous prigs who preach climate change, and then jet off over the horizon to their vacation home. Their wealth made it workable to live a "coked out" life of excess at *Club 54* in NYC, until assigned probation by the court or went into rehab in the Hamptons or Martha's Vineyard. The educated played to excess with a protective net to catch their fall.

At the same time, their policies make it nearly impossible for the middle class to own a home, educate their children in a safe environment, and stay married. Elites, tabloid headlines aside, created stable families, got married and stayed married much more than the poor. Their attempts to help others by creating a climate of victimhood have created the greatest degradation of the family, the quality of home life for children, and locked the majority of poor in a welfare system that has sentenced them to generations of subservience.

The greatest predictor for young people's ability to succeed is a solid two-parent home. The divorce rate and the percentage of single women raising children alone have never been higher. Add to this the rising crime rate and the lack of will on the part of politicians to police and prosecute local crime has combined to sentence the next generation of the young and unprotected to a life of failure and drug addiction. Yet, the progressive left's crusade goes on unabated like it is working and like it is true. We all must remember this—victims do not lead, victims are not brave, you can't count on victims as long as they remain victims. The elite's lust for power has destroyed normal life for everyone else.

They, in effect, are saying, that *you, the general populace, live with less and we get more!* More power, more wealth, more of a world that we can control. The sexual revolution was the easiest way to get *their* way because sexual freedom is very appealing. It's fun, so why not get as much as you can, when you can, and worry about the rest later?

All this nonsense will end when we implode under the weight of our own decadence and have to fight for our survival. By then we will be too weak to win, thus, history repeats itself. Babylon, the

Persians, Greece, Rome, the Soviet Union, and many a lesser power have failed because, as a people, they failed. We will only tinker with perfection while we are rich and safe. When that is gone, we are gone. The progressive left is no longer the revolutionaries, they *own* the culture, they *run* the government, they *control* major industries.

The new revolutionaries are Christians and those with a Biblical world view. The old sexual revolution has been won by the progressives—now for the new revolution—the one that is different and one that cleans up after itself.

Another approach to the sexual revolution

Men have always been sexually aggressive, which is why most Bible studies on lust are addressed to men. Rarely will you hear a ripping sermon at a women's conference called, *Ladies, Stop Lusting* with a call to resist that uncontrollable urge to merge with everything that moves. The sexual revolution changed that, at least on the surface. The feminist movement said, "Ladies, become more like men. Men sleep around, you should sleep around. Men get drunk and do crazy things, so should you." This is a new sexual age, men and women are equal, and you can be equally as disgusting and irresponsible as the guys. You have birth control, and if that doesn't work, you can kill the baby. You can live a full, free, and fun life, get drunk, sleep around, get pregnant, kill the baby, it will be a wonderful life."[1]

Now for the new revolution.

"You have heard the commandment that says, 'You must not commit adultery.' But I say, anyone who even looks at a woman with lust has already committed adultery with her in his heart. So if your eye— even your good eye—causes you to lust, gouge it out and throw it away. It is better for you to lose one part of your body than for your whole body to be thrown into hell. And if your hand—even your stronger

---

1   Andrew Klavan, Speech @ Iowa State University, 2022.

hand—causes you to sin, cut it off and throw it away. It is better for you to lose one part of your body than for your whole body to be thrown into hell." [2]

Jesus launched his revolutionary idea about true sexual freedom by referring to the Old Testament sex ethic. *"You must not commit adultery."* The theme of the entire *Sermon on The Mount* is found in Matthew 5:20:

"But I warn you—unless your righteousness is better than the righteousness of the teachers of religious law and the Pharisees, you will never enter the Kingdom of Heaven!" In other words, your spiritual life must come from inside you, very deep inside of you, and *that* righteousness is *not earned*, it is *not* from your better nature, it is from something *only I, God* can provide for you.

To go both higher and deeper, Jesus upgrades it by saying, *no sex outside of marriage!* No sex outside the covenant that exists in marriage. A *covenant* is a category higher and deeper than a contract, agreement, or handshake. It is a lifetime commitment to another person. It is based on our commitment to God and the integrity of both parties' trust in God and each other. A *contract* will get the most for me in the negotiations regarding the relationship, and when it is over and I no longer benefit, I'm out! In the covenant of marriage, each is saying, "I will adjust to you," and we move into a secure zone, no longer needing to use sex as marketing or campaigning for the position of husband or wife. No more spinning or selling. This is why cohabitation is an insult to the person you are living with. "I haven't made up my mind about you yet, so I will live with and use you because perhaps I will need to find a better option."

In the covenant of marriage, the husband gives himself to his wife and she to him. No one is keeping score, at least on most days. You get the most when you give the most. But breaking through the barrier of keeping score is necessary to get there. Then, there are children. Parents give, give, and give some more, and never give up no matter how hard it gets. The kids can never catch up, no matter

---

2 Matthew 5:27-30 New Living Translation

how hard they try, kids will always be in a deficit position with the parents. The beauty of it is that parents never stop giving until they breathe their last. Quite often, parents require outside intervention to keep them from giving too much— especially when it comes to grandchildren—but for most grandparents, the only way to stop them is to seal the casket, put them in the ground, and cover them up with dirt. Google John Rosemond for parenting advice—he's on Substack, too.

In the covenant context, there is true sexual freedom. When you make the promise, you say your vows and sex becomes a sacrament. It becomes a physical symbol of a spiritual reality, of oneness. In marriage, I am giving my whole life to another person. And as partners age, performance can wane, but satisfaction can increase because of the intangibles. It continues to provide life's greatest consolation, that being the love and adoration of your most precious and dearest friend. You may think this unrealistic. You may lament your present state, you may have been betrayed by a spouse, these are all possible outcomes. But let's look a bit deeper at what Jesus called lust.

What does it mean to "lust" after another person?

The word Jesus used was επιθυμησαι, which means craving. It has a relationship to greed, to want to have what is not yours. It includes fantasy, longing, and self-absorption, often, enhanced by pornography. In Jesus' time, there was ample time and occasion for men to indulge their sexual fantasies, but more in real-time with real women than today, with the alternative of the internet. It means much more than attraction. It is also quite separate from acknowledging the beauty of another person. Beauty is, in fact, evidence of God's beauty. Of course, through jest and casual comment, a woman's beauty can be used for baser reasons. But to be attracted to another person is not a sin and not what Jesus is talking about. Jesus is talking about "I've got to have that. I will have that!" Then, instigating a fantasy life and even a strategy, or worse, a stalker mentality. This is particularly damaging when it begins to damage and dull the affection and desire for one's spouse. It threatens the covenant and everyone who lives under the protection of that covenant.

Drastic action

Jesus said when you get caught up in lust, take radical action. He doesn't want people to cut off their hands or pluck out their eyes. But whether it be a real person or a creation of the internet, the danger of fantasy is that it destroys the real. Here is what fantasy and lust can do to damage a person, a family, a community, a culture:

Creates unrealistic expectation. I recall a woman in divorce proceedings who, while she remained attracted to her former partner, wasn't willing to become a "French whore" to stay married. Her husband had watched so much pornography on screen that he thought his wife should perform acts that he had grown to see as normal. This included other partners for three-way sexual experiences and orgies.

Diminishes interest in normal relationships of marriage. This refers to not wanting to be with each other, not doing normal family activities, and not having the simple enjoyment of each other's company.

The woman forced to dress like his fantasy women. This kind of behavior began with husband buying clothes and outfits for his wife that he found provocative and that looked good on others about whom he was daydreaming.

Don't go to Hell!

This belies the idea that pornography is a victimless crime for adults because it threatens to destroy the covenant of marriage. Jesus says it is better to rid yourselves of this problem by taking radical action than have your *"whole body to be thrown into hell"*—your entire body, your spouse, your children, your career, your community—all cast into hell with you. *You're the whole body in Hell* is an image, γεενναν, a word with a history. It was the garbage dump outside of Jerusalem. It was this place that produced the frightening phrase from the lips of Jesus, *"where the maggots never die and fire never goes out."*[3]

Hell is real, but I don't believe Jesus is describing the ultimate Hell as a garbage dump. The real Hell, the final Hell is a place created by God, therefore it is good! God reigns in Hell. He guards his repository for evil and evil's founders, Lucifer and his legions.

Jesus created it for the devil and his angels.[4] In the parable, those who claim knowledge of God but don't live it, who lie about it, are thrown into this Hell with the Devil and his angels when it is all said and done. And when they protest Jesus' answer is chilling:

And he will answer, *'I tell you the truth, when you refused to help the least of these my brothers and sisters, you were refusing to help me.' And they will go away into eternal punishment, but the righteous will go into eternal life."* Matthew 25:45,46

Hell is the end of God's mercy. Until our last breath, he is ready to forgive, and we can enter in. We repent of our sins and acknowledge our need. But as scripture says, *"It is appointed for every person, once to die. And after that the judgment."* (Hebrews 9:27) After that, God's mercy is closed, we are shut off from his mercy, from repentance and will be locked up in Hell.

I know we have conveniently dropped this teaching from our churches in recent years. But we have no reason to think God has dropped it. And think of it this way—I love C.S. Lewis' *The Great Divorce* and his fantasy depiction of Hell. He mentions that Hell's gates are locked from the inside and they get out on weekends to visit Earth and ride buses toward heaven, a wonderfully contrived tale it is. I so wish it were true, but that is not going to scare one person outside of Christ. I think one of the reasons that the church is waning is that without Hell, the exclusiveness of Jesus, and the standards for sexual morality, there is nothing at stake with the church, at the church, or because of the church. So why bother?

---

3   Mark 9:48 NLT.

4   Matthew 25:41

5. GREED

The Eye of the Needle

"I tell you the truth, it is very hard for a rich person to enter the Kingdom of Heaven. I'll say it again—it is easier for a camel to go through the eye of a needle than for a rich person to enter the Kingdom of God!"

—Jesus of Nazareth

Those who accuse others of greed are never greedy. At least you get that impression hearing their screeds. They attack the educated elite who they claim have most of the wealth and selfishly hoard it. Angry people attacking others for being greedy is proof that they are particularly greedy. Isn't wanting what someone else has earned referred to as coveting, as theft, as a cultural shakedown? I am talking now about those who don't have and who want.

Politicians have their own philosophy on greed which of course, reveals they are greedy for power. They want all the power they can get, and they don't plan on sharing it. In fact, they have a very interesting financial plan for you and your money. If you go to work, get paid, and then have the audacity to keep it and spend it any way you want, then you are greedy. If, however, you go to work and earn your money, they take your money and spend it the way *they* want to spend it, then *you* are generous. The plan is they take your money and use it to buy votes which makes them more powerful.

This system also creates what is commonly known as welfare psychosis. You don't need to be on welfare to have it. It spreads virally through the human heart catalyzed by ungratefulness. Welfare psychosis is when you start to believe that you deserve the money that is given to you which was earned by some other person. You might even complain, "Where's my money?" You don't need to be rich to be greedy, those most greedy often are those without money. It is to live a life based on psychosis which by definition, is to deny the reality around you. It ruins your life because it creates in you a sense of entitlement.

Charity, however, is different. Charity is when you desire to give what you have earned, and you give to those in need. This allows you to sacrifice and enjoy the benefit of caring for others. It ennobles both the giver and the receiver because it helps those who receive to develop gratitude. The gratitude then develops a spirit of giving in the receiver. To fully understand greed and its devastating characteristics and the benefits of giving, we again cite the revolutionary teaching of Jesus of Nazareth.

The rich young man/ruler

Someone came to Jesus with this question: "Teacher, what good deed must I do to have eternal life?" Jesus answered, *"Why ask me about what is good?" There is only One who is good. But to answer your question—If you want to receive eternal life. Keep the commandments."* "Which ones?" the man asked. Jesus replied, *"You must not murder. You must not commit adultery. You must not steal. "You must not testify falsely. Honor your father and mother. Love your neighbor as yourself."*

"I've obeyed all these commandments," the young man replied. *"What else must I do?"*

Here is a person who had life wired. He was like a Rothschild, Rockefeller, or Vanderbilt. His family probably had a foundation and already was doing a great deal of moral good. He is not standing there alone—behind him was his family and his reputation. You just didn't get rich fast and easy in first-century Israel. Wealth was a family tradition. He was rich, he was young, he was a man, and he was ruler—he had it all. He sounds like a well-meaning, good-hearted, highly ethical person. He represented a lot of good history and he could say with great confidence, I and my family, have done all these things, we are doing them even now.

Let's face it, we all sort of believe, even though we don't like to say it out loud, that moral goodness is linked to financial success.

And that somehow it seems that people who suffer more are linked to poor decision-making. Standing there, his entire life seemed to announce goodness, great decisions, acts of charity, and good character. But he wasn't sure he would enter the Kingdom of God. He wanted to know how to seal the deal and if he still lacked something. But he was talking to the **revolutionary** Jesus. The *real* Jesus, if you like, the One who smashed all the categories and was about to tell him what would send him packing with his head down and disappointed.

Jesus told him, *"If you want to be perfect, go and sell all your possessions and give the money to the poor, and you will have treasure in heaven. Then come, follow me."* "*If you want to be perfect.*" Jesus seems to be saying, "I *know* you want to be perfect, but just to prove to you that you are not and cannot be perfect, try this out!"

This is a revolutionary way to provide a new stock portfolio for an entire society. The sloppy reader, the activist reader, immediately jumps on this to mean, "Hey rich guy, sell your stuff and give it to the poor!" That is the revolution that comes from advocates who would like to drain the rich's bank accounts dry and redistribute the vast wealth of a nation. Wouldn't that be what Jesus is calling us all to do? I hate to burst your little utopian bubble, but NO, Hell NO. This is the only person Jesus ever told to do this. And aren't you glad it wasn't you? *When the young man heard this, he left sad, he was grieving.* He realized he wasn't up to it, he couldn't do it, and he didn't have it in him. He wasn't perfect, not even close. **Jesus knows how to make self-salvation beyond our reach.**

Christianity is different than any other religion or philosophy

This is when the young man heard bad news: **he couldn't save himself.** This *getting into heaven project* was above him, beyond him, he didn't have enough money to give to this, and he did not have, even though very rich, enough resources to get admission. If Jesus had given him a lower price, then the young man would have asked about the VIP lounge in Heaven. If you can earn your way in, then you can earn your way up, from gold, to platinum, to Super Diamond, *et al.*

He was sad and grieving because it demanded more than he thought. When people learn that the gospel says they can't earn it or achieve it, they get offended. The rich in particular, like to give tokens of their appreciation to the gods. But not to *this* God! Oh, let's see, 5k to United Way, 2k to the neighbor's GoFundMe, 15k to Samaritan's Purse. None of that will gain entrance. For the rich young ruler, building a new synagogue, purchasing new vestments for the High Priest—nope.

Jesus is not only revolutionary, not only does he shock religious sensibilities, he gets *very* personal.

This was the only time he required this of anyone, but it was the primary breaking point for this young man. Peter didn't have any problem leaving the fish behind, or even his boat. I didn't suffer by giving up my life as a poor college student when I started following Jesus. But then Jesus said, *"After you have done all that, then Come follow me!"*—such high standards are beyond basic human nature, and the requirements ensure that few show up to follow Jesus. You will never be able to follow Jesus on your abilities.

This is a power struggle with God about our dreams. We are greedy for *our* goals, for *our* dreams, for *our* schedule, for *our* modern identity. God is in effect saying, "You will get new treasure in the Kingdom of God. Let me decide how rich you will get! And Jesus then issued a statement that even scandalized his faithful disciples.

"I tell you the truth, it is very hard for a rich person to enter the Kingdom of Heaven."

Isn't it interesting that you don't hear much about ministry to the rich? Probably, for two reasons. First, it is difficult to raise money around helping those whom most believe don't need help. Second, those who are called to such a mission are embarrassed to speak of it. Nothing like a holiday on the *French Riviera* with rock stars and troubled captains of industry to spice up your ministry newsletter. I recall philosopher Dallas Willard often saying, "Don't forget the rich, it's harder for them to get into heaven." It is true, but so few want to help the greedy. Yes, common folk always think that the rich are greedy, they live behind high walls with security systems, servants, and valet health care. One thing is for sure, you have to dig deep to feel sorry for them. Jesus even bangs his boys up with a little stinger metaphor, *"It is easier for a camel to go through the eye of a needle than for a rich person to enter into the Kingdom of God."* His disciples were scandalized—they wanted to know more about this crazy theology of their leader.

The Disciples protested, "Now wait a minute!" They complained, *"Who then can be saved?"* Jesus' answer is what should be shouted around the world, *"Humanly speaking, it is impossible. But with God, everything is possible."* The disciples were confused because Jesus seemed to be saying that even the best among us—the elite, the morally superior, the nobility—if they can't make it, if they are not good enough, then who is? Jesus admits it, humans can't do it, no one can make themselves a Christian, no one can reach God, please God, satisfy God, or be good enough for God. It takes a miracle, a miracle of new life, a new heart, **a rebirth.**

Peter, in particular, seems both confused and wondering if, all things considered, this is equitable. **He asks Jesus a rather cheeky question,** *"We've given up everything to follow you. What will we get?"* This reveals a lot about us doesn't it? Even after three years of being intimately close to God, Peter wants to make sure he gets his fair share. This, my friends, is greed. Greed is usually the rich's problem. And who is rich? Someone with more stuff than you! That is why we never confess to greed or do so readily. This rich, young, ruler, this guy who can't fit through the eye of a needle is not going to make it. He isn't going to show up and join the band of followers. Jesus, you told him he would get heavenly treasure—could we review our retirement portfolios with you? Please remind us of the benefits package.

Jesus responds by reassuring them that **whatever they have invested will be returned to them many times over.** And he reminds them that the kingdom's pecking order, who gets the *Pulitzers, Nobels,* and *Oscars,* will be topsy-turvy, a glorious world, built upside down.

Contemporary disciples, you and I, must be reminded that this following Jesus thing is not a negotiation—it is a surrender. Then we will be able to slip through that needle, even with unanswered questions, knowing that whatever it is, it is a miracle of God.

SEVEN DEADLY SINS

6. SLOTH/LAZINESS

Most of us know of the animal known as a sloth because of zoos and TV. Mainly we are fascinated with its amazingly slow-moving life up in the canopy of the rain forest. They don't do much, because they sleep 15-18 hours a day and climb down to the rainforest floor only once a week to defecate. It is a mystery what sloths are for. Certain important bugs crawl up into their fur and grow and those bugs are important to the environment.

What you can say about the sloth is that being slow, nocturnal, and sleeping most of the time, it is doing what sloths were created to do. Therefore, being a sloth is not a sin, but being a human and imitating a sloth *is* a sin. Laziness, the modern equivalent, gives sloths a bad name. Sloths are offended by slothfulness. Even sloths would accuse a human imitating a sloth of slothfulness. Sloths have risen up and protested such an aspersion on their family. As a result, from this point forward, we will refer to this problem of slothfulness as **laziness.**

What makes a person lazy?

My personal experience was a lack of direction and a weakened desire to please my family or authority figures. It has been discovered that teens are not sleeping more just to irritate their parents, but because it is a hormonal time-shift. It can also be a lack of structure and accountability which can trouble us in every phase of life. Jordan Peterson mentions that the two greatest predictors of successful people are intelligence and conscientiousness. I would add to that a foundation of moral conviction because some things are right and other things are wrong.

My wife's aunt was called lazy until she was an adult when it was discovered that she had a congenital heart defect. Sometimes a person will be accused of laziness, but the *lazy* person might not be interested. For example, a spouse could accuse their counterpart of being lazy because they don't want to work in the yard or fix a lawnmower. It could be that the spouse is a very hard worker but would rather lie on the couch and read a book than plant a garden. Laziness has always been associated with youth, but youth have always seemed to have plenty of energy to do the many things they desire. Therefore, it is highly unlikely that the young are naturally lazy, but they could be naturally at cross purposes with authority figures starting with parents and teachers.

The real challenge of parenting is getting children out of laziness and into responsible adulthood. This usually involves instruction, discipline, repetition, and parental diplomacy. If laziness persists and turns into drifting, a lack of ambition, and living a parasitic lifestyle, then you've got a problem! When one encounters this problem, the question becomes, *who has the most to gain by creating a cultural ethos that produces a new lazy generation?* Many places in the Bible condemn laziness and describe its ill effects.[1]

We have all heard the term, failure to launch

Many pathologies can destroy people and countries. Among them is one new generation after another producing lazy youth. The truth is, our villain once again is Lucifer. His dedication to the destruction of God's work and people is without exhaustion. It has become obvious that in the last twenty years, a new generation has entered American life which is at times productive, but society in general is growing more lax because hard work and accomplishment are optional.

You can be unsuccessfully successful and admired for having influence but for no other reason than celebrity. This could be categorized as useless, aimless, and destructive to people and institutions, but beneath it all is the destructive nature of a fallen human. The Apostle Paul addresses the deepest part of our being when he attributes the source to Lucifer's malevolent power.

Paul begins by spotlighting the law. The law he is speaking about is Israel's code of conduct and priorities. The law was a stan-

---

1 Proverbs 19:15-25

dard given through the Ten Commandments. It was codified, and stamped into the nation's soul and every Jewish heart. It was what the nation and its citizens were to live up to—it provided them with a standard. This kind of moral ethos is present in most societies, but we will stick with Paul and Israel.

"*So the trouble is not with the law, for it is spiritual and good. The trouble is with me, for I am all too human, a slave to sin.*" Romans 7:14 NLT.

Paul confesses that he is a "slave to sin." To be a slave is to be owned by some other person or entity.

"*I don't really understand myself, for I want to do what is right, but I don't do it. Instead I do what I hate.*"

He is befuddled that he can't seem to do the right thing and he ends up doing the opposite.

But he gets even more precise:

"*So I am not the one doing wrong; it is sin living in me that does it. But I know that nothing good lives in me, that is, in my sinful nature. I want to do what is right, but I can't.*"

Sin is not only an action in the same way that faith is not only an action. Its reality is revealed in action, but the source is very deep and mysterious. Paul is saying something that we all know is true from our experience. We are a slave to sin and that sin has a power and it has a will. That will, unchecked, will badger, confuse, tempt, and then ruin our life. Every time we sin in our minds, in our emotions, or in our body, sin does damage.

The way out is found in Paul's words:

"*I have discovered this principle of life—that when I want to do what is right, I inevitably do what is wrong. I love God's law with all my heart. But there is another power within me that is at war with my mind. This power makes me a slave to sin that is still within me.*" Romans 7:21,22

Finally, Paul has had it, and he cries out!

"Oh, what a miserable person I am! Who will free me from this life that is dominated by sin and death? Thank God! The answer is in Jesus Christ our Lord. So you see how it is: In my mind I really want to obey God's law, but because of my sinful nature I am a slave to sin.

Paul goes on to proclaim: *So now there is no condemnation for those who belong to Christ Jesus. And because you belong to him, the power of the life giving Spirit has freed you from the power of sin that leads to death."* Romans 7:24-8:2

Paul went deep into the inner maze of human conflict and confusion. He emerged confused, covered with the muck of battle, but with a deep yearning for God's love, acceptance, and forgiveness.

Laziness is a spiritual problem

Yes, behavioral modification, structure, accountability, exhortation, and discipline are all necessary to make laziness an only occasional menace for most people. These are all part of the toolbox for helping people overcome it. Most of the time those addicted to laziness, meaning it is a pattern, will defend their position against all threats, foreign and domestic. Here are some steps to help a person who seems to drift through life at half speed.

1. Admit, repent, and confess to the failure of running your own life. As Jesus said, *"If anyone wants to come after me, deny yourself, take up your cross and follow me."* Luke 9:23. It is a fool's errand to hold on and control one's life. Luke 9:24,25.
2. Realize that once we fling ourselves onto the mercy of God, all condemnation is gone. *"There is now therefore, no condemnation for those in Christ Jesus."* Romans 8:1
3. Get involved with others who live by covenant—meaning clear purpose, mutual support, expectations, and accountability. Hebrews 10:24,25 and I Thessalonians 5:14.
4. Remember with God, your record is clean, it is a fresh start—no condemnation.

SEVEN DEADLY SINS

7. GLUTTONY

It is the just doom of laziness and gluttony to be inactive without ease and drowsy without tranquility.
—Dr. Samuel Johnson (1709-1784)

With all due respect to Dr. Samuel Johnson's great wisdom, he was renowned for his oversized body and appetite. He had genius-level capacities in his knowledge of the English language. His most famous biographer, James Boswell, chronicled Johnson's great struggles and personal battles.[1] He was a poet, playwright, literary critic, preacher, and lexicographer. He is one of history's characters called Doctor even though he couldn't continue his studies at Pembroke College, Oxford University because of a shortage of funds. His genius was universally accepted by some of his contemporary greats like Charles Dickens, James Boswell, and Edward Gibbon.

His greatest achievement was the completion of the *Dictionary of the English Language.* The project was given the funds and three years to complete the task. He ran out of money and it took ten years. But it is clearly understood that no one else could have done it as well as Johnson. He was considered the life of the party and a great conversationalist. He struggled mightily with his health which was due to bad luck and bad conduct because he spent many hours in pubs. He comes to mind when I think of excess. I'm sure I am being unfair to some degree, but he fits the image of a patron of an old 18th-century English pub crammed with patrons of every ilk. You may recall those Tom Jones films portraying men with one hand eating meat off a large drumstick, holding a beer in the other, and a wench on his lap.

Gluttony isn't just about food, even though that is part of it.

---

1 The Life of Samuel Johnson, was written in the late 1700s. Published in the United States, 1992, Alfred Knopf Books.

Gluttony is taking something good and necessary, like pizza, and eating the whole thing. *The Seven Deadly Sins* were named by the *Catholic Church* and exegeted and explained by medieval theologian Sir Thomas Aquinas (1225-1274). Aquinas remains the Catholic Church's most respected theologian. He influenced a variety of fellow medieval scholars. They broke down eating and drinking into categories. You could eat ***excessively*** by demanding too much. You could eat ***sumptuously*** by demanding the richest or best foods. You could eat ***daintily*** by demanding only the perfectly prepared food. Finally, you could eat ***impulsively*** by demanding the food right now.

It is obvious, isn't it, that the opposite of gluttony is self-control?

Gluttony works much like other addictions—gambling, alcohol, or even now more pernicious addictions like sexually related problems. It has a lot to do with the process of temptation. **Dallas Willard's temptation example was—the Twinkie.** In case you have just appeared from the cave you've been living in, it is a rectangular yellow cake-like object with vanilla crème filling. Ben and Jerry's fancy ice cream flavors come and go, but the simple, boring vanilla Twinkie has been passed on from generation to generation at birthday parties, weddings, and gas stations for almost 100 years. I confess to driving cross-country late at night and stopping for gasoline, grabbing a pack (or two) for a snack, washing it down with a Coke, and driving on. It is tasty, gives you energy, and can even survive war. Twinkie's are tough—they last.

According to Dallas the problem with the Twinkie is that it lives in the imagination. You can pass by the Twinkie table, but as you walk around the fair or the event, that Twinkie lives in your mind. You crave it, it calls out to you, and you must have it. Finally, you grab it. Somehow your imagination—your craving, your lack of self-control positioned your body in front of it and you took it. This happens every day all over the world in millions of minds.

The Bible tells stories about it. Achan comes to mind because he was drawn to the booty of war and took what he craved.

Israel was distinguished in war because they were not allowed to take the personal possessions of the citizens of a conquered nation. God told Joshua that the covenant had been broken and to discover the guilty. Everyone knew the covenant and Achan didn't even argue his case before Joshua when he was found out. "It is true! I have sinned against the Lord, the God of Israel. Among the plunder I saw a beautiful robe from Babylon, 200 silver coins, and a bar of gold weighing more than a pound. I wanted them so much that I took them. Joshua 7:20-21 NLT

Joshua's soldiers went to Achan's tent, found the buried spoils, and brought them to him. Achan, his family, and even his livestock were stoned to death for his offense. This is one of those events in the Bible that modern people can't accept or understand. Some call it a fable, but the total historic exegesis of the passage persuades me that it is an actual event. One must understand the nature of a pre-modern world, its ethics, its procedures, and how God was working through that world. The progressive revelation of God to the human race must be considered.

This is part of what Hebrews 1:1-3 is explaining:

"Long ago God spoke many times and in many ways to our ancestors through the prophets. And now in these final days,[2] he has spoken to us through his Son. God promised everything to the Son as an inheritance and through the Son he created the universe. The Son radiates God's own glory and expresses the very character of God and he sustains everything by the mighty power of his command. When he had cleansed us from our sins, he sat down in the place of honor at the right hand of

---

2 "final days" is understood as the capstone of revelation in Christ. In that Christ can return at any time. See Matthew 24:14 as a time frame.

the majestic God in heaven. This shows that the Son is far greater than the angels, just as the name God gave him is greater than their names."

Whether it be ancient more primitive times or the most current high-tech world, the same principles apply. Gluttony is a sin that reveals the inner strength or weakness of a person to exercise self-control.

Gods revelatory context was introduced in Athens to a pagan/secular culture.

"From one man he created all the nations throughout the whole earth. He decided beforehand when they should rise and fall, and he determined their boundaries. His purpose was for the nations to seek after God and perhaps feel their way toward him and find him—though he is not far from any one of us. For in him we live and move and exist. As some of your own poets have said, 'We are his offspring.' And since this is true, we shouldn't think of God as an idol designed by craftsmen from gold or silver or stone. Acts 17:26-29 NTL

This one man of course, is Christ, who is clearly named here in Paul's sermon, and in his writings in Colossians 1:15-20.

The inner process of temptation or "Twinkie Theology"

"If you think you are standing strong, be careful not to fall. The temptations in your life are no different from what others experience. And God is faithful. He will not allow the temptation to be more than you can stand. When you are tempted, he will show you a way out so that you can endure. So, my dear friends, flee from the worship of idols." I Corinthians 10:12-14a.

1. Everyone is at risk, common nature, common enemy, common tendency

Paul warns about thinking certain sins can't get at you. The old saying is succinct, "pride goes before the fall." The reason is that the same temptations are in front of us daily. The entire human race encounters the same temptation—and that temptation is to want something so badly you will violate your integrity, even all you have, as Achan did, to get it.

William Temple, one time *Archbishop of Canterbury*, spoke of the Solitude Test. It was simple, what do you think about when you don't need to think about something else? Where do your relaxed thoughts go? He said, "Religion is what you do with your solitude." What have you programmed yourself to desire or crave—that becomes your god? A career, a person, a dream of more money, or power of some kind?

Another test is what the late Tim Keller called the *Unanswered Prayer Test.* "God, if you don't give me this, we are through!" What would it take to get you to leave God? Whatever it is, there is your idol, the object of your worship. It is what you want more than anything—beware, you are vulnerable.

It has been said that the only way our minds can be released from the grip of a beautiful object is an even more beautiful object. What is that object?

2. God is faithful

A bit trite, you might say. Isn't that a good slogan on a religious site? Ok, you have a point. But look at the specificity of the promise. *"He will not allow the temptation to be more than you can stand."*

God is promising that he will give you the strength if you ask and want it. Turn now to that Twinkie. It could be that you should eat only one a week, or something quirky like that, but whatever it is, that intense desire can be defeated. A more serious temptation is to abuse yourself or others with irrational behavior with sexual desire that is all-consuming. When you think you're on the brink of giving in, stop and pray and ask God to help you overcome it, run from it, and get away if you can. Remember that more beautiful object we are looking for?

Remember this about Jesus:

"So then, since we have a great High Priest who has entered heaven, Jesus the Son of God, let us hold firmly to what we believe. This High Priest of ours understands our weaknesses, for he faced all of the same testings we do, yet he did not sin. So let us come boldly to the throne of our gracious God. There we will receive his mercy, and we will find grace to help us when we need it the most." Hebrews 4:14-16 NLT.

The beauty of Jesus is he understands weakness. He stands alone among all religious leaders or proposed gods to our world. Jesus must either be believed or discarded, there is no middle or moderate with Jesus. Either we are all in or not in at all. This is the uniqueness of incarnation, the logos, the logic, and the word from God is the Word Himself. God has spoken with such a profundity that it defies human vocabulary. As John wrote, "We beheld his glory full of grace and truth." Remember Jesus in Gethsemane? The agony, the pain, the prayer, indeed he understands. The only God who came to us and died for us. And yes, we are guilty, and yes, evil is terrible, and yes, you may be suffering today as you read this. But he understands. He understands our weakness—so go boldly to God—he is gracious, he will help, he will provide a way of escape. That is his promise, he is faithful to be with us and helping us endure.

Christ gave himself for you and for me. Why did he do that? Because he loves us completely, fully, eternally. Because you and I matter. I can't understand it, I can only embrace it. I heard it said recently that a former glutton attempted to explain why he now could control his appetite. He said he had eaten enough, and he was saving some room for dessert. He went on to say, "I've heard that a great feast, the marriage supper of the Lamb, will be taking place in heaven, I am leaving room for dessert."

SEVEN DEADLY SINS

05

THE CHURCH THAT CAME IN FROM THE COLD

THE CHURCH THAT CAME IN FROM THE COLD

"The ultimate reality is no longer something available to reason and to the mind of the philosopher. It is to be known by accepting and following the core of Jesus. The answer to the question what is the ultimate secret of the universe is the man Jesus." [1]

—Lesslie Newbigin

The 1963 John Le Carré spy novel, *The Spy Who Came in from the Cold* told the story of a British intelligence agent working behind enemy lines. "Cold" was a useful metaphor because East Berlin is cold, but more importantly, because working undercover in hostile environs is inherently dangerous. Hearth and home imply warmth. Operating daily with tension in your body, looking over your shoulder, the weight of pretending to be someone else, is cold and inhospitable. Then there is the constant possibility that you will be found out, tortured, and shot. Even worse, repeatedly tortured, then tortured some more, then shot.

When the church is being the church, it is out in the cold. Its members are constantly in danger because we are strategically placed in a hostile culture. Placed by the Holy Spirit, that is what is behind the prayer, *"Lead me not into temptation."* Culture is what shapes you without you knowing it. It makes you what you are without permission. We buy hot dogs when we go to a baseball game, not because they are good for us, but because that is what we do when we go to baseball games. Then we eat peanuts and wash them down with a twenty-dollar beer. I don't even like beer. We go to the ballpark because that is Americana, it is who we are. "Jesus Saves" is an American cultural artifact, part of the scenery, believed by many, ignored by most. Properly taught pastors "shoo" their members out of the church so they can become the church. "Go

---

1 Nihilism, Lesslie Newbigin

out there and be the church, be faithful witnesses of Christ our Lord." Christ ordered us to *"Go and make disciples of every ethne or people group."* [2]

But the Americana many of us love is breaking down, it's being deconstructed by the nefarious efforts of those who seek to create a new utopia, a secular age, an age of reason alone, even though none of these advocates can run their daily lives by reason alone. If that were the case, none of them would order french fries. But they do order french fries, hey do top off their lattes with whipped cream, and borrow money via credit card for Christmas presents so family feelings won't be hurt. Regardless, even if these advocates of reason alone (little Descartes if you will, "I think, therefore I am" types) lose daily battles with their appetites, they insist on making the rules that will help create their utopian world. They can hate, which is fine as long as you hate the right people. They can ruin cities, facilitate crime, and corrupt youth through a vast educational system, but it's for a righteous cause. We are called to make disciples who reproduce, but we are doing a poor job of it. They are called to "make victims," which is easier, and they are having great success.

It is a world that advertises itself as better, more caring, and where everything is shared, but as Alexander Solzhenitsyn said, "We have placed too much hope in political and social reforms, only to find out that we were being deprived of our most precious possession: our spiritual life."[3]

They have designed a world where God has been forgotten, or a god emptied of its content, intention, and meaning. This is a world that has turned cold for Christians, and clearly inhospitable to the gospel. The good news is that it is dawning on the general population that such naiveté regarding human nature among elites is not working. One need only view the rubble of the former Soviet

---

2 Matthew 28:19

3 Alexandr Solzhenitsyn, "A World Split Apart," speech delivered at Harvard University, June 8, 1978

Union and the bloody body count of the 20th century to know that any endeavor that violates human nature will fail.

What does it mean to come in from the cold?

As long ago as 1989 the highly respected missionary statesman and intellectual, Lesslie Newbigin, considered former Christendom, or as we might call it, Western Civilization, was the most resistant culture to the gospel. He challenged the church to establish what he called a Missionary Encounter with the culture. He said the encounter would not be a withdrawal from the culture, or assimilation into the culture. It would be to confront the culture, name its idols, create conflict, and then coverts would follow. Newbign's advice hardly sounds like a call for all deployed disciples to come in from the cold hard and difficult work of confronting a society run by a powerful elitism—a power that controls most of the major institutions, businesses, entertainment, and media platforms. You find yourself as a faithful witness competing by the elites' ground rules—what it rewards and what it punishes—what it promotes and what it seeks to destroy.

Coming in from the cold means to stop playing by the culture's rules.

It means to stop looking for innovative solutions based on the latest technology, rather to use technology for a greater purpose. It means to return to home base, the church, where a renaissance in learning and practicing the ways and means of Jesus take center stage. Lutheran theologian, Andrew Root, advocates such an action by stating that church growth/health literature in the past fifty years have largely misdiagnosed the decline of the church. He claims, *"The answer to the problem is not more and faster."* [4] Clearly,

---

4 Andrew Root, Blair Bertrand, When Church Stops Working (Brazos Press, 2023), page 2

the dominant definition of the problem is decline. Most mainstream or historic denominations have experienced a dramatic decline in worship attendance, membership, funding, and cultural influence in the last five decades.

Root and Bertrand see numeric decline only as a symptom.

When one reads research by Barna, Gallup, and other pollsters, it screams decline, but it is only the symptoms, its pain. Most consultants measure, they quantify, but they find it much more difficult to go deeper into the problem. It is a decline in people, funding, and progress that alarms church leaders and causes them to call in experts who are accustomed to solving measurable quantifiable problems. Most advice is do more, do it faster and better, be more relevant, change your branding, refresh your mission statement, get a motto and go for it. Maybe change your language, create a new culture, hang a few banners, penetrate the corridors of power, et al.

Root and Bertrand go on to say, "Effective innovation has not stopped the crisis in the church because the crisis comes from the very place that effective innovation comes from: the secular age. Instead of helping the church, effective innovation actually worsens the crisis by driving us deeper into the secular age we find ourselves in."

The cold is the secular age and all its premises, assumptions, prescriptions, that are at war against Christ and his church. Pascal reportedly said, "Men despise religion, they hate it and are afraid it might be true."[5] It is quite true that even in its decline, the church stands in the way of the luciferin effort to turn light into darkness and darkness into light.[6] They are trying to remove Christianity from the culture, but it is like extracting flour from a baked cake, it's a fool's errand.[7]

---

5   Blaise Pascal, Pensees (Oxford Press, 1999), page 46. [Pascal lived in the 1600s]

6   Isaiah 5:20

7   Cake without flour analogy courtesy of Root and Bertrand.

Why the Church needs to come in from the cold

Because as long as we use the metrics of the secular age, we will be their prisoner. We will not find the solution to our problem of decline in the innovation of the best counsel money can buy. This is because what lies behind the secular age and its commitment to use technology, reason, and transhuman intelligence, A.I. to move from the human world to a new transcendence. This effort is hurtling at breakneck speed away from the ancient world in which Christianity was birthed and its founders who wrote the Bible. The disciples of Jesus will never feel entirely at home in the secular age—it is pedal to the metal in the opposite direction. But we are on board with the culture, we are traveling along, and we need something to stabilize us, a place to stand. We can't continue to let the secular age be our masters, we can no longer play by their rules.

Skepticism and doubt as superior to faith

This is just one example of how different the secular age assumptions differ from a biblical world view. The underlying assumption of the secular mind is what is called the critical theory. Critical theory is the basis of what later would be applied to race. Critical theory assumes that anything that qualifies as knowledge must survive the gauntlet of deconstruction that is based in skepticism. A story in the Bible such as Jesus feeding the 5000 with two fish and five loaves of bread is surely false. It must be rejected and cast aside as a serious idea. Therefore, it cannot be included in the public domain as real knowledge. The critical theory is the jewel in the crown of western scientific civilization.

The idea is that skepticism and doubt are superior and more intellectually sound that faith or belief. But who decides that? And on what basis do scientists hold that science itself isn't based on faith? The critical faculty can only operate on the basis of beliefs which are held uncritically. When someone criticizes a proposition, one has always to ask, what are the assumptions which are not criticized when the critical move is made? It does not occur to most that faith is based on spiritual knowledge that is just as real and useful as the study of gravity. Scientists believe in gravity, but even today if you are having dinner at high table at Cambridge University and ask the most brilliant physicist in the world, "Could you explain gravity, its origin and how it works?" They couldn't do it.

Belief precedes doubt, because you must have something to doubt. In fact, if we doubt everything, we will never come to know anything. We cannot begin our quest for knowledge by doubting, but by believing. Faith is primary, doubt is secondary. This is really a debate about how one knows anything. But if the church agrees to argue its case in the secular age that is based on the critical theory, then there is no way to fully and fairly determine knowledge. Knowledge of persons, tastes, geography, scenery, history, languages, families, relationships, and yes, of God's reality in a person's life must be included. They all are vitally important to the way we live. A simple proposition would be, "The Bible is true, it presents knowledge that is crucial to human life, death, and answers the primary questions of meaning. To begin with the assumption that the Bible is true is a level playing field.

In future columns I will discuss what we are actually to do when we come in from the cold. They are as follows:

- The actual problem
- The solution
- The product
- The process
- The new delivery system

THE CHURCH THAT CAME IN FROM THE COLD

THE CHURCH THAT CAME IN FROM THE COLD: PART 2

The Actual Problem

> *"A widespread transformation of character through wisely disciplined discipleship to Christ can transform our world—disarm the structural evils that have always dominated humankind and now threaten to destroy the world."* [1] —Dallas Willard

So, let's say a local church decides to come in from the cold. They have chosen to give up on secular solutions to spiritual problems. What comes next? What is the actual problem it faces? Why was it in decline? Why had they lost touch with the reality of the culture? Why had their disciples failed to engage the people and to make progress in keeping friends and neighbors, even themselves, from becoming disciples of the secular age? First, these questions need answers and second, require a leadership willing to ask and answer them regardless of embarrassment. The following represents a look inside the church. Most pundits read research by polling organizations, which normally analyze churches as a group or genre, and does not include a deep dive into the beliefs and practices of a particular congregation. I want to make some observations from an insider point of view—who has been up to his eyeballs in the church culture—and emotionally connected to every action, disagreement, conflict, heartache, and achievement.

We intentionally withdrew from participation in shaping the culture.

Many, if not most, conservative evangelical churches intentionally separated themselves by not participating in any activities that seemed dangerous or questionable.

---

1   Dallas Willard, The Spirit of the Disciplines, 1989, Harper & Row, page xi

"Don't team up with those who are unbelievers. How can righteousness be a partner with wickedness? How can light live with darkness? What harmony can there be between Christ and the devil? How can a believer be a partner with an unbeliever? And what union can there be between God's temple and idols?" [2]

These remain vexing questions for contemporary Christians. Let's say you encourage young adults 21+ to engage their friends. This may include joining clubs and organizations where the worldviews, premises, and assumptions are antithetical to biblical truth. The young adults become colonized by those friends and organizations. In other words, the Christian witnesses became more like their friends than their friends became like Christians. That is precisely the fear the church had—more afraid of the culture than those in the culture feared the church.

This fear has gone away except in parental hearts, as their emotions betray them, desiring their children to be successful more than holy. Thus, the statement, "My child isn't going to church, but is very bright and successful." The church fears they will lose their young much earlier and for different reasons. They don't fear that they will go over to the other side because in habit, mindset, and practices, they are already on the other side. Now the church is trying to figure out how to stop the bleeding. This is a defensive posture which seems a long way from:

"You are my witnesses, in Jerusalem, Judea, Samaria, and then the world."

The key could be found in the simple observation that Jesus attended Matthew's party, but he didn't stay, he didn't join that society—but he did influence them.[3]

We, the church, have succumbed to the intoxicating aphrodisiac of being loved by the cultural elites, their leaders, their rewards, their status

---

2 2 Corinthians 6:14-16 NLT

3 Matthew 9:9-13

This does seem contradictory to the previous diagnosis of cultural withdrawal. While the first is a withdrawal based on the fear of spiritual corruption, *this* is based on the fear of being an outcast in career, family, or social connections. There is an element of "cool" in evangelicalism that desires to be part of the real action of society where the strobe lights shine. Being an "insider" among the cultural elite is such a *coup* for the church one could reason. There is the glamour that goes with being the Chaplain of an NFL or NBA team or a Presidential advisor. A *Grammy* is better than a *Dove*, a *Nobel* better than the *Christian Writers Association* annual award, and a *Pulitzer* trumps the *Christianity Today Book of the Year*.

All this is of negligible importance *except* when it comes to being colonized by the culture or discipled by its assumptions that caused Christians to soften or abandon clear moral or ethical standards of scripture. This problem is so obvious when Christians begin their comments by stating, "I have no problem with the transgender or the LGBTQ+ communities." Can that really be true if one reads and understands the teaching of Romans 1:18-32? Yes, there are differences in interpretations and valid nuanced understandings of the passage, but to say there is nothing that concerns you about degraded perversion, as a representative of the gospel, is at best, disingenuous, at worst, a falsehood. I recommend you spend a bit of time reading Isaiah and Jeremiah.

In summary, it could be said of these first two points that we have done our best to look and sound odd and to separate ourselves from the culture. At the same time, like befuddled magicians, somehow, we managed to capitulate to the secular age by trying to appease and please them so they would like us and recognize our achievements. I think this second point is more a practice of the academics or scholarly elements of evangelicalism. Our institutions have chosen to be accredited by the standards of the secular age. This accreditation is not only official but more powerfully practiced unofficially via trimming back and curating opinions so as not to offend the evangelical elite. The evangelical elite doesn't seem to have a problem—in their self-righteousness—to attack the more conservative members of the movement.

It does seem, and please excuse my unvetted opinion, that anyone among evangelicals who supports Donald Trump is looked at as less worthy and lower on the evangelical totem. The former President has now become a metaphor for love/hate, good/evil, predator/victim. He may be a SOB, but he is *their* SOB. And their rationale as Christians for supporting him is as good as the other more self-righteous opinions being put forth considering him unworthy. I pray for better leaders—I desire that—but many are forced to make choices that they don't want to make so as not to do further harm to the land they love. Do progressive evangelicals believe they are more worthy of thinking, writing, speaking, and ruling the world?

"We are all infected and impure with sin. When we display our righteous deeds, they are nothing but filthy rags." [4]

So much for the problems, what should the church that has come in from the cold do?

Change your ask—curate your message

Every tribe or community asks for something from its members. In ancient times it was more about *being* something.

Today's culture is much more superficial, detached, individualistic, and about *believing* something. The church is about both.

It is based on the *belief* that Christ is our savior and leader, thus, we are to follow him and *become like him*. Most people will confess to not being perfect and it is rare to hear anyone claim they are like Christ. It is common for a person to say they are not like Christ as a prelude to the excuse to not even try. The dagger in the church's heart is when the leadership says, "OK, you are fine, you are loved, you can be one of us and enjoy all the benefits of the church, and not be a practicing or serious member." We even have a category called "inactive member." The cure for such sickness is to change

---

4   Isaiah 64:6 NLT

the ask. Ask for more—at least ask what Christ asked.

"If anyone will come after me, let him deny himself, take up his cross and follow me."

This is being a Christian 101. It is the ticket into the community. If the church drops the most basic requirement, the whole thing falls apart.

To curate the message means to rebuild an inadequate gospel that doesn't deliver anyone from anything and demands nothing—not even repentance and a desire to follow. To curate means to attend to and carefully define the salvation vocabulary: *grace, faith, obedience, reborn, trust, et al.* Cut the taproot of a highjacked gospel built for quick and easy decisions and replace it with Jesus' call to follow him. Then ask people to repent of their sins, believe the good news, and follow him in discipleship. Reset the ask then start acting like it is true.

Address the problem directly through preaching

Communities live or die based on their leader's power of address. The tribal leader defines reality week after week based on the authority of the Bible. For example:

"This is why we are here. This is how we relate to the watching world. These are our responsibilities. We are here to prepare to take our message to the world. This is our mission."

Preaching must address the real-life drama of living as a Christian in a hostile environment. Goals are set, stories are told, heroes are made, the challenge is issued—Go! Get out of the church and be the church. Great preaching is not just technique, talent, and oratory. It is the fire of expectation, it is the courage to call people to burst through their fears and to be brave in speaking up, standing up, and refusing to support the big lie that humans are in charge and society can save themselves. This is about expectation! Every Christian is a disciple, a student, an apprentice. All who are called to salvation are called to discipleship, no exceptions, no excuses.

Leaders repent and lead by example

No leadership team wants to ask, *"How many new disciples have we made this past year through our programming, not counting our children?"* Of course, our children are top priorities, but doing all we can to reach them is a given, isn't it? And wouldn't you do that even if your church was doing nothing, you would do *something*—right?

Many surveys and research projects have studied data around the question, but they still missed the answer to the question asked above. Churches measure baptisms and baptisms include new disciples, but many baptisms are rebaptisms of long-time Christians who finally got around to it. Research also measures new members, new givers, new families, and new attenders with a bottom line—net growth for a given year.

What must be faced is *how many new disciples.* Since disciples and Christians are the same when you define the gospel properly, it is really asking, are we, as disciples, *proving that we are* by introducing and teaching new people who are now following Christ? I recall a standard statement from the 1970s and 80s which said, "In America it takes 100 church members 365 days and $100,000 to make one new disciple." It is a sobering reality and I don't believe the numbers have improved. Yes, there are great exceptions to this average and yes, they are good examples for others to follow. However, it must be admitted that good examples are not much help when, for them to work, they need a highly charismatic leader who can make pigs fly.

A leadership team will need to humbly seek God, reverse engineer their process, and try to find the source of the problem—why so much effort, personnel, and resources are wasted—and then decide to change and to be living examples of the change they advocate.

Build an infrastructure that demands more and produces something better

The final point to make is: create a support structure that makes the new goals a reality. In order to do this clarity will be essential. You need a clear definition of what you plan to make. A disciple is … fill in the blank. Next, what are the activities that a person needs to engage in to become that disciple? If part of your definition is that a disciple interacts with God through the word and prayer, then how will you teach them to do that? How long would it take? How often would you meet? What assignments and projects would benefit them the most? There is one thing that people know about life, but like to ignore, in the spiritual life.

You can't make disciples without accountability and you can't practice accountability without structure.

I have never known this to be untrue or to be disproven. And I know that it has been proven in every person I have ever known or worked with.

Results will never get better unless you believe and practice this principle

I've had people say that it doesn't work because people can just lie. That is true if you are talking about a question like, "Did you watch porn this past week." But you will be found out if your training leaves the academic and gets into tasks, fruitfulness and actually doing mission together. If you don't get them out of a Bible study, small group, or home group, or classroom, it won't work anyway—you need to do something brave together with live armed resistance before it means anything anyway. Don't get me wrong, something brave could mean you are the hand someone in pain can hold, the arms to embrace brokenness of neighbor, or providing a meal for a hungry person—it doesn't require headline news. I recall Hall of Fame football coach, Tom Landry, saying,

"The job of a coach is making men do what they don't want to do in order to achieve what they've always wanted to be."

THE PASTOR/CHURCH THAT CAME IN FROM THE COLD: PART 3

...about a man who did the right thing at the wrong time...

> *"Faith in Jesus Christ is to learn his ways by going and doing them, not trying to understand them first."*
>
> —George MacDonald

> *"I don't think I have fully implemented my own strategy as a pastoral leader. I haven't been the man I wanted to be long enough to get it done."*
>
> —Bill Hull

What kind of leader will it take to create a disciple-making movement? We have thus far discussed why the church needs to come in from the cold. The cold is defined as the secular age, and its premise is, that given enough time, humanity can figure out its problems and construct innovative solutions. Additionally, the secular city has rules—that public and useful knowledge is based on reason, rationality, and the STEM[1] sciences—and that faith is not useful in the public square, spiritual knowledge is not knowledge, therefore, not to be taken seriously.

Christians who are Christians first can benefit from human progress, but when it comes to what it means to be a follower of Christ, it is only logical that learning Jesus' ways and *doing* them is priority *one*. Fundamental to all Christian thinking is that spiritual knowledge is *real* knowledge. As real as any other knowledge so the church should attempt to master it. The church does come in from the cold, but as modern humans, we stay out in the cold in our living. We have talked about what the church should do in previous columns. The question before us today is who will lead them?

---

1 STEM is an acronym for Science, Technology, Engineering, and Math.

The Leader in a Hurry

Carl Jung said it, "Hurry isn't of the devil, it is the devil." Jung was not a theologian but had clear ideas about the destructive nature of anxiety, fear, and confusion. If you prefer the opinion of pastors and theologians, John Wesley, who traveled 250,000 miles on horseback, carriage, and sea, kept a superhuman schedule. He would often preach a 5:30 AM service in a village, spend the remainder of the daylight getting to the next town, preach an evening session, minister until the late hours and do the same thing day after day. Additionally, he wrote many commentaries, Bible studies, and church policy documents for the Methodist movement. He made an important distinction that Jung did not.

Wesley said, "I am always busy, but never in a hurry."

I would define hurry as an attitude, a frame of mind that crams anxiety and fear into a person's schedule. Sometimes it manifests itself as drive or ambition, and by a person not being able to stay put long enough to accomplish something important. Staying put in this context could mean a geographic place, or it could mean the same project, or kind of work, such as a writer, an artist, or a politician.

Regardless, as the late philosopher Dallas Willard told a friend, "Ruthlessly eliminate hurry from your life."

Willard was a man who did not fret or worry, attempt to control or manipulate results, and accepted the results of his efforts, for good or ill. One thing evident from Jung, Wesley, Willard, and other leaders of accomplishment, they all found a way to have a satisfied soul. A satisfied soul is the primary trait of anyone who expects to create a disciple-making movement among local church members.

Talent and God-given abilities certainly enhance a leader's chance to make their impact large and newsworthy, but frankly, that is around 1% of leaders. Yes, statistics say that large churches are getting bigger and small churches are getting smaller. But all that means is that crowds chase talent and seek anonymity as they consume the crème de la crème from the best and brightest. What tastes good, however, isn't always good. But making headlines is different from making disciples. You can make disciples and not make headlines. In fact, the Jesus revolution quietly takes place behind the scenes—not newsworthy in the city of man. What is needed is something within the reach of the 99% of leaders who can turn their attention to making disciples. But first, every leader must deal with themselves.

The Unsatisfied Soul

The "But first" in the previous sentence is a bit misleading because the secret to a person dealing with themselves is *not* to stop and work on themselves. The idea that you must sort yourself out before you reach out is bad advice doled out by the therapeutic industry. Going monastic is only helpful if you are working on something challenging that tests you. Part of the "me first" movement is to love yourself, then you can love others. It is tripe and it is self-destructive, as is the idea that once you understand yourself, then you can discover how God wants to use you. I would recommend the George MacDonald school of thought presented in a quote at the top of this column, "Faith is going and doing his ways and means, *not* trying to understand them first." In fact, the only way you can understand them is *by doing them.*

All the treasure with God is found on that path of obedience.[2] It might be helpful for you to know that MacDonald, a man of the 19th century had eleven children, five of whom died of illness. He was a man of sorrows in some respects but was a major influence on C.S. Lewis. Sabbaticals, the practice of the religious and academics are quite dangerous, particularly to driven leaders—because it asks them to STOP and punish themselves for a few months by getting to know themselves and plan the next year of their lives—which takes about a week.

I told you, don't get me started. If you are tired, take some time off until you feel better and call it whatever you want. In ancient times they called it a vacation. If you are a writer and claim you

---

2 John 14:21

don't have time to write then you're not a writer. If you are a writer, and in rare cases, you truly don't have time to write, then change jobs. I would suppose, however, that you need to know the difference between having the ability to write and those who are called to write and can't stop writing.

Ok, I will stop now. My point here is your soul will continue to be unsatisfied as long as you concentrate on it, think about it, pray about it, and ponder it. For the gospel's sake, forget about yourself and follow Christ—that is the way your soul will be satisfied. Let me explain.

The Satisfied Soul

"The Lord is my shepherd, I lack nothing. He makes me lie down in green pastures, he leads me beside quiet waters, he refreshes my soul. Psalm 23:1-3a NIV.

David, the author of the most famous lines in all of poetry, was a shepherd before he was a king. I will assume for a moment he wrote this once people became interested in what he had to say, probably after it was known he would be king. The imagery is built on the ancient relationship of sheep to shepherd that he knew something about. I take these words as comforting to a sheep. I understand that we are all like sheep, we share some common attributes with our wooly friends, but it must be granted there are some differences. I, along with you, live in a secular age, one where there is much chaos, moral confusion, accelerated decadence, and spiritual destruction to our souls.

The test from this text for a satisfied soul is "I lack nothing." It seems the cure for the sheep is green pastures and still waters, and then on his command you follow the shepherd on good paths. It is the satisfied soul that provides the patience, dedication, and grit needed to start and establish a disciple-making movement. This is a good place to define a disciple-making movement.

A Disciple Making Movement

A disciple-making movement, in biblical terms, is where a group of people living by covenant, usually a church, are making disciples through at least four spiritual generations.[3] I would base this on the four generations mentioned by Paul to his young pastoral protégé, Timothy. **Paul**, the first generation said to **Timothy**, the second generation, *"And the things you have heard me say in the presence of many witnesses entrust to **reliable people** who will also be qualified to teach **others**."* 2 Timothy 2:2 NIV.

The third generation are the "reliable people" and the fourth generation are the "others." I will not fully explain it here, but some key ideas that will unlock multiplication are "heard," "witnesses," "entrust," "reliable," "qualified," "teach." Skipping any of these vital traits will mean failure in reproduction and multiplication. The important thing for us now is how do we pull this off. It will take knowledge, skill, grit, wisdom, and time. Time that can only be provided by a leader with a satisfied soul.

A journey to a satisfied soul

Who can pull this off? Only a leader with a satisfied soul. Only a satisfied soul will permit the leader to forget about self long enough to concentrate on others, take up his or her cross, and serve. A satisfied soul allows all one's dreams of self-importance, fame, recognition, and comfort to be laid aside. The greatest fear for many is anonymity, lack of recognition, a life absent of the "green room" and the luminous lights of fame.

The deadliness of a soul nourished by toxins is the holding back, never releasing your total self to Christ and his people. This is be-

---

3 I will eschew the Missional definition of a Disciple Making Movement proposed by missiologists based on the experience of leaders and movements in other countries and cultures. My reason for such an omission is based on their definition of a church, the vast differences in the secular post-Christian age of former Christendom, and cultures where a different set of assumptions form a basis for such an approach. Paul's very statement was made in a very different world, an ancient world that was as wild and wooly as ours, it was a pre-Christian world, and we operate in a disabling affluence that is secular and post-Christian.

cause if you fail, you will disappear into the world of average, and this is a fate worse than purgatory because it reveals that God is simply not enough for you—you are an addict. Therefore, you live life with an escape hatch. When your real gods are revealed and you are in danger, you pull the red lever, and out you go. I should know, that was me, in fact, it is still me, just less so, but still so.

The gospel begins to penetrate when one day you realize, "I'm the schmuck," "I'm the idiot," "I'm the jerk," "I'm the sinner." G.K. Chesterton entered the *London Times* inquiry contest to the general public, *"What is wrong with the world?"* Chesterton answered, "I am." One day it was a revelation to me, "What is wrong with this congregation?" The answer came to me, "I am." This revelation started a journey for me to have a satisfied soul.

As Jesus said, *"If you continue in my word, then you are truly my disciples, you will know the truth and the truth will set you free."* John 8:31,32.

President James Garfield, a devout man, added, "Yes, the truth will set you free, but first it will make you miserable." I don't think I had fully implemented my own strategy as a pastoral leader. I just wasn't the man I wanted to be long enough to get it done.

The Pastor Who Came in From the Cold
by doing the right thing

There they stood, 83 new church members, certificates in hand. What a grand scene of success on the platform. The Congregation

was beaming, filled with pride, we all felt it. "We are doing really good." The *Knights of the Holy Grill*—don't laugh—a very serious and potent ministry in our community by members of our church. Those mighty knights in aprons had prepared a sumptuous meal for over 500. The smell of ten+ turkeys cooking outside was wafting through the sanctuary. What a great day! Then I stood to give the sermon. I was introducing a new series called *Choose the Life*. It is now a book with a ten-week curriculum and videos, but that day it was just an idea.[4]

What I heard coming out of my mouth was something like an urge that had built up inside me for years. I was trying to keep it down, but I knew what was in my soul or my immaterial nature's executive center was a question and suddenly I heard myself asking it. **"Do you think it is a good idea to bring 83 people into something that is not working?"**

There, I had done it, I had spoken the truth. I had ripped my mask off and the congregation's smile turned to a frown. Of course, it was my unsatisfied soul attempting to take a shortcut to success, but still, it was true. By every measure, we were successful, but it didn't seem to matter that we were. Something was wrong. We were highly programmed, and our discipleship was sophisticated and based on solid biblical exegesis, but all that activity lacked one thing—transformation. I mean, real attitudinal and behavioral change in our membership.

Our discipleship was superficial. People were finishing curriculums, passing tests, had their minds filled with the right thoughts. There was, however, little evidence that people were being reconciled, and we saw very little that reminded us of the events described in the book of Acts. I felt something like Karl Barth as a young minister who didn't think he had anything to offer his congregation. He likened it to blowing as hard as he could into a trumpet and no sound coming out.

In all of this, I knew that my competence had failed. That is how people described me, I was really good at a lot of things, but

---

4 See Choose The Life book and curriculum by going to www.billhull.com

something was not right. I was becoming painfully aware that it was my unsatisfied soul was unwilling to release itself fully to God. I wanted to hang onto my identity as a writer, speaker, church consultant, smart guy, and didn't want to disappear into what I feared most, being normal, average, regular, nothing but a flickering light. My frustration was that "the people" were not helping me reach my goals. I was using God, not serving him—this is painful to write.

Deeper Issues

I was hooked on results, wanted to control outcomes, and desired recognition. The funny thing is that I had plenty of recognition, but plenty is not enough when you are unsatisfied. This is when God impressed on me a most glorious revelation, "Bill, don't run, I'm going to break you." I stayed put, I waited, and it happened. Meaning that even though my attitude and relationship to others was deepened through the series of messages that became *Choose The Life*, the conditions of ministry did not change a great deal. In fact, there was a backlash, some people didn't like my vulnerability, they thought it unseemly, it revealed weakness. For some vulnerability is blood in the water, it is an opportunity to make a grievance.

Seat # 50

A number of our Church staff were attending a seminar. They had attended and were recommending it to me. I don't like being put into situations where I am asked to do silly things, where there is great pressure to conform. An odd hang-up for a pastor, but I have found that is not rare. Jane and I decided to attend a seminar, even though it was four twelve-hour days. The seminar was a series of behavioral exercises that challenged the basic premises and assumptions of the attenders. You could say that it bordered on some cultic, manipulative techniques. You could leave at any time and was based on biblical texts, but it was confrontational, and it spared no one. After two days of what I considered somewhat manipulative, even childish activity, I was tempted to leave.

On day three, as I recall, there was an exercise where all members were asked to evaluate their fellow participants. If you thought a person was a giver, you would give them a popsicle stick. If you thought they were a taker, you would simply say, "taker" and not award a stick. You had a limited number of sticks, so you had to make choices. I was awarded 1 stick. The 54 participants were then placed in a horseshoe configuration with the person with the most sticks in seat #1 and going around to seat #54. I found myself in seat #50. Through an unusual set of circumstances, my occupation was revealed. One member was baffled by the irony of my being a clergyman and that I scored so low that I was in seat #50. She asked me, "Given you are a pastor, why are you over there in that seat?" I told her I didn't know. As it turned out I asked a few people later why they had not given me a stick. They all gave the same answer, **"You didn't appear to me to be interested in us."**

Over a few hours, it became clear to me what the problem was—again, it was me. I had taught over the years that Jesus loved and we are to love as Jesus loved. Any minister worth his pay will teach that because it is clearly in scripture.[5] And the reason we were in that room together was that Jesus loved us in such a way that we "got it" that he loved us. I claimed to love people, and my heart and intention was for them to know it. But I was not getting through, they were not getting the message. I was holding back, something I have been really good at. During the closing of that seminar, I committed to love as Christ loved by loving people until they got that I loved them.

I returned to the church, I confessed my sin to the entire congregation, and I began my quest to love from a satisfied soul. I have made progress in the decades that have passed. But as I must confess, even as I write these words, I am reminded that I am the problem. And I can't give myself fully until I have put my gods aside and get on my knees, lift my hands, and confess, "Oh God, be merciful to me a sinner." I have slowly become the kind of leader who can lead a disciple-making movement. I hope this helps you get started.[6]

---

5   John 13:34,35

6   https://www.christianitytoday.com/ct/2023/june-web-only/thailand-missionary-bible-school-doctor-church.html

06

SALVATION BY…

SALVATION BY REASON ALONE

"Reason is the devil's whore."

—Martin Luther

"One word of truth (λογος) outweighs an Empire of Lies." [1]

Luther's sentiment concerning the master of deceit in the 1500's certainly proved itself true in Paris a century later. There are two ways of knowing. They are reason and faith. Another way it could be put is reason and revelation, reason and myth, reason and religion, ritual, white magic, doctrine, icons, and saints. We humans like and use them all. In that lecture hall in Paris, circa 1628, it was clear that French clergy and scholars were tired of reason and philosophy as their only path. They wanted, as the late Francis Schaeffer wrote, to *Escape from Reason*.[2] They seemed to be looking for a way out of the self-imposed philosophical *cul-de-sac* that led to anxiety, purposelessness, and despair.

Everything was going along fine, until...

Aristotle, via Aquinas, had a strong grip on Catholic theology. Aquinas' five arguments for the existence of God were standard fare which claimed that God could be known through reason alone. This is why most seminary students, even to this day, are schooled in Aquinas' arguments.[3]

---

[1] A combination of Aleksandr Solzhenitsyn's speech, One Word of Truth Outweighs the World, of Andrew Klavan's Empire of Lies concept and the λογος is, of course, the idea from John 1:1 that God in Jesus is the Truth itself spoken most powerfully in the person of Christ. A word so profound that it cannot be answered by human reason or normal explanation.

[2] Francis A. Schaeffer, Escape from Reason (Inter Varsity Press: 1968)

[3] https://philosophy.lander.edu/intro/aquinas.shtml#:~:text=The%20arguments%20are%20often%20named,(5)%20argument%20from%20design

Luther believed that reason is always looking for a way to sell itself to humans, especially religious leaders. We are told to follow the science which is far different than putting your trust in the scientist, let alone in one of the many other forms of knowledge and truth available to us. The knowledge of persons, of course, being a major player in human life.

Back to Paris in 1628. The room was filled with Priests, none more impressive than the Archbishop of Paris. They were confronted with the vice-like grip that philosophy, reason, and the other limits of human knowledge had on them. The arguments from reason had to be airtight, but of course, they were not and still are not. Reason didn't qualify as proof.

There was a guest speaker that day and he offered an escape from skepticism because he proposed that probability would be sufficient and could serve as proof of God. The address was a big success and he received a standing ovation. But one young man did not stand or applaud. The Archbishop asked him, "Why do you not applaud?" The young man, René Descartes said, "Because if you follow *my* method, you can have certainty."

Grasping at reason…

As a result of the conversation, the Archbishop gave Descartes a commission, (authority/funding/time) to prove through what is called probability, the law of non-self-contradiction. Using logic, you could be certain of the existence of God. Descartes claimed that to prove certainty, we must begin with something that cannot be doubted. Thus, the famous, *I think, therefore I am.* Descartes said that he could not doubt his own existence. His argument proceeded to use mathematics and could build a structure of proof for God—and then that all truth claims would be subjected to the critical principle or gauntlet he had built. A bulwark against all falsehood.

Here comes trouble...

This opened up the door for the separation of faith from knowledge. Of course, the problem being that salvation by reason alone treats faith as a luxury, a ride-along, a parasite, and depends on the reliability of the human brain to work logically and without fault. This doesn't even include the problems such as why do you need a Pope, a church hierarchy, and as Luther pointed out, why would working people buy indulgences to avoid purgatory and Hell? Then the Pope turns around and cuts backroom deals with political and religious figures to fund Saint Peters in Rome—it's all dribble, piddle, and drivel. All of this remains an unproven premise that is self-contradictory.

But Descartes' scheme took hold and it has left us with nihilism which led to the philosopher, Fredrick Nietzsche. When you throw out Biblical morality, Nietzsche asked, what do you replace it with? The answer is the general decadence of contemporary society—nihilism—or in plain English, nothing but a sappy, selfish world of personal opinion detached from reality. Nothing on which a life can be based.

A Walk Across Campus with Dallas Willard (Along came Dallas...)

This reminds me of walking across the quad at the University of Southern California with the late great philosopher and Christian writer, Dallas Willard. I had just attended his undergraduate class on logic. It was a beautiful day and Dallas had a stack of papers and folders tucked under his arm—very professorial. As we made our way by the school Mascot, *Tommy Trojan*,[4] we talked about how this great university had separated faith from knowledge. He had been a professor since 1965, and in those forty years, he spoke

---

4 https://usctrojans.com/sports/2018/7/25/usc-history-traditions-tommy-trojan-statue.aspx

of the disappearance of moral knowledge[5] on the campus. He said the university and the church had made a deal. It wasn't official, as most of these cultural decisions are never formalized. The university or academic world said, "Church and religion, you take faith, the university, we will take knowledge." A separation of realms, powers, world views, if you like. The deed was done and the whore of reason had found herself a home. The reason Dallas chose the academy for his career was because he knew that if he went into the church as a career the university would be closed to him. But if he chose the university, the church would remain open to his work. He was so right—and we thank God.

As we made our way to *Mudd Hall*,[6] the home of the School of Philosophy, he told me another story pointing me to a dedication plaque near the entrance. When entering this replica of a Romanesque Revival style building, I was struck by its beauty and elegance. The building was built in 1929 and the main donor was Seeley Wintersmith Mudd. Dallas told me that Mudd had a son who was a student at USC and a Methodist clergyman helped his son a great deal while there. As a result, by funding the building, Mudd was saying thank you to the University for helping his son.

Dallas told me USC was once a small Methodist College where they played a little football on Saturdays. They saw it as their mission to pass on a body of moral knowledge to each generation. But sadly, that has faded into the cultural mist. We continued to his office, one of the great wonders of the professorial world. He had been working on chapters to a new book and his office was stacked with books, piles of papers, and stacks on top of filing cabinets. There was a small space in the 10x12 room for him to sit, and a

---

5 The Disappearance of Moral Knowledge. A Book that Dallas started but did not finish. It was finished by three colleagues; Edited and Completed by Steven L. Porter, Aaron Preston, and Gregg A. Ten Elshof. (New York and London: Routledge Press, 2018).

6 https://www.trojans360.com/trojans360posts/history-and-hidden-stories-of-usc-a-glimpse-into-the-history-of-mudd-hall

chair for a guest. Every other space from floor to ceiling was taken. It wasn't filled with plaques, pictures of famous friends, or any form of self-homage. It was about his work.

He gathered up fragments of his new work and filled my arms with various chapters of *The Disappearance of Moral Knowledge*, anxious to get my opinion. I think he was just being nice. I did read them and did send my opinion. There we stood in a building dedicated to philosophy, *i.e.,* the lovers of wisdom, who do their best to explain reality. A building dedicated to reason, yet the most respected philosopher in the building, the one most loved, was a man of faith. There are many great minds at USC and in the general population. Dallas, however, had the most beautiful mind I've encountered. It combined a high IQ, wisdom and humility, and a great deal of knowledge. His faith was not parasitic to reason, or just along for the ride. It was a faith at the center of his being. He sought to teach his students that when you reason without revelation you are lost at sea on a ship of fools.

The Prospect of Salvation by Reason Alone

The missionary stateman and scholar, Lesslie Newbigin, spoke about this idea of the separation of faith from reason.

The idea that there is available to us a kind of truth that does not depend upon a faith commitment is an illusion. If the universe were a collection of things, then it would be true that by observation and reason it would be possible to find out what it is and how it works. If the universe is, as we believe and as Christians think it is, the creation of a loving God, or to be more precise, that the love of the triune God, the love of Father, Son and Holy Spirit, that endless ocean of joy and bliss, of love given, and love enjoyed, has been spilled over in order to create a world which would be a theater of his glory and the human race who would voice the praise of creation. If that is true, then the only way to understand the universe would be to respond in love and faith to the one whose universe it is…

> *...if you are walking along a road and see men at work and cement mixers turning around and bricks being piled up you know that a building is going up. How do you discover what the building is going to be? Is it to be a church or a factory or an office or a home? There are two and only two ways to find out. One is to wait on the roadside until the building is complete and you can then, by observation and reason, discover what it is, a home. The other is, if you can't wait long enough, ask the builder. He must tell you and you will have to believe him.*[7]

The idea that there is available to us a kind of knowledge that is not dependent on faith is an illusion. That illusion has led the modern world to into nihilism, from the Latin, meaning *nothing*. Salvation by reason alone doesn't exist.

---

7   https://www.youtube.com/watch?v=5WyrC7JVd5Q

SALVATION BY...

SALVATION BY MYTH ALONE: C.S. LEWIS

The old myth has become fact

"Do you mean, he asked, that the death and resurrection of Christ is the old 'dying God' story all over again?" "Yes," Tolkien answered," except that here is a real dying God, with a precise location in history and definite historical consequences. The old myth has become fact."
—J.R.R. Tolkien to C.S. Lewis on Addison's Walk

"We must not be ashamed of the mythical radiance resting on our theology. We must not be nervous about "parallels" and "pagan" Christs. They ought to be there—it would be a stumbling block if they weren't... if God chooses to be mythopoeic—and is not the sky itself a myth—shall we refuse to be mythopathic? For this is the marriage of heaven and earth: Perfect Myth and Perfect Fact."
—C.S. Lewis[1]

There is a natural impulse among my tribe, conservative biblically based Christians, to think of Greek mythology as an argument against Christianity. That is why Socrates, Plato, and Aristotle have not been widely taught in such circles, even intentionally avoided by many. It's all a bunch of godless tripe critics say, made-up stories to make up for their general ignorance of the biblical narrative. Let the English majors and philosophers study it. They can all don their togas, from Socrates to Julius Caesar to John Belushi in *Animal House*. We have more important things to do—just preach the gospel!

C.S. Lewis, himself an Oxford and later Cambridge professor of Mediaeval and Renaissance Literature, didn't see the connection between mythology and Christianity. Not until that night on Addison's walk, a one-mile circular road near Magdalen College, that *Lord of the Rings* fame, J.R.R. Tolkien, who through a conversation

---

1   C.S. Lewis from God in the Dock.

that lasted until after 1:00 AM, connected the two for him. Two colleagues who loved and respected each other—two great writers of myth. That night Lewis came to believe that Christ was not just one of the dying god myths, but indeed was in history and reality, the God who died and was resurrected.[2]

All Aboard with Odysseus's adventure, singing sirens and all

Venturing into myth, fantasy, imagination, and the arts makes many nervous. It's like the land dweller going out to sea. The Bible even warns Christians not to be tossed to and fro by every wind of doctrine.[3] Lots of bad stuff happens on and in the water. To deny, however, that knowing God does not come with mystery and requires imagination, is to sentence one to a weak doctrinaire, even inhuman faith. Life, especially the abundant life in God with all its richness, includes all elements of how God has fearfully and wonderfully made us. Dreams, visions, story, feeling, mystery, and knowledge that are deeply embedded in one's soul, require more than a boxed-up ready-to-wear theology. Yet, since transformation's home base is in what the Bible calls the mind, we must return there for a moment.[4]

The mind—just as an aside—is more than one's brain. Eventually, it will occur to most of us that the brain is not always needed. For example, there is no reason to believe that God the Father has or requires a human brain.[5] The same could be said for the Holy Spirit. Jesus, however, is a different matter, he had needed a brain as the incarnate God/Man. Whether he still needs it is too far afield for this column. The mind is something both material and imma-

---

2 Addison's walk is a must do for any Lewis fan. Much has been said about it, probably some of it wrong and certainly of legend. But well worth the experience, I've done it twice. Once with my wife, Jane, and once on my own.

3 Ephesians 4:14.

4 Romans 12:1,2

5 John 4:24

terial. The immaterial nature of a human cannot be scanned, photographed, weighed, or found through exploratory surgery. It exists primarily and first in the mind of God, in his person before the creation of any human. Myth seems to appeal to the larger spiritual mind and capacity to understand spiritual meaning and truth that is common to all people.[6]

The Purpose of Greek Mythology as General Revelation

Myths speak to the common truths revealed in all human experience. From the experiences of joy, sorrow, suffering, war, and death emerges ethics, wisdom, and some attempt to answer the big questions. Why are we here, what is a good person, what is a good life, and who or what is behind it? You can think of this history as follows.

Socrates, who never wrote anything that survived antiquity, walks up to a big whiteboard. On the whiteboard are notes and ideas that preceded him. He wipes the board clean and starts asking people the big questions. In the marketplace, he asks the politicians, poets, artisans, and craftsmen questions. He was such a threat that he was forced to drink the hemlock.[7]

His most famous disciple, Plato, came along and wrote the answers on the whiteboard. He answered the questions, much of it recorded in his *Apology* and *The Republic.*

Then came his disciple, Aristotle. He was an abstract thinker and systematized the collections of thought and wisdom. He became the teacher for Alexander the Great and much later Saint Thomas Aquinas assimilated Aristotle's work which became an important part of Catholic Theology.

---

6   Philippians 2:5, I Corinthians 2:10-16

7   Socrates was convicted of corrupting the youth of Athens and introducing strange gods. He was sentenced to drinking poison hemlock. Rather than flee the city, he decided to voluntarily do so as a lesson to his disciples. He was a threat because his questions shook the premises and presuppositions of his critics.

The limits of general revelation, or what God has revealed to all humans, are historically displayed in people like Alexander the Great who had a ten-year reign as leader of an empire that made many mistakes in its treatment of conquered peoples.[8] Aristotle and his pupil, Alexander, came up short as they had only what was generally revealed to all people.

The historian, Tertullian, asked the famous question, *what does Athens have to do with Jerusalem?* In a way, the question was what does *general revelation,* Athens, have to do with Jerusalem or special revelation? All humans look through a glass darkly, his is the summation of the Apostle Paul, but for those outside of special revelation, the underside of truth is even darker.[9]

Special revelation is more specific. God spoke to Abraham and the story of God's special relationship to the Jewish people began. God revealed himself gradually, culminating in Christ, and the story, prophecies, prophets, priests, and pastors unfold in the inspired text. Athens and Jerusalem came together, particularly in the Gospel of John and the Book of Hebrews.[10] What the Greeks called *logos* was revealed in the person of Christ, a first-century Jew.

The myths of Ancient Greece, including over 80 gods and goddesses, from Zeus, Achilles, Aphrodite, and Diana, conveyed the great truths of human experience. Whether it be Icarus flying too close to the sun or so low that he would disappear into the sea, or the hell of Sisyphus pushing a rock up a hill every day, what was generally true of life emerged.

The Mystery of Faith

It has become an article of faith which admits that reality defies human ability to grasp God fully through reason alone. It is

---

8   Romans 1:18-32

9   I Corinthians 13:11-12.

10   Book of Hebrews is quite Platonic as it is a book of shadows, of earthly symbols that represent perfection on a new and higher level. This begins with Christ himself and is pictured in the complete sacrificial system of the Jewish festivals and rituals.

commonly called "the mystery of faith." The mystery is what Plato could never imagine, God becoming a man and living and then dying for his creation. This idea of God dying for you and me will never make complete sense to us. Why would he do it? There will always be a *what is going on here on planet Earth, anyway* element to it. And we find ourselves somewhere between wonderment, befuddlement, anger, thanksgiving, tears, and laughter.

Finally, we are on our knees with hands in the air, praising him because what else can we do? Whenever you drive by a house of worship, you nod your head, tip your hat, pull off the side of the road, breathe more deeply. The whole idea arouses something deep inside that is holy. Don't try to explain it, embrace it. It is what makes life rich and abundant.

C.S. Lewis's conversion to Christ was a process. Lewis was a skeptic, atheistic, with a head full of assumptions. It was Tolkien's conversation, friendship, and academic credentials, that allowed Lewis to relax and consider this great mystery. Many have speculated about when Lewis actually made his decision. The mystery is that only God knows, possibly even Lewis came up short on his own understanding. He spoke of the long conversations with the *Inklings*,[11] and the reading of each other's work in the group. He speaks of riding in the sidecar of his brother, Warnie's motorcycle, and finally something about a bus ride to the Zoo.

Regardless, the myth and the mystery of faith have came together and transformed a man's life. He spoke the words of hope to a confused nation during World War II on the BBC—he had been chosen to define and declare to the British people, the gospel, or what he called, *Mere Christianity.*[12]

---

11 An informal group of literary friends usually associated with C.S. Lewis, J.R.R. Tolkien, Charles Williams, Owen Barfield, Hugo Dyson and others. They were part of Oxford England and the academic community.

12 Mere Christianity is Lewis' most famous book. Nearly 100 years later, there is nothing quite as clear and good as the essence of Christianity. It nourishes mind and soul and clears the head of unnecessary accoutrements.

THE COST OF CHEAP GRACE

BILL HULL & BRANDON COOK

RECLAIMING THE VALUE OF DISCIPLESHIP

SALVATION BY DISCIPLESHIP ALONE

The book no one wanted to publish

> *"The only person who can be justified by grace alone is the man who has left all to follow Christ. Such a man knows that the call to discipleship is a gift of grace and that call is inseparable from grace."*
> —Dietrich Bonhoeffer: The Cost of Discipleship

Caliente! "This is a hot one," said the publisher who recruited me and a colleague to write the book we named *Salvation by Discipleship Alone*. We live in a Salvation by Grace alone, by Jesus alone, world. Jesus Christ + nothing." And when you believe that, that is what you get, nothing! Nothing like Jesus intended. The publisher wanted the book, so they set out to move ahead. But for the first time in their history, the board of directors of the parent organization pulled rank and the publisher canceled the book. The book was published under a different title, *"The Cost of Cheap Grace."*

It doesn't really have the NO sign on it, but it may as well. After it had been neutered and transitioned into the harmless little book on discipleship that it became. I know where you can get five copies at a local *Barnes and Noble*. It is flanked by Joseph Campbell's *The Hero with a Thousand Faces* and Joel Osteen's, *Your Best Life Now*. Get there before market realities close the store and workers throw the unsold copies into the dumpster outback.

It is true, no one dares publish a book that challenges the prevailing winds of the Gospel Americana[1] that, in effect, teaches you can become a Christian and NOT follow Jesus![2] But that is what

---

1 Americana refers to the cultural artifact that the gospel has become across the American church landscape. For a further explanation, please see page 33 in my book, Conversion and Discipleship. Also, the introduction to I Will Not Bow Down, published 2023 on Amazon.

2 Noted exceptions in the recent past have been The King Jesus Gospel by Scot McKnight, Salvation by Allegiance Alone, by Matthew Bates, Conversion and Dis-

we've got and that is where we live. It's more than semantics or even wordplay. It seems we have been trained to talk out of both sides of our mouths. On one hand, books are written, and sermons are given on how we can do nothing to save ourselves. And then other books and sermons tell us all the things we must do to prove that we are saved. I must confess I am part of all this and find myself befuddled and confused by salvation itself. But there is such a fear of that word, *alone*, at the end of the heart cry of the Reformation: *sola scripture alone, sola Christ alone, sola fide:* faith alone, *sola gratia:* grace alone, and *soli Deo Gloria:* glory to God alone. Therefore, I've decided to consult with our leader, Jesus the Christ from Nazareth.

The first to teach salvation by discipleship alone

Jesus warned *his disciples* not to tell anyone who he was. "The Son of Man must suffer many terrible things," he said. "He will be rejected by the elders, the leading priests and the teachers of religious law. He will be killed, but on the third day he will be raised from the dead." Luke 9:21, 22.

Jesus restricted this terrible news to his closest followers. Not sure if this included his larger group of disciples numbering slightly over one hundred. It easily could have, and it wouldn't change anything because it is very likely they never heard the last part after the word, "killed"—the part about being raised from the dead three days later. But they understood to some degree what it meant to live this new "saved life" it would be very costly. It would cost them everything. I think this is what Dietrich Bonhoeffer was getting at when he spoke of being justified by grace alone:

"The only person who can be justified by grace alone is the man who has left all to follow Christ. Such a man knows that the call to discipleship is a gift of grace and that call is inseparable from grace."

---

cipleship, You Can't Have One Without the Other by Bill Hull, and The Discipleship Gospel, by Bill Hull and Ben Sobels. There are others as well, but these were all preceded by Dallas Willard's, The Divine Conspiracy. These books go upstream to the source of the problem which is theological and philosophical.

Jesus' disciples, at least those who appear and perform in the Acts of the Apostles, understood that they could not have done anything without having left everything behind and having answered the call to discipleship. Because faith and following, believing and acting, were all the same thing, there was no separating them. And if you tried, and oh how we have tried, you get something that Paul called dung and Jesus called manure.[3] We call it something else. It is what so many avoid, it makes people hold their noses. Unfortunately, when society decays, there is more of it everywhere.

Discipleship alone is the road to salvation and Jesus wasn't afraid to say so

"Then he turned to the crowd. If any of you wants to be my follower, you must turn from your selfish ways, take up your cross daily and follow me. If you try to hang on to your life, you will lose it. But if you give up your life for my sake, you will save it. And what do you benefit if you gain the whole world but are yourself lost or destroyed?"

This is the kind of message many leaders have kept from their followers. In our lust for more people, prestige, and power, we have reduced the requirements so that more people can easily be assimilated into our religious communities. It is this kind of capitulation that has caused throngs to take Lucifer's invitation and jump off the pinnacle of the temple and grab for the kingdoms of the world.

Jesus' teaching also is a message for the general populace in more ways than first appears. In this statement, Jesus proclaims he is the only way because there is salvation in no other. There is no other way to know God or to enter into a relationship with God, except by Him. We seem to get stuck or limit the conversation at this point, as to the difficulty of following Jesus.[4]

The call to discipleship is the same as the call to salvation

---

3 Luke 14:34, 35 and Philippians 3:8

4 John 14:6, Acts 4:12.

The most obvious point here, however, is that Jesus turned to the crowds. The point is made both here and in Luke 14:25, that clearly distinguishes Jesus' disciples from everyone else. This calling that Bonhoeffer speaks of—and that Jesus himself gave—is one to believe and follow Jesus. Belief and following are the same thing, not distinguishable from each other. This is why Bonhoeffer wanted to unify justification and sanctification under the single rubric of discipleship.

This mystery of will mixed with action, of faith, and following, is just too much for most of us. We like to box things up, systematize them, and market them so we can measure some results. That way everything can be monetized. Foundations insist in all presentations that the mission organization, the grantee, provide measurables so the foundation can determine if they should invest in the project. Churches count baptisms, budgets, square feet, staff ratios, etc. Jesus, however, asks for only one measurable—100% of us. And this is not a message for the elite, the preternatural religious types, this is the gospel for everyone. Jesus is doing evangelism, it is not a high-commitment conference, it is the only commitment Jesus offers.

He started with: "If any of you, meaning no exceptions, no VIP section, no valet service, no fast lane, everyone stands in the same line. His next statement takes us back into the first-century context. He didn't ask if any of them wanted to become a Christian, because there were no Christians—they didn't exist at the time. He called his disciples "followers" or "my disciples." He then said, "You must turn from your selfish ways." This clearly means to repent and lay aside selfish ways. Turning/repenting takes but a moment, laying aside selfish ways takes a lifetime.

Losing the plot

As one turns, follows, and becomes Jesus' apprentice, that process begins. It is one single action or motion. The one single-motion idea reminds me of slow-motion video, or in sports, the replay. If we slow down the video, break it down into various parts, and take it apart frame by frame, the commentators and game officials can review it while the fans sit and wait. The players only have opinions, usually accompanied by passions and score, ego and contract negotiations. This is what we have done to Jesus and his call. It has taken us two thousand years to confuse everyone and lose the plot.

Life is lived at full speed and it is what we call conversion that naturally extends as a whole to the entire process of learning, following, failing, succeeding. It's called discipleship—and it is the only way to follow Jesus—and is the only way to know God. This both clears up and cleans up the mess we have made of the gospel and the church. It strips the church and its members of all pretensions, customs, rituals, and nonsense that obscures the call to become what we now call a Christian.

Enough said?

Enough said, a pretty stiff tonic, isn't that enough? It seems Jesus is just getting started. He brings up the fact that there is a cross somewhere with your name on it. Look around, it's nearby, pick it up, you will need it every day. With all apologies to Dolly Parton who tells people who are feeling self-pity to "Come down off that cross of yours." This is not a cross you get on—it is one you pick up and carry. It represents the mission God has given to each of us. The mission is individualistic, tailored to each person,[5] but it's all the same because it requires dying to self, putting aside our selfish ways, and following Christ.

How life works

Jesus finishes his call to the human race with how life works. *"If you try to hang onto your life, you will lose it."* I certainly sympathize with hangers-on because I've done a lot of it myself. But then

---

5 Ephesians 2:8-10.

you lose a lot and miss even more. Now to be fair, we are eternal beings, made to live for eternity.[6] Jonathan Edwards said, "Lord, stamp eternity on my eyeballs." We are celestial prisoners trapped in a human body. That is why we fight to live. It is basic to being human. Living life to the full, the kind Jesus promised,[7] is only found in relinquishing life to Christ. He then asks the question, *"And what do you benefit if you gain the whole world but are yourself lost or destroyed?"*

So what?

Because the gospel we believe in determines the disciple we are, get, make, and reproduce. The world is awash with disciples of every kind. Every possible realm you can name makes disciples—from the arts to plumbers. The church is for discipleship and is to develop and deploy well-formed disciples into all societal realms. If the church does a good job, then the entire society benefits. Our artists, our films, our institutions, our journalists and yes, even our politicians will be better. Policies matter, but character matters more. There is a lack of good character in the political world. Many are corrupted in practice and are unsatisfied souls whoring about for nourishment. Therefore, understanding the foundation of what it means to follow Christ is paramount for the church.

Jesus was a great teacher and his calling to be his disciple was clear and demanding. Yet, there was something about him that made him more than a teacher. He was God become man and he came not only to live but to die. The source of life, himself[8] became one of us and was different from any other religious figure. He came to save us, save us from what we call sin. But not only sin but its companion, death. He had to eliminate sin and to do so, he

---

6   Ecclesiastes 3:11

7   John 10:10

8   Genesis 2:7 "God breathed into man the breath of life and he became a living being."

became sin. As the scripture says, *"When Adam sinned, sin entered into the world. Adam's sin brought death, so death spread to everyone, for everyone sinned…there is a great difference between Adam's sin and God's gracious gift. For the sin of this one man, Adam brought death to many. But even greater is God's wonderful grace and his gift of forgiveness to many through this other man, Jesus Christ."* [9]

Buddha sat under a tree and got fat, Mohammad spent his time abusing women and spreading his misery among the nations. Jesus got busy loving, sacrificing, teaching, healing, and finally, being brutally abused, wrongly tried, and killed. If you are considering whom to follow, no one compares. He stands head and shoulders above all figures of human history. He was a dying God. Nietzsche was right, God is dead, but after three days Nietzsche was wrong because then He was alive. And when he was dead, when the cause was lost, and hope went away, darkness descended on the earth and in life. Like David requested when his world went dark—he told God, *"Leave me alone so I can smile again before I am gone and exist no more."* [10] Like Heman, the Ezrahite, lamented, *"You have taken away my companions and loved ones. Darkness is my closest friend."* [11] Have you ever been there? Did you somehow think it wasn't fair or right that you were?

Light overcomes dark

Remember this, what you think is happening is not always what is happening. What can seem like your darkest hour actually can be the most wonderful miracle ever. Think of this, *"At noon, darkness fell across the whole land until three o'clock. At about three o'clock, Jesus called out with a loud voice, "Eli, Eli lema sabachthani, "My God, my God, why have you abandoned me?"*[12] *…Then Jesus shouted*

---

9   Romans 5:12,15

10 Psalm 39:13.

11 Psalm 88:18

12 Matthew 27:45, 46.

out again, and he released his spirit. At that moment the curtain in the sanctuary of the Temple was torn in two, from top to bottom. The earth shook, rocks split apart and tombs opened. The bodies of many godly men and women who had died were raised from the dead. They left the cemetery after Jesus' resurrection, went into the holy city of Jerusalem and appeared to many people.

Jesus didn't go quietly into the night. He fought his Father for life in his prayer in Gethsemane. He cried out in agony from the torture of the Cross. In that moment he became sin, he became a ransom, he became the lamb of God who was slain, and we get life, we get his righteousness, we become his family, and God becomes available to everyone for the asking. That is why discipleship matters, because when this gospel of the kingdom is preached to every nation, then the end will come.

"And when the Good News about the Kingdom will be preached throughout the whole world, so that all nations will hear it; and then the end will come." Matthew 24:14.

SALVATION BY...

SALVATION BY WORKS ALONE

"What good is it, dear brothers and sisters, if you say you have faith but don't show it by your actions? Can that kind of faith save anyone?... So you see, faith by itself isn't enough. Unless it produces good deeds, it is dead and useless." [1]

"We are saved by faith alone, but not by a faith that remains alone."

—Philip Melanchthon (protégé of Martin Luther)

"When a person only looks through one eye you can't see the varmint you're trying to shoot, two eyes are required to create true depth perception."

—Rooster Cogburn (*True Grit*)

Martin Luther had a knack for getting himself into trouble. He didn't mean to create such a fuss on October 31, 1517, when he took his little hammer and nailed a document to the village bulletin board, the chapel door of the church at the University of Wittenberg. It was just an ordinary Wednesday. Not much was happening in the dull life of a typical Augustinian monk, but he was fed up with the church's abuse of selling indulgences so they could fund the Pope's new church, St. Peter's in Rome. He posted the now-famous 95 Theses in Latin. It was meant to assemble a group of interested scholars for a discussion. Later, because it was translated into German and, with the advent of the printing press, the document was published and it set Germany on fire.

History tells the story. The reformed world celebrates October 31st as Reformation Day. Everyone else calls it Halloween. Thus, we now live in the shadow of the Protestant Reformation. Luther was a special man with extraordinary gifts, such as shooting off his mouth. And that brings me to the Epistle of James which begins

---

1   James 2:14, 17 New Living Translation.

this column. Luther didn't like it because it screwed up his narrative. It seemed to have contradicted his emphasis on salvation by grace alone, in Christ alone. He called James' epistle an "epistle of straw." He thought it should not have been included in the canon of the New Testament. He also didn't care for Jews once they rejected Christ. Strange, because Christ was as Jewish as they come.

Luther was a great man who, alone, did for Germany what it took five or more men to do in England. He translated the German Bible, wrote the music and the liturgy, provided a new form of German language, was its primary theologian, led a movement that became the Lutheran Church, and spent time in exile. He checked all the boxes. The same accomplishments in England required Thomas Cranmer, Samuel Johnson, John Newton, Wycliffe, Tyndale, the Wesley brothers, George Whitfield, *et al.*

The problem is no one does anything alone but God himself. Let's face it, doing anything alone is quite untenable, even for God. The triune God is one, yes indeed, but Jesus is praying to his Father and talking of and promising the ministry of the Holy Spirit. Somehow, God himself is not alone in the saving of his creation.[2] Salvation by anything alone is to misunderstand salvation. That reality underlies this entire series of columns which, even as I sit alone writing, is not a column by Bill Hull alone. Beside me, behind me, or in me, is a large chorus and I only sing my part.

A Salvation without works is not Salvation at all.

George MacDonald, the great writer, father of eleven, philosopher, and mentor to C.S. Lewis, sums it up quite well:

"Instead of asking yourself whether you believe or not, ask yourself whether you have this day done one thing because He said, *do*

---

[2] It is quite human to slip into an unintentional Modalism, which means that God manifests himself in three forms switching from Father to Son to Holy Spirit depending on the situation. This idea, common as it is, can't stand up against the smallest of Biblical scrutiny.

it, or once abstained because He said, *do not do it.* It is simply absurd to say you believe, or even want to believe in him if you do not do anything he tells you. If you think of nothing he ever said as having an atom of influence on your doing or not doing, you have too good a ground to consider yourself no disciple of his. But you can begin at once to be a disciple of the Living One by obeying him in the first thing you can think of in which you are not obeying him. We must learn to obey him in everything and so must begin somewhere. Let it be at once, and in the very next thing that lies at the door of our conscience."[3]

The American church is allergic to works even though it measures itself *by* works. This allergy is in its head. It is the theological condition. But in its heart, we all know every pastor, elder, leader, and even the casual parishioner, is measured by and measures the church itself, by works. You don't hear people say things like, "I go to this church because it doesn't work." We want things to work—the garage door, our cars, the electric toothbrush. Now this may seem like double-speak to you. Theological works, you might protest, are different than whether my lawn mower works or doesn't work. You are right, but humans can't function without working, whether it be pre-fall or post-fall. After all, God worked for six days and created our universe. Then he rested from his work and he looked at all his work and said, it was "very good."

Why can't we just admit that work is God-given, that if we don't do it, we can't even enjoy pleasure or rest? Is it possible that when Paul says, "Work out your salvation with fear and trembling"[4] he is getting at something everyone down deep inside understands? Working is integral to salvation—you can't enter into and enjoy your salvation without it. Only when you work in your salvation can you rest with pleasure that God alone has created in you the need for work. And the longer you live in this reality, the more you

---

3   George MacDonald, Creation in Christ, published on page 60 of A Guide to Prayer for Ministers and Other Servants, The Upper Room: 1983. Nashville, TN. 1983.
4   Philippians 2:12.

are convinced that Grace is the only way you can work that hard and long in the service of Christ.

What are we to do?

There I go again, talking about doing instead of being. I think there is too much talk about *being*, loving oneself, taking tests that get us to examine ourselves, and find our true selves. These are just exercises in self-indulgence. And really, who cares? Aren't you finished and fed up with you? Self-focus is a disease, and when you get older and everything begins to hurt, the harder it can become to focus on others. But as Jesus said, as a man in his early thirties, "turn from your selfish ways."[5] The joy is found in focusing on others. Forget yourself as much as you can, and you find out you hurt a little less, your ears quit ringing, you forget you're wearing support socks, and you skipped your medication.

Jesus said to his disciples, "I have told you these things so that you will be filled with my joy. Yes, your joy will overflow!"[6] When you see a smile on a child's face who has just been fed or is happy for a few minutes while undergoing medical treatment, it gives you, the person who put in the work, the joy Jesus is talking about. Jesus wants us to be other person oriented.

What's the Point?

James now has Martin Luther's attention and certainly our attention. I think he is being intentionally outrageous. His comments are upsetting to our grace-alone/by-faith-alone culture. James knew Paul's theology of grace. Paul claimed to have been taught by Jesus himself. This was discussed and the gospel was agreed upon at the *Council of Jerusalem*[7] before the writing of the letter we know

---

5 Luke 9:23.

6 John 15:11 NLT.

7 Council of Jerusalem: Acts 15:1-15. Paul, Peter, and James were there. James presided over the meeting. An agreement was reached.

as the *Epistle of James*. There are some ways to reconcile the differences.

One way is to contrast faith alone and works alone by thinking of wages and being an heir. Wages are based on what you have accomplished. An inheritance is based on family. You earn a wage for the work you have done, but as an heir, your money is already in the bank. Whether you are a Rockefeller, a Vanderbilt, a Getty, a Gates, or an heir to billions, what you will do with it and whether you can make your life mean something is the greatest challenge.

James makes it quite graphic. He tells us if we see people in need and don't help and if our faith doesn't respond to human need, then our faith is dead, useless, not real. He wants us to emphasize what saving faith is—as compared to merely complying with a set of principles or statements. James calls our bluff. Show me. Prove your faith is real by how you act—what do you do!

You say you have faith, for you believe that there is one God. Good for you! Even the demons believe this, and they tremble in terror. How foolish! Can't you see that faith without good deeds is useless? [8]

The demons have been to the best Divinity School that exists, the one in Heaven. They, as created angelic beings, have seen the power of God. They believe the right things, but they choose to align with Lucifer. They know the truth about God and they shudder and are afraid. They respect the power of God. They have had more truth shown to them than any human, but they have not bowed the knee.

James then uses the father of the faith, Abraham, as an example, who through his willingness to sacrifice his own son Isaac, was someone who was justified by his actions. Another way to put it is that Abraham's actions proved, or completed, his faith. And he concludes, "So you see. We are shown to be right with God by what we do, not by faith alone." James' words are a rebuke to the church that was caught up in disputes about right thinking—and it was really about right living.

---

8   James 2:19-22.

James takes it down to the bone when he brings up the Harlot of Jericho, Rahab. This is a well-known story to the recipients of this letter, the twelve scattered tribes of Israel. His famous words were, "She was shown to be made right with God by her actions when she hid those messengers and sent them safely away by a different route." Rahab was courageous. Abraham was God's friend. They both *did something* that God valued and proved their faith as real saving faith.

Being a Friend of God

The demons believed in God and were in awe of his power. But they were not in love with God and didn't see his beauty and didn't think of themselves as his friend. Many people respect their enemies, even are afraid of their enemies, but loving one's enemies, well … that is out of the reach of most. Friendship is what God invites us into via obedience to his will and it is special and distinct even from associations with others and collegial feeling. For example, I might say about a colleague or associate, I have tickets to the World Series or a great Opera, how can I use this event to further my career, or get the contract, or some other advancement? While this is not an evil thought, it is how business works. But it still would be different from friendship. Friendship is more like, I would like to spend time with my friend, so I'm going to figure out how to make that happen. The best way I know to be a friend of God is to go where God goes, be where God is, and get in on what God is doing.

And when that friend is Jesus, and I think about his spilled blood, "Now I know he loves me." And I feel it because my friend took my place. He paid my debt, he suffered, and when he cried out, "My God, My God, why have you forsaken me?" I know in that moment he went to Hell, he became sin, and he was separated from his own Father.

When we become friends with God, then what James was talking about becomes real. Not long after he wrote his letter to the church scattered, as recorded in Acts 8:1-4, he was killed by Herod Agrippa. Acts 12:1-3. And he joined his friend Jesus.

Dear Brothers and sisters, when troubles come your way, consider it an opportunity for great joy. For you know that when your faith is tested your endurance has chances to grow. So let it grow, for when your endurance is fully developed, you will be perfect and complete, needing nothing. James 1:2-4

SALVATION BY POLITICS ALONE

"Politics are downstream of culture and culture is downstream of theology."[1]

Moses and Aaron Discussing Truth and Politics

"When they came near the camp, Moses saw the calf and the dancing, and he burned with anger. He threw the stone tablets to the ground, smashing them at the foot of the mountain. He took the calf they had made and burned it. Then he ground it into powder, threw it into the water, and forced the people to drink it." Exodus 32:19-20 NLT

Moses' reaction to appeasement

Moses had disappeared into a cloud at the top of the mountain. He had been gone nearly forty days. The people were told that they dare not ascend the mountain or they would die. They waited and waited. How long does it take to hear from God? They complained to Aaron to provide some way to break their boredom, to meet their immediate needs. Aaron, like many needy leaders lacking confidence, gave them what they wanted—a party—an experience where they could dance the night away. The hell with the next morning.

Moses burned with anger, smashed the tablets, and asked his brother to explain his very odd, weak actions. Aaron's answer describes the nature of humans when we forget God.

"Don't get so upset, my Lord." Aaron replied. You yourself know how evil these people are. They said to me, 'Make us gods who will lead us. We don't know what happened to this fellow Moses who brought us here from the land of Egypt.' So, I told them, 'Whoever has gold jew-

---

[1] I Will Not Bow Down and No Longer a Bystander, By Bill Hull on Amazon.com. Chart for Downstream/Upstream found in The Bonhoeffer Project Curriculum, page 8. Copyright Bill Hull and Brandon Cook, 2020.

elry take it off.' When they brought it to me, I simply threw it into the fire—and out came this calf!" Exodus 32: 22-24 NLT

What a weasel! Talk about magic—what a story! Easy for us to look back at Aaron's foolishness, naivete, and weakness. Aaron had done what any good politician would have done. He had "reached across the aisle" and found a solution that made everyone happy for a short time. He didn't think it through or consider long-term consequences. Most of all, he abandoned his commitment to God and his first principles, namely, the Ten Commandments.[2] What happened was that Aaron ceased to be a leader, a second in command to his brother Moses. He became a politician. Confronted with 400 years of Egyptian culture that was now part of the Jewish soul he compromised and folded in the clutch.

Theology and the mighty Mississippi

Theology determines culture and culture determines politics and controls the work of politicians. Think of the world of thought and the behavior of human beings as all part of a river. The headwaters are often small and insignificant to public notice. When describing the mighty Mississippi River rarely does anyone mention its source. It is a mere 18-foot wide, knee-deep river flowing from Lake Itasca, a small glacial lake in Minnesota.

Most culture talk begins with various factors that have shaped and changed, even controlled, culture. Choose your significant data, wars, the rise and fall of kings, countries, and worldwide powers. Some choose significant atrocities, massacres, the growth of knowledge, plagues, or medical advances. One can point to obvious cultural changes; the railroad, the steam engine, electricity, the telegraph, the phone, the internet, the iPhone, soft-serve ice cream.

Missed at the headwaters of this river is theology. Question

---

2   I must reference comedian Mel Brooks' parody of this event when he toted three tablets down the mountain with five commandments on each tablet = 15 commandments. He accidentally dropped one tablet, and thus, it became ten commandments.

yourself: *"Whatever comes into your mind when you think about God is the most important thing about you."* [3]

If your thought is an impersonal force, a raging or angry God, or a weak God who cannot control all things, and who, itself, himself, herself, doesn't know about or can shape the future, all of that determines how you interpret and explain the world. The answer to the question is your theology. Even if you believe in no God at all, you have the problem of declaring dead a being that must exist to deny its existence. Oh well… This belief, whatever it is, is the lens you must look through and the filter you use to define and explain the culture in which you live.

A common theology

The most common theology is a pragmatic one. It is built in, factory installed in the human heart. People want to be free to pursue a *good life*. Everyone needs to answer the big questions. What is a good person? How does one become a good person? Everyone needs to answer those questions, but most do not answer in any formal way, so their culture answers for them through societal norms. In one culture a good person believes in Jihad, in another, diversity where they can prosper and love and live with whom they like and not have others cram their lifestyles or beliefs down their throats. Most are somewhere in between. They just want to live quiet and peaceful lives and believe in peaceful protests and freedom of speech. There are enthusiasts and there is also freedom of religion.

The majority of cultures are not free. The people rationalize and cope based on legends and religions. Most are willing to put up with religious zealotry—evangelists reaching out and trying to save them—as long as it doesn't get out of hand. If they are free to

---

[3] "Whatever comes into your mind when you think about God is the most important thing about you." Quote from A.W. Tozer's little masterpiece, The Knowledge of the Holy.

say *no* without repercussions, then fine. Again, in more cultures than not, the citizens are not free to publicly hold any belief they want. They must conform.

People believe in certain kinds of absolute truth. Potato chips are better than liver, a massage is more desirable than shingles. If you don't believe in absolute truth or an infinite personal God who is there and has spoken, you are adrift. You are forced, like a wayward Aaron, to seek a political solution, and when politics becomes your religion, your salvation will come in some political movement or personality.

America is divided

Everyone knows America is divided. It can be seen in many ways. It is divided economically as the middle class shrinks and leaves a chasm between the wealthy and the poor. It is divided by the states we live in, Blue or Red. It is divided philosophically between the cultural elites who hold the high ground of culture's institutions and the working class. And there remains what is left of the middle class who are also highly educated and have money. The strongest division is not as much political as it is religious. It simply reveals itself politically, as politics give people a chance to be on a team and fight for their point of view.

There is also a division between those who see politics as a means to an end and those for whom political policy is the end itself. Politics provides a release valve, a way to empty out a person's passion and bone-deep beliefs. Let's pick an issue as an example:

Climate change

I believe there is plenty of evidence that climate gradually changes over long stretches of time. There is a difference between climate change and weather. Weather lends itself to anecdotes, climate change, to long-term study. Climate change used to be called "Global Warming" until there was "Global Cooling." Now no one seems to know what to call it, so "Climate Change" is the current rubric. Temperatures rise in cities where large groups of people pack in together surrounded by cement. There are other factors such as technology, energy, and disposal of waste products, etc. This is of some concern to me, but I don't believe it deserves to be called an *existential threat to humanity.*

The threat is gradual and computer models don't provide much help. Disaster will come *if current trends continue,* we are warned. One thing that history proves is that current trends never continue. Just as it is certain we will eventually run out of space, *if current trends continue,* technology will certainly solve many of the problems. It is a natural progression given enough time and patience. In summary, I think it is good to study it, to be good stewards of the earth, and to do what we can to preserve the best parts of it and keep it healthy.

The deification of the earth

But for many, the salvation of the earth is paramount. This is because they believe that the earth is permanent, and humans are temporary.[4] I believe the exact opposite. The earth is temporary, and humans are eternal. Salvation, for those who are uncertain about God and retreat to theistic evolution or worse, the natural route becomes the deification of the earth and of the human species. Biological life is the only life, and granted, it is a mystery they might say, so do the best you can and leave the earth better off than you found it. For those of this ilk, politics then becomes the means of salvation of all that exists. This kind of difference then is argued and fought out on the political battlefield.

---

4 The temporary nature of the present heavens and earth: see 2 Peter 3:3-13, and Revelation 21:1. Regarding the eternal existence of the human being: Hundreds of scriptures, promises, and the entire thesis of the Bible itself are of eternal life and also somewhat quite different, the eternal existence of all humans. John 3:16, John 10:10. John 5:16-30.

There is a certain desperation in those for whom this or any other means of salvation for themselves or the earth can be found in politics alone. Yes, this issue is nuanced, and I am speaking in generalities. But then my subject is general and broad.

The big surprise, I suppose, is that salvation by politics alone can be found on both sides of the Climate Change issue because there is the secular[5] view on both the left and the right. There is a religious side to both the left and the right. My worry is for those who find their only hope to be the political one.

The Perplexity

Oliver Wendell Holmes, former Chief Justice of the United States Supreme Court said it well, "For the simplicity on this side of complexity, I wouldn't give you a fig. But for the simplicity on the other side of complexity, for that I would give you anything I have."[6] I can see that a Supreme Court Justice would treasure a simple answer to a complex issue. Perplexity comes to us because we are Christians. Christians on either side of the political divide. Where is the simplicity we need?

Simplicity in the middle of complexity

Jesus is the most complex being to ever live,[7] but he provides the simplicity we need right now. Jesus had a way of being very clear with his followers and an astonishing enigma to his critics. You might recall the story from the gospels when the Pharisees plotted to trick Jesus over a political issue that could get him arrested. They attempted to get him to commit to a political movement around

---

5   Secular as a lexical matter means "the span of a human life."

6   https://www.goodreads.com/quotes/44564-for-the-simplicity-on-this-side-of-complexity-i-wouldn-t

7   It took the early church seven major councils to sort out Jesus. And of course, they failed. No one or group should ever be expected to get it exactly right. They found agreement in this: he is "Fully God fully man united in one person forever."

paying the "Head Tax" to the Romans. Among the Jews, it was very controversial whether they should pay a special tax to the Romans for the privilege of being subjects of Caesar. They could trap Jesus if they could get him to commit to a side. Jesus called his accusers out and asked for a coin. Not just any coin, but a denarius, not a lot of money. It was the exact amount each subject of Rome was to pay annually. The image was that of Tiberias Caesar and the inscription read, "Tiberias Caesar, Son of God, High Priest."

The coin was Caesar's property, the coin having been minted from Caesar's silver and gold. The coins were distributed around the Roman world. It was Caesar's money. It belonged to him. If Jesus answered don't pay the tax he became a revolutionary. Twenty-five years earlier an insurrectionist named Judas rebelled against the Head Tax. He entered the Temple with arms and claimed that God alone was King and he would bring in the kingdom of God. He was arrested and executed. The similarities with Jesus were startling. But so were the differences. For the Pharisees, if Jesus said, no, don't pay, he could be executed. If Jesus said, yes, pay the tax, then his entire movement, his teachings, his examples, and his kingdom would have collapsed. His followers would have considered him a fraud and just another huckster.

He took the coinage of the day and asked them, *"Whose picture is imprinted on the coin?"* The Pharisees fell into Jesus' trap, *"they answered Caesar's." "Well then," he said, "give to Caesar what belongs to Caesar, and give to God what belongs to God." His reply amazed them, and they went away."* [8]

What does this astonishing statement mean? It means the coin belongs to Caesar as his image is on it. Give it to him. But Jesus also means, that God's image is on you, give your life to me. So, Jesus said neither but said both. Two groups represented the extremes that must avoided: The Essenes, a monastic group that dropped out, refused to pay Rome, and left civilization, and the Zealots who refused to pay but revolted with arms and politics.

---

8   Matthew 22:20-22 NLT.

Jesus is not telling us to be uninvolved in politics. In fact, as Christ changes us, we are much more likely to care about and participate in politics. What must be rejected is the belief that our salvation is political, legislative, or through the courts. Yes, work and fight for what we care about, but first, we are to seek Christ and his kingdom, and with love and determination, seek justice, show mercy, and walk humbly with our God.

Show respect and love for those with whom you disagree. But please don't be a moderate. Moderation is for those who live in fear, who can't make up their minds, who want to be left alone. You can't be a revolutionary in the tradition of Jesus and just rearrange the deck chairs on the Titanic while the orchestra plays on. The Church is sinking—what are you going to do about it?[9]

---

9 Thanks to the late Tim Keller for his insights on this passage. Nothing is word for word or needs a footnote. As always, however, his insights seem better than mine. I have always joked that he was trying to put me out of work. I hope to join him one day.

SALVATION BY PHILOSOPHY ALONE

"Man can will nothing unless he has first understood that he must count on no one but himself; that he is alone, abandoned on earth… Philosopher Jean-Paul Sartre (a leading figure in 20th-century French philosophy and Marxism, 1905-1980)

"Everything is meaningless," says the Teacher "Completely meaningless!"[1] King Solomon of Israel

"Vanity of vanities, saith the Preacher, vanity of vanities; all is vanity." King Solomon in the King James Bible

"Well, but mustn't the churches adapt Christianity to suit the ideas of our time? No, they must not. Our ideas are killing us spiritually. When your child swallows poison, you don't sit around thinking of ways to adapt his constitution to a poisonous diet. You give him an emetic." Joy Davidman, Mrs. C.S. Lewis[2]

"So where does this leave the philosophers, the scholars, and the world's brilliant debaters? God has made the wisdom of this world look foolish." I Corinthians 1:20 NLT.

Philosophy is an exercise in vanity. You get philosophers when you lack enough information to answer life's most important questions. As Solomon himself concluded at the end of his treatise:

"The words of the wise are like cattle prods—painful but helpful. Their collected sayings are like a nail-studded stick with which a shepherd drives the sheep."[3]

Now you know why you disliked that philosophy class you took and why you were lost in the hopelessly confusing theories by the

---

[1] "meaningless" is in Hebrew Havel or "smoke/haze. Something akin to Paul's looking into a mirror in the dark or with very little light. I Corinthians 13:12. Ecclesiastes 1:2 begins the world's greatest book on philosophy by its wisest man. Solomon, if you think about it, is a wonderful example of the world's wisest man because he was seriously flawed and not so wise.

[2] As seen in Megan Basham, Shepherds for Sale, Broadside Books, Harper Collins. Introduction.

[3] Ecclesiastes 12:11

gloomy logic of Nietzsche, the despair of Sartre, and the debauchery of Michel Foucault. If you liked that class or thought it made sense hopefully you moved on before it ruined your life.

Then there is the classification of those among us who liked it. May God have mercy on your souls. You couldn't get enough of it, it's almost like God gave you a special hunger, the ravenousness of a wolf. You ended up a poorly paid professor of philosophy at some small college in a shire or a better paid one at a prestigious university. You may have worn the academic robe of a Don—or even worse—a dreaded amateur like yours truly, doing the work without the credibility or the pay, an addict for which there are no meetings in which to confess sins. There is one conclusion that all of us have reached, it didn't save us! I mean in the truest sense of the word, saved! Saved from powerful forces that cause confusion of the mind, lamentable thoughts, uncontrollable urges, the deterioration of the body, and finally, death.

Religion and Philosophy

Religion has been defined as "man's best effort to reach God." Philosophy, of course, means "lover of wisdom." Is it man's best effort to answer life's biggest questions when you don't like the ones God has provided? What are life's biggest questions? You already know, but for the record, "who started this thing called life? Why? What is going on? How will it end and then what happens to all of us? Or something like that. For extra credit, where does evil come from? Where does good come from? This problem of good does not seem to trouble anyone—why not? Why do we think something is good, or bad? You know the rest.

Philosophy needs a foil. It is usually God, who either does or doesn't exist. If he does exist, he isn't very nice and cooperative, so we construct him and then deconstruct him. We put him on trial and then execute him. Atheists wouldn't have anything to do all day if God didn't exist. God is always lurking just beneath the philosophical discussion. Philosophy is beguiled by the questions but doesn't want answers. There is great disdain for any answer because any serious answer is a threat. A real answer puts them out of business.

We look at the life and writings of Saul of Taurus, the Apostle Paul, a bona fide intellectual, and a great philosopher in his own right. Saul was dangerous to the Christian cause because he was brilliant and well-taught in both Hellenistic/Greek culture and Jewish/Pharisee theology. His personality was type A, very driven, bordering on fanatical in some respects. His conversion with Christ was arranged by Christ himself, who changed his name to Paul and set him on fire, and redirected all his gifts.

Paul was schooled in Solomon's wisdom, even Solomon's cynicism and portrayal of life "under the sun" and his deep dive into what life is like and would be like without God. He had a great deal more information than Solomon. Solomon looked forward to Messiah, but Paul not only met the Messiah, he was privately taught by Messiah and he had a name—Jesus. During his missionary journeys, he had a few days to wait in Athens for his protégés, Timothy and Silas, to join him. For 21st-century "disciples," a few days in Athens calls for touring ancient sites, eating at great restaurants, enjoying the ambiance of warm nights, and soaking up the culture of Socrates, Plato, and Aristotle. And with a little too much Ouzo, throwing plates into the fireplace and dancing the night away as Zorba the Greek.

Paul, however, had a different reaction. He was no tourist. Paul was "deeply troubled" by the ubiquitous idols in the form of sculptures and the ones chiseled in stones and monuments. Another way to say it was that he was provoked, angry, pissed off.

I watched the *2024 Olympic Games Opening Ceremony* shown live from one of my favorite cities, Paris, France. I have been there many times as a tourist or on short stopovers. I have many fond memories. I loved being there. I missed the very beginning, so my first reaction was, "This is so great, the teams boating down the Seine, WOW, look at how they are assimilating the games into the already magnificent architecture and familiar structures of the city."

But then later I saw troubling scenes, the celebration of debauchery with Bacchus, one of the gods of perversion and excess. The display was proudly called, *The New Gay Testament, The Last Supper Staged on the Seine*. It was so morally foul that it was repudiated around the world. *The International Olympic Committee* apologized for their blasphemous display and removed it from YouTube. Elites never seem to get it until they get smacked upside the head. Next, there was the celebration of a "ménage à trois," a cascading of shameful desires, vile and degrading—the misuse of everything human and finally, the encouragement of such depravity. It was the moral fall of a society being celebrated and encouraged with a sense of mandate. This was not something a family could watch together.[4]

Even more disturbing was that the networks, the commentators, and the entire entertainment establishment had flushed itself down the toilet of such grotesqueness. The revulsion I felt sitting in front of my television was something like Paul must have felt every day he was in Athens. What should get our attention is that the trashing of Christianity got a sign-off at the highest level of the French Government along with NBC. They had bowed the knee to Caesar, to this trashy LGBT mockery of the Christian faith.[5] [5]

Paul was disgusted and his nature was to confront the idols and to take his ideas to the marketplace. He spoke daily in the market to anyone who happened to be there. Because he was effective, he was taken to the city council who shuffled him off to the philosopher's area, Mars Hill, the Areopagus. In London, it would be Speaker's Corner; in the United States, there is no equivalent. Free speech is in its last days and we see its death throes daily as life is squeezed out.

---

4 Romans 1:18-32 chronicles the moral depravity of the human race. This is happening right now, here, not somewhere else.

5 For more commentary, please see A Civilizational Suicide Note on the Seine. Rod Dreher, as found in Europeanconservative.com https://europeanconservative.com/articles/commentary/a-civilizational-suicide-note-on-the-seine/

Cultural Idols

Paul presented them with a fully contextualized thesis, rich in mystery and context for the philosophers. He agreed they were very religious with their many gods. Divine ambiguity is a philosopher's paradise. But Paul pointed to their "Unknown God" which keeps philosophers working, paid, and respected—the god that now could be known.[6] Paul introduced himself, who he was, his name, and what he had done. In the final analysis, this is everything important to our world, our lives, our fates, and our future—that our God has done.[7] The response was laughter and mockery and they discounted him as a hayseed, a middlebrow, a commoner, the bourgeoisie. But some wanted to hear more—in other words, there were converts.

When you confront and identify cultural idols you will be hated and opposed, but then you will have converts. You will have established a missionary encounter. You have started a church because you are the church. You are the church getting out of the church—to be the church.

Isn't this the best response to cultural decadence? We are swimming in spiritual waters dirtier than the Seine. We are to love the world as Christ loved it by telling it the truth and giving ourselves to its salvation. Christ said, "I am the way, the truth, and the life and no one comes to the Father but through me." It's not a popular message, it's not the spirit of the age, but it is the one that is true, it is the one that works, it is the one that saves.

There were thousands of Christians in Paris during the Olympics. They were there not to eat good food, enjoy the cocktail circuit, or rub shoulders with the stars. They stayed at cheap hostels

---

6 Dallas Willard warned that Christian philosophy is largely in a defensive position because we have become apologists, responding to the cutting-edge leading secular philosophers, examples of Kant, Hegel Husserl, Jaspers, Heidegger, Jean-Paul Sartre, Albert Camus, etc.

7 Acts 17:22-31

in outlying towns far away from Paris. They slept on the floor of churches and in private homes. They were young and old, people of many colors, from every inhabited continent, had taken an oath, had been baptized, and were on a mission. A mission to make new disciples – many new disciples. Not just any kind of disciples, but disciples of Christ. They were afraid, they were brave, they were prayed for, they were walking in obedience. And don't forget the athletes, the coaches, and the officials, for Christ was among them— they were the insiders. God used them all.

I hope they saw some events and ate good food in the City of Light. But no city is darker spiritually. In all the decadence that surrounded these dedicated followers of Jesus, may these words of Jesus be ever present in their heads, and in the hearts of those to whom they witnessed, "And be sure of this: I am with you always, even to the end of the age."[8]

---

8 Matthew 28:20

SALVATION BY SCIENTISM ALONE

Adobe Stock, "Charles Darwin with a lookalike ape." Date: 1874. By Archivist

All that we call human history—money, poverty, ambition, war, prostitution, classes, empires, slavery is the long terrible story of man trying to find something other than God which will make him happy.
—C.S. Lewis, Mere Christianity

I think the world needs to wake up from its long nightmare of religious belief; and anything that we scientists can do to weaken the hold of religion should be done and may, in fact, be our greatest contribution to civilization.
—Nobel winner Steven Weinberg (Good Reads Quotes)

Scientism: **The belief that science and the scientific method are the best and only way to render truth about the world and reality.**

*Jesus said, I am the way, the truth and the life. No one can come to the Father except through me. If you had really **known me**, you would know who my Father is, from now on, you do know him and have seen him!*
—John 14:6,7 New Living Translation

*"… and **we know** that God causes everything to work together for the good for those who love God and are called according to his purpose for them."*
—Romans 8:28 New Living Translation

In 1859 Charles Darwin published *The Origin of Species* and the unbelieving world celebrated. Not that it proved or claimed much more than that birds within species made slight adjustments to external conditions over long periods of time. Nevertheless, the intellectual elite in England ran, with scholar's robes flowing, toward the new loophole, a way of maintaining their societal status, and saving their jobs at Oxford and Cambridge. They were easily led through any opening that would excuse them from continuing to be dominated by the Church of England and its requirements to sign the thirty-nine articles of faith[1] required to keep their academic positions.

Of course, they did not celebrate alone. All atheism, agnosticism, and unbelieving society joined in. As C.S. Lewis cited, humans are always on a quest to look for any meaning or explanation for life—other than God—for God requires us to bow the knee, to submit, to admit we need him, to humbly worship him. We must lose to win.

Darwin's book, based largely on small changes in various sea life off the coast of Ecuador produced Darwinism, the confident assertion that people could actually know something, something that would be true, that could be classified as knowledge.[2] Even a knowledge to build a life on, to construct an edifice complex for life without God. But the edifice crumbled because it sat on a foundation of sand, rather than the rock of knowledge. Darwin's ideas became Darwinism, and science became scientism. *Ism* means ideology, it means zealotry, it means what once had value becomes a religious cult.

Knowledge, belief, and commitment—the differences

Knowledge includes truth, accuracy, evidence, and insight. Belief is different. It can come from many sources and emotions such

---

1 The Thirty-Nine Articles of Religion, 1571, Book of Common Prayer (Anglican Church in North America 2019). page 772.

2 Darwin's Finches are an example of giant leaps over unknown abysses. I would recommend Nancy Pearcey's book, Total Truth. Specifically, the chapter on Darwin Meets the Berenstain Bears. 153-178.

as fear and hatred. People believe many things that are not based on knowledge—I'm the smartest, dumbest, fastest, best looking, *etc*—just because I think so, or my parents or friends say so. Commitment is highly valued, but we can commit to causes we don't believe in. People can make religious commitments for personal gain, yet not believe the teachings of that religion. People have pets and spend thousands of dollars on their purchase and care, yet do not like animals. They do it because someone close to them does care about animals. Christians profess to believe the Nicene Creed or the Methodist Book of Worship, even pay homage to the Archbishop of Canterbury or the Pope, yet not agree with the church's teachings. It could be said that even the Archbishop or Pope don't believe their own stuff.

Scientism rules the roost

Scientism is quite powerful in contemporary society and is a means of salvation for all those looking for loopholes, excuses, and personal autonomy. We are confronted with it regularly and distinguishing it from science is difficult. Let's say your physician provides you with a negative test finding. The doctor recommends a medication or procedure or even a more radical intervention. The medical facts are in front of you, that is the science and you thank God for the science. But the doctor doesn't have all the truth or knowledge. You may have held back vital information or hedged your bets. The doctor doesn't have context, knowledge is limited, and he or she is operating on numbers, trends, medical literature, and percentiles.

Some cultural elites and organizations go with them and tell you, "Follow the science, believe the science." But to make the decision using only science is to decide without a vast realm of other forms of knowledge. In fact, unless other forms of knowing are considered, a science-only decision is a bad decision. To allow science to take the dominant position is scientism and everything else serves it.

Not long ago I sat in a doctor's office and was told, after flunking my cognitive test, that I was entering the early stages of dementia. I was in a bad way because after surgery I had experienced brain fog. I had symptoms that looked like I was in some serious trouble. My wife was there, as she had been my keeper for several weeks. The doctor suggested seeking the help of a specialist and moving into preparations for my decline. I sat silently for a moment and finally said, "I want to give God a chance." I wanted to give God a chance to heal me and bring me back. I had other forms of knowledge that made my decision a completely contextualized choice. It took three months, but slowly I got better until one day someone plugged my brain back in. Based on all my underlying foundations and knowledge base, that someone was God.

I want to be clear, if I had a broken leg, a hip so bad I couldn't walk, then *ipso facto,* I needed to fix it. But there are times when contemplation, prayer, and knowledge about oneself and overall reality take the lead. I did tell my doctor that his diagnosis was a reasonable one, but unless he could come live in my body for six months, he couldn't really know me. And the only one who knew what was going on inside of me was God. I likened it to incarnation—God became a man to inhabit time and space—he became one of us. Another way to understand this is to introduce Grandpa's Box of Knowledge.

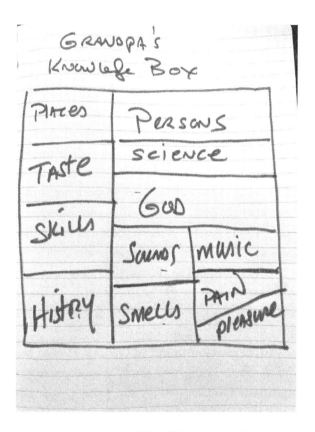

Drawn by Bill Hull for James Hull

As you can see, there are many forms of knowledge. Science, while important, is not the most crucial or lead dog. My oldest Grandson, when in Junior High, was being taught scientism, *i.e.* science is the societal god, follow it and it will lead you to all the truth, at least into any truth that can be known or worth knowing. I wanted my grandson to understand knowledge comes in many forms and that the most important knowledge is knowing people and knowing God. We know people, the sound of their voices, their personalities, and none of this by the scientific method. Even the most ardent atheists can't possibly live the way of life they champion. Science is so limited that it cannot answer a ten-year-old's most important questions. Why do we exist? Why are we here? What happens to us after we die?

These same champions of despair need a reason to tell their children to play fair, not to hate, and give them a reason to excel. They don't tuck their preschoolers into bed at night and say, "Honey, sleep well, I know that you are just flesh and bone, that your life has no meaning, there is no God or eternal life, there is no reason for you to be moral because without God everything is permitted." No, they don't say it because they can't stand their own philosophy. Reality is too stark and ugly for them, so they piggyback on Christianity and its meaning, its protection, its benefits, and its ethics.

Knowing persons, especially knowing God, is no less knowledge than knowing about gravity. I recall the great apologist, Professor John Lennox of Oxford University, asking his colleagues a simple question. This is the question he asked the greatest scientists and philosophers he knew or was acquainted with: "Can you explain gravity, how does it work and why?" Not one person could answer, and still, no one can answer his question.

The only answer is God found in Genesis 1:1 *"In the beginning God created the heavens and the earth."* Gravity keeps everything from flying apart. God created it, the Lord Christ continues to hold it all together, and there is your answer.[3]

Scientism will not save the earth or its inhabitants. Science without the elite demigods helps if you consider the benefits of technology such as air-conditioning and fossil fuels that have delivered a reliable power grid for billions of poor people and raised their standard of living worldwide. Scientism, however, is despotic, *1984* turbo-charged, and it violates human nature. Nearly everything it predicts turns out wrong. From climate to creating a new life that is actual life, its servants continue to force a ruinous and wrong reality onto the populace. One thinks of the falsehood that a man can become a woman, menstruate, and give birth to a child. All you need to do is declare it as true by human fiat. It's true because I say it's true. It leads to the scandal of the bodily mutila-

---

3   Colossians 1:15-20. Not a satisfying answer if you want to prove it in a test tube or lab. But if you want the answer outside of science itself, it is quite satisfying.

tion of children, a horrendous evil in our society. If a five-year-old boy says, "I'm a pirate," should we poke out his eye, amputate one leg beneath the knee, and fit him with a peg leg? Unthinkable, this is Dr. Josef Mengele, "The Angel of Death" stuff.

Jesus said, "I am the way the truth, and the life, and no one comes to the Father but by me."

There it is, the total truth based on a very broad knowledge in Grandpa's Knowledge Box. And unlike Pandora's box from Greek Mythology which released sorrow, disease, vice, violence, greed, madness, old age, and death, Grandpa's box is the knowledge of places, persons, tastes, science, skills, God, sounds, music, history, books, smells, aromas, pain, and pleasure. All of these stimulate and inform our minds, which are different than the human brain. The "mind of Christ" is advocated by Paul and, of course, revealed in Christ himself by his ways and teachings.[4]

Salvation by Scientism alone is a lie. It rules in our world which is now an empire of lies. The secular elites are like Lucifer in John Milton's masterpiece, *Paradise Lost*. Satan finds himself fastened to the floor of Hell. A place he claimed he would rather rule than be in Heaven where he would be a servant. He would make Heaven out of Hell. Until he realizes that he, himself, is Hell. They proclaim from the heights of culture that they can transform their dystopian dreams into a more enlightened utopia. Yes, people will need to be eliminated, the unborn and the unwanted. Yes, they will need to restrict and punish misinformation. Yes, they will need to shove history down the memory hole and rewrite it.

If you are a biblically based Christian, it may seem as Shakespeare wrote, *"Hell is empty and all the devils are here."* But one day all truth will be revealed. Their utopian dream will be revealed as a dystopian nightmare. As my Uncle Gibb used to say, "Reality is a bitch, Christ is coming back, and boy will he be pissed!

---

4   The Mind of Christ: I Cor. 2:16, Philippians 2:5. Matthew Chapters 5-7 & the gospels.

SALVATION BY MONASTICISM ALONE

During the winter of 1940–1941, Dietrich Bonhoeffer spent some months at the Ettal Abby monastery as the friend and guest of the Abbot. While there he worked on his book, Ethics.

In 1937 Dietrich Bonhoeffer gave the world his book, The Cost of Discipleship. It was a masterful attack on "easy Christianity" or "cheap grace." But it did not set aside—perhaps it even enforced—the view of discipleship as a costly spiritual excess, and only for those especially driven or called to it.[1]

The restoration of the church must surely depend on a new kind of monasticism, which has nothing in common with the old, but a life of uncompromising discipleship, following Christ according to the Sermon on the Mount. I believe the time has come to gather people together to do this.[2]

What can save Christianity or at least make it better? Many, I concluded, have said, work harder at it! Get serious! Some even say, go monastic. Historians champion the role of monks and monasteries for saving the church from its wholesale debauchery and decadence toward the end of the Roman Empire. From the Third century Monks copied, preserved, and cared for the biblical manuscripts and attempted to live simply, powerfully, and separately from the normal population. Some early desert fathers such as the Egyptian St. Antony, (251-356) like Jesus, went looking for the devil in the desert to fight and defeat him. Many others followed, were killed by the elements, others by wild animals. Finally, they moved in together behind walls for protection. Within these walls, they separated themselves so they could be alone, together.

---

1 Dallas Willard, The Spirit of the Disciplines, San Francisco, Harper and Row, 1989, page 262, 263.

2 Eric Metaxas, Bonhoeffer, page 260.

The separated life does not work for most people. After all, someone needs to make money so the group can be Monks. It's nice that they can read, meditate, garden, make great wine, and even broaden their skills to make many commendable products. To be fair, the same could be said of pastors and politicians. This may be where Bonhoeffer's New Monasticism, nothing like the old, came in. Few are attracted to self-flagellation, crawling stairs on one's knees, or setting world records for living on top of pillars.[3]

Humans seem to be drawn, as a form of guilt mixed with worship, to find a way to deprive ourselves without it hurting too much. We like pain that doesn't hurt, a depression that is not too deep, a deprivation that is planned and short. We walk a tightrope between the flesh and the Spirit. The church has assisted us in this quest for a deeper spiritual life. There are special seasons when we can deny ourselves wine and chocolate until the forty days of Lent are complete and then "as you were."

One innovation might be to permanently deny ourselves real sins that actually matter. Gossip? Malice? Envy?

The reason we don't is character sins don't just go away, they take time to get rid of and then effort to keep away. Being a Christian is quite a mystery. We are adopted as sons and daughters and vested with the full heavenly inheritance. The money is already in the bank with our name on it. Yet, we are expected to live up to the expectations of the family—and to constantly strive to live up to

---

[3] Excess among Monastics is legendary. From Saint Antony selling all his possessions and heading out to the desert, or Simeon Stylites, living atop a pillar for 36 years. And Saint Ignatius of Loyola stripping to his waist and exposing his torso to the sleet and cold of a winter's day to identify with those in Hell—apparently, a case of global warming becoming an ice age event—Hell did finally freeze over, and the Eagles reunited in 1994. Even Martin Luther, yes, the unintentional leader of the Reformation, as a Monk, climbed the steps of the church, Scala Santra, on his knees in 1510 and repeated "Our Father" on each step. Today it is a tourist attraction and the steps are covered by wood to protect the marble. This is the theater of the absurd, excessive indeed, and does not impress God in the least.

and achieve very high goals on a platform of discipline—giving our all—holding nothing back! Confused yet?

Dallas Willard's analysis of Bonhoeffer's most famous book, *The Cost of Discipleship,* enhanced the popular view that discipleship is excessive and therefore only for those specially called to it. "Discipleship" or believing, living, loving, and leading like Jesus is out of reach. Therefore, when the clergy or someone like clergy calls all to discipleship, we in the pew can sit back, cross our arms, and say, "It's not for me, they really don't mean it, I'm still going to heaven." So, the pendulum swings, the battle continues, and minds are confused, "as you were."

Dietrich Bonhoeffer was clergy. At age 25 he was ordained at Old-Prussian United St. Matthew's Church near his home in Berlin. Earlier, after his graduation at age 21, he spent a year in America at Union Theological Seminary where he repudiated modern Americana liberal theology and yet, through his exposure to an African American congregation in Harlem, experienced a personal conversion to Christ. He returned to Germany a different man—one who read the Bible and received communion. He had served as a youth director, he had been an intern in Barcelona, Spain in a German-speaking congregation. He had been a pastor in a German congregation in London. (1933-35) While in London he would arise at 11:00 AM and go to bed at 3:00 AM. He enjoyed his theaters and restaurants, but he did have a practical side—as far as a patrician son of the privileged elite could. He also had fought the fight against the most liberal and compromising German Lutheran Church which capitulated to the National Socialists and their leader, Adolf Hitler.

He had a double PhD from the University of Berlin, and at 25 was granted the position of lecturer. He was already considered a troublemaker, an agitator, part of the Confessing Church which separated itself from the German Evangelical Church. He spent four years in his "Grand Experiment" teaching in an illegal seminary for the Confessing Church. The first 2.5 years at a campus in Finkenwalde, the next 2.5 years in various locations, and underground meetings in various venues. He wrote two books during this period.

The First was *Discipleship,* which is known in the English-speaking world as *The Cost of Discipleship*. And a smaller volume, *"Life Together,"* which describes his and his 23 students' lives together. Bonhoeffer attempted his "New Monasticism," nothing like the old, and his many insights from it before the Gestapo closed the seminary.

A New Monasticism, Nothing Like the Old

The new monasticism was admired and hated by Bonhoeffer's 23 students, and finally, it exposed Bonhoeffer as a highly revered figure, but flawed, inconsistent, and even hypocritical. It was nothing like the old or almost nothing like Luther's Augustinian order. But still, it was living by covenant, "Life Together."

Bonhoeffer reached his breaking point early on in the community. His students were also under a lot of pressure. The students hated the 30 minutes of silence in the morning. They would rather be smoking their pipes or doing something useful. Instead, they were required to sit and concentrate on something spiritual. They were academic in orientation and wondered what this had to do with becoming pastors and scholars. They complained and frankly, some chose not to do it. One evening after dinner, Bonhoeffer let it be known that he would be cleaning up the kitchen, assuming that others would join him cleaning. No one did, so he locked himself in the kitchen and did it all himself.

Bonhoeffer's training was distinguished by his two-hour lecture on discipleship each weekday morning. The material used became the foundation for his famous work, *The Cost of Discipleship.* Every day began and ended with worship services and the infamous 30 minutes of meditation before the lectures. They prayed the entire book of Psalms weekly. On Saturdays, he would deliver a commentary and on Sunday there would be a full worship service and a sermon. Afternoons provided time for exercise, free time, walks, gardening, and leisure.

It sounds rather intense for the non-monastic mentality. This new monasticism was much looser than previous forms, but still more structured in overall life than German students were accustomed to. But there was unspoken dissidence among the community. Virtually the entire student group lived by rule and by the fact they had no money or transportation and were restricted to the seminary campus. But not Dr. Bonhoeffer. His very powerful and wealthy father had presented Dietrich with a new Mercedes that allowed him to travel to Berlin for weekends, special meetings, and of course to the theater, the opera, and his favorite restaurants.

Bonhoeffer's best friend was student Eberhard Bethge. Liberal scholars have gently nudged history toward the conclusion that possibly the relationship was a bit more than was publicly acceptable in those days. But this is a heinous theory and only taken seriously by the more decadent and dishonest scholars who have a contemporary political agenda. Bethge was admitted into the Bonhoeffer family and was by Dietrich's side during much of eight years stretching from the beginning of the seminary until Bethge entered the German Army.

Dietrich always had money. His family made sure he had all the special tennis clothes he needed in Barcelona, membership in the right clubs, and access to the German elite wherever in the world he went. He invented missions connected with leisure and travel. This is very popular among American Christians today. He was a hard worker but, also not hesitant to spend weeks traveling, sightseeing, and retreats at his family cottage in the Hartz Mountains. A son of privilege, accustomed to the good life, he was out of sorts when his creature comforts were missing. He was the kind of guy who accepted an internship and explained that he could not begin for nine months and would also need a few weeks off for a tour with his brother Klaus. He was human, flawed, and fallen, but with positive qualities. Like so many of us, he was an anomaly.

Brilliant and brave, when it counted, he stepped up in a way that many, if not most, would not. He was principled, mentally and emotionally tough, and thought of discipleship as standing between the oppressor and the oppressed. In his case, between the Nazis and the Jews. He fought for the church to be independent of government power and any restraining of the preaching of the Gospel. In 1939 he went to New York City at the behest of his friends to sit out the coming war in safety. But he could not stay. Only 26 days after arrival, he left New York on a ship back to Europe—just before Germany invaded Poland—the beginning of World War II.

He refused military service. He worked behind the scenes to oppose and finally, to attempt to kill Adolf Hitler. He was imprisoned and was a true pastor to his fellow prisoners during his last two years in prison. Bonhoeffer lived a sacrificial life as best he could, based on how God made him, where he placed him, and the opportunities he had to preach the gospel. He was a martyr driving a Mercedes with a cigarette hanging from his mouth, dressed in the latest fashion, with a case of champagne in the boot, *la bonne vie*. He lived life to the full and embraced it when he could. He died a hero, by order of Hitler at the foot of the gallows on April 9, 1945. He said in effect, "This is not the end of life, it is a beginning."

The New Monasticism

When your pastor or someone you listen to tells you to get serious about following Christ, it has to be based on how God made you. So, drop all the stuff about imitating the mystics, the monks, the missionaries, even the highly disciplined guy sitting next to you in church with a trim body and youthful look. When you hear that fasting is feasting and silence is essential, or that certain practices are essential, ask yourself this question, "Did Jesus do it or practice it?" If the answer is yes, then introduce the spiritual practice that would address your greatest problem. Don't attempt them all, you might not need half of them in your life because God made you in a way that some of them are not compatible and the chances that you would do them are quite remote.

What to do?

Often a mystic will say something like, "It's not what you do, it is what you are." Or someone else will ask what God gets out of this whole thing called life—it's the people we become. It all sounds nice, even poetic, but doesn't help much past a warm feeling that lasts a few moments.

Historically, there are several spiritual practices and I put them in two categories. *A spiritual discipline is a practice modeled by Jesus that sets spiritual forces into motion creating Christ-like character.*

1. **Disciplines that remove negative character traits.**
   Silence works against addiction to noise,
   Solitude against crowds,
   Fasting against food addiction,
   Frugality against materialism.
   Chastity against lust,
   Secrecy against being indiscreet,
   Sacrifice against self-indulgence.

These disciplines work to free us from the grip the "flesh" has on us.

2. **Disciplines that connect us to God.**
   Study addresses ignorance,
   Worship battles independence,
   Prayer against passiveness,
   Celebration against a sadness,
   Service works against self-interest,
   Fellowship against isolation,
   Confession against hiddenness,
   Submission battles rebellion.

Bonhoeffer kept his eye on the ball. Everything from the *Barmen Declaration*[4] to his walk up the gallows steps was about one thing, the freedom to preach the gospel without restraint.

---

4   The Barmen Declaration was a document announcing that a new group called the Confessing Church would fight for independence to preach the gospel. It was largely authored by Karl Barth, the most influential theologian in Europe during the 20th century.

Don't lose sight of the goal

Christlikeness is the goal. And why is it the goal? Christlikeness is Godliness—and that makes for an abundant life full of meaning, joy, and doing God's will. That is why we are here—it is the masterpiece that God has made each of us and which he planned before the foundation of the world.[5] You can't go it alone, all this must be done in community because as the great John Calvin wrote, "The ruin of a man is to obey himself."

---

5 I Timothy 4:7, Ephesians 2:10, John 10:10b

SALVATION BY FAITH ALONE

In the beginning was the Word.

Then God said, "Let there be light."

Many of his disciples said, "This is very hard to understand. How can anyone accept it?"

Nothing comes alone, salvation didn't arrive on our planet for free, it combined the work and sacrifice of others. It was presented to a particular people at an appointed time and place after centuries of planning and preparation. When an evangelist sums it up with what is called in the trade, *the close,* or *the invitation,* or *the ask* the usual closing is: *God sent his son to save us, Christ died on the cross for our sins, now all we need to do is pray and ask God to come into our lives. He alone can save!* the preacher is not wrong, not right— but deceptively naïve, or uninformed, like describing the reason for the collapse of the Twin Towers on 9/11 as gravity.

God began His work before time and space before the earth existed. In an existence where life didn't have a before or after, but only now, only "I Am," God decided to create. There was a beginning because God willed it. He spoke it into existence with words. Words are the genesis of action and creation. Just as the incarnate "Word of God." Jesus is the consummate, most complete Word. In the way that DNA underlies all matter and meaning, it is information, a code, a knowing about something. "In the beginning God created the heavens and the earth." And he spoke and said, "Let there be…" and there was. And then he said, "Let us make human beings in our image, to be like us." And the human being was created. "Us" means the Triune God. I won't go into the plural "us" within a singular person or one God, it's a bit much for here right now.

Then after a few bumps in the road, man fell, creation was cursed, and as early as Genesis 3:15[1] the reclaiming, the redemptive plan was predicted and set into motion. Yes, a great deal of planning and work went into all of this thing called salvation.

So, when a young boy or girl kneels at an altar and "gives their heart to Jesus" they board a train already packed with the "saved" from previous generations. One can see the countless heads through the windows in the cars that have preceded them, those saved by the messages of Abraham, Isaac, Jacob, Joseph, Moses, Joshua, the judges, the prophets, and kings. And then, of course, Jesus himself. God became a person and because he was worthy, he was the lamb that was slain, he was the one as the old hymn says, "paid it all." The others prepared it all, and now we join it all by praying, and then following Jesus as he leads us all into the future.

So, all this nonsense that salvation by anything alone must go! It isn't by scripture alone, Christ alone, faith alone, grace alone. Salvation is through Christ alone but so much has gone into it. To treat it like a simple transaction is blasphemy. I should know, I'm an old blasphemer and was pretty good at it in years past.

I think it is fair to say, faith alone is a modern theological construct driven by market forces to produce easy converts to keep the church up and going. It is a modern capitulation; our weakened wills and bodies have made it necessary for us to lower the standards of following Jesus. Sympathetically I must say, it is the easy way, it is alluring, it works, and it appears to be proof that we are headed for Shangri La. Unfortunately, Jesus wouldn't have any of it and sent packing those who didn't like his kind of discipleship. Yes, Jesus would send most of us packing. Salvation is an all-in proposition, if you aren't all-in, you are out!

---

1 Genesis 3:15 describes the hostility between Lucifer and Eve's offspring which means Jesus, the Messiah or anointed one. "He will strike your head, and you will strike his heel." In other words, Satan's head strike will be fatal to his plans and desires. The strike to Christ's heel will end differently.

The decision

Jesus had over 100 men and women following him at the time of this episode in the gospel of John. He had announced he was the "bread of life" and had introduced them to what is called "Holy Communion" or "Eucharist." He was speaking about drinking his blood and eating his flesh. They obviously understood it to be symbolic on some level, but it was mysterious and seemed a bit crazy to many of his followers. He was actually saying, *are you all in? If so, a decision had to be made.*

[60] Many of his disciples said, "This is very hard to understand. How can anyone accept it?"

[61] Jesus was aware that his disciples were complaining, so he said to them, "Does this offend you? [62] Then what will you think if you see the Son of Man ascend to heaven again? [63] The Spirit alone gives eternal life. Human effort accomplishes nothing. And the very words I have spoken to you are spirit and life. [64] But some of you do not believe me." (For Jesus knew from the beginning which ones didn't believe, and he knew who would betray him.) [65] Then he said, "That is why I said that people can't come to me unless the Father gives them to me."

[66] At this point many of his disciples turned away and deserted him. [67] Then Jesus turned to the Twelve and asked, "Are you also going to leave?"

[68] Simon Peter replied, "Lord, to whom would we go? You have the words that give eternal life. [69] We believe, and we know you are the Holy One of God." [a]

All in or all out?

Everyone who has ever made a difference in the kingdom of God was all in, how about you? Jesus confronted his disciples with a new level of following him that offended many of his best fans and admirers. They had followed him everywhere, they were elite, they had been chosen to become part of his band of "true disciples."

But when Jesus started talking total consumption of his person, they were offended, shocked, and put off. Some of them did not believe in him. This reveals that Jesus seemed to be less concerned about non-disciples than he was with false disciples. He told them they couldn't pull off following him on their own. "Human effort accomplishes nothing," he said. (John 6:63) Many of his disciples left him. Jesus said even harder things before he was finished. He declared that no one could do this unless the Father drew them to Him as a disciple. And finally, as though the whole thing were an object lesson or test for the twelve he had first appointed, he asked, "Are you also going to leave?"

Peter's reply revealed how you know you are all in, *"Lord, to whom would we go? You have the words that give eternal life. We believe and we know you are the Holy One of God."*

There is no going back! At one time his true disciples were lost without him. Now they would be lost again without him. This episode reveals a stark contrast between what the contemporary Christian faith considers disciples and discipleship and what Jesus actually lived and taught. Being all in now doesn't look from the outside what it looked like then. Jesus isn't here in the flesh, he doesn't lead a band of a few followers around Palestine. There are more than a few now, over 2 Billion who claim Christ in some way.

But when you start thinning the herd via Jesus' demands, false disciples by far outnumber true disciples.

Many years ago, I was a member of a study group that flew regularly to meet and discuss the question, *What is wrong with the church?* We had written several papers and published a book together.[2] A curious seatmate on one of my trips asked me why I

---

2 The Kingdom Life https://www.amazon.com/Kingdom-Life-Practical-Discipleship-Spiritual/dp/163146678X/ref=asc_df_163146678X/?tag=hyprod-20&linkCode=df0&hvadid=693512208602&hvpos=&hvnetw=g&hvrand=16183543551187617013&hvpone=&hvptwo=&hvqmt=&hvdev=c&hvdvcmdl=&hvlocint=&hvlocphy=9031088&hvtargid=pla-491550933296&psc=1&mcid=8f-593c5544403c0dad1eea8957dddfa1

was traveling. I put it succinctly for him. We fly from all over the country to discuss a problem. What problem? he asked. I explained that in America we preach a gospel that states, *you can become a Christian and not follow Jesus.* It is the normative default position of the contemporary church. It has led to what I call the *Gospel Americana. This is because the gospel you preach determines the disciple you make.* Therefore, if we normalize non-discipleship Christianity, you get what Jesus feared—false disciples who represent Christ, but don't believe him and won't reproduce anything else except more people like them—in other words, it's a disaster.

Then he wanted to know the solution. Interestingly, Jesus didn't give a solution in this passage primarily because the answer was unfolding every day in their discipleship. And because the story wasn't over yet.

I heard a speaker recently wondering if the Eucharist was more important than the Resurrection. I don't think they compete, but I would say Jesus' disciples would have nothing if they were following a dead leader. Christ on the cross can be inspiring like any sacrificial act or martyrdom. But resurrection lights up the world, graves are opened, bodies are transformed, death is put to death and eternal life begins. That is what I told him.

But I told him something practical for right here, and right now. **The Solution** *is for the church to reorganize its life around the practices of Jesus.* Yes, we look back and can declare the Gospel **about** Jesus, but daily, it is the Gospel **of** Jesus, meaning following him, learning from him, and engaging in the practices he modeled. The man turned, leaned his head on the window and began to quietly cry.

ABOUT BILL HULL

Bill Hull is an untroubled writer who refuses to leave his home in downtown Babylon, California. He is pastor to a congregation he has never met, his readers. He has held important jobs, has written many books and has been given impressive awards, including the highly coveted Dragon's Head award, but humility prevents him from naming the others. You know, like book of the year stuff. Even though he has been asked not to mention it, he is a graduate of Oral Roberts University and later, Talbot School of Theology, where he taught for several years before they found out. Bill does have a family, but they have chosen to remain anonymous.

Just joking. Bill is the happy husband of one wife, proud father of two sons (and loves their wives), and crazy about his three grandsons.

BILLHULL.COM

- Books, study guides, and resources

- Links to Bill's podcast, videos and socials

- Contact Bill

- Book Bill to speak or consult with your church or organization

BillHull.com

BILLHULL.SUBSTACK.COM

Many of the chapters in this book began life as articles on Bill's Substack channel.

No Longer a Bystander is for activists who are also seeking spiritual solutions to personal and societal problems. If you are looking for sappy devotional thoughts, you are in the wrong space and need to move on. Martin Luther said, "If you want to change the world, pick up a pen and write." Every article will challenge conventional thinking and provide a knowledge base that will make you rethink the world around you—and if applied, will change ideas and behavior. The subjects live at the intersection of religion and culture and how it is reflected in religious bodies and contemporary culture, which, by default, includes political leadership.

Read & Subscribe at billhull.substack.com

OTHER BOOKS BY BILL HULL

THE COMPLETE BOOK OF DISCIPLESHIP
On Being and Making Followers of Christ

NO LONGER A BYSTANDER
A Radical New Way To Look At Our Christianity, Our Culture, Our Future, And Our Legacy

CHOOSE THE LIFE
Exploring a Faith That Embraces Discipleship

CONVERSION & DISCIPLESHIP
You Can't Have One Without the Other

THE CHRISTIAN LEADER
Rehabilitating Our Addiction to Secular Leadership

CHRISTLIKE
The Pursuit of Uncomplicated Obedience

THE COST OF CHEAP GRACE
Reclaiming the Value of Discipleship

THE DISCIPLESHIP GOSPEL
What Jesus Preached—We Must Follow

JESUS CHRIST DISCIPLEMAKER
Emulates Christ's model for reaching the lost

THE DISCIPLE-MAKING CHURCH
Leading Others on the Journey of Faith

THE DISCIPLE-MAKING PASTOR
Leading a Body of Believers on the Journey of Faith

https://amzn.to/3O2vB3t

Made in the USA
Middletown, DE
11 April 2025